"Parenting is arguably the most challenging journey we ever embark on, especially alongside nurturing a couple's relationship. The book offers a compelling collection of essays that brilliantly bridge the gap between couples' dynamics and effective parenting. It's more than a guide – it's an essential read for professionals. By transcending the dyadic, this unique book champions a holistic view across a wide range of contexts, spotlighting how relationships influence relationships. The book will take your approach for the betterment of both children and parents to a new more sophisticated level!"

*Professor Peter Fonagy, OBE FMedSci FBA FAcSS, Head of the Division of Psychology and Language Sciences Director, UCLPartners Mental Health and Behaviour Change Programme Chief Executive, Anna Freud National Centre for Children and Families National Clinical Advisor on Children's Mental Health, NHS England*

"The transition from coupledom to parenthood can prove immensely challenging. Fortunately, Kate Thompson and Damian McCann have curated a beautiful, ground-breaking book documenting the ways in which experienced couple mental health specialists can prevent families from exploding. I warmly recommend this deeply important, clinically original, and highly readable text to all psychological professionals and, moreover, to parents as well."

*Professor Brett Kahr, Senior Fellow, Tavistock Institute of Medical Psychology, London, Honorary Director of Research, Freud Museum London, and Past Chair of the British Society of Couple Psychotherapists and Counsellors*

"Clinicians and parents will find this interesting and intelligent book incredibly useful. So many parenting books overlook that adults are also navigating their own relationship as they go about the task of bringing up children – this excellent volume really addresses that gap."

*Susanna Abse, Psychoanalytic Therapist and author of* Tell Me The Truth About Love: 13 Tales from the Therapist's Couch

"*Couples as Parents* fills a void in the fields of family and marital psychotherapy. Writings about couple therapy have focused on marriage as a thing in itself, and family therapy has focused largely on interaction between children and parents. This encyclopedic book puts the microscope on the parenting function of couples, and thereby gives new perspective on a wide variety of largely unexplored dimensions crucial to family well-being. It is a most welcome addition to our knowledge and ability to help a wide variety of families."

*David Scharff, MD, Co-Editor, Psychoanalytic Couple Therapy and Co-Founder, International Psychotherapy Institute*

"*Couples As Parents* is truly an insightful delve into parenthood and partners. Experienced therapists share their observations of working with parents in conflict, expertly unpicking the knots of discord to deliver understanding, and in turn build the foundations of good communication. A brilliant read for anyone working with or interested in couple and family dynamics."

**Sally Land**, *Agony Aunt for* The Sun

"This book tackles some of the hurdles facing parents from the moment they decide to try for a baby to the moment their child flies the nest. It maps the different stages of a couple's life together and traces them as they intersect with their child's developmental trajectory. I wish it had been to hand when we set out on our parenting journey."

**Tracey Camilleri**, *parent and author of* The Social Brain

"This very thoughtfully written and edited book describes how even planned and welcomed babies challenge the couple relationship as two become three, and intergenerational precepts around childrearing come into play. One of the unique contributions of the book is that the baby as well as the couple is held in mind by the authors. The various chapters make for surprisingly easy reading while dealing deftly with complex issues. I have come away enriched."

**Tessa Baradon**, *Consultant Infant, Child and Adolescent Psychoanalytic Psychotherapist*

# Couples as Parents

*Couples as Parents: Explorations in Couple Therapy* explores the complex task of parenting from the perspective of the couple relationship.

A book for clinicians and parents alike, it describes problems that can occur during the transition to parenthood and the initial decision to have a child to raising young children and adolescents. The book offers a comprehensive exploration of the nature and patterns of intimate partner relationships and how they can be affected by such things as the loss of a baby, raising a child with autism or adoption. Chapters delve into issues unique to same-sex parents and those facing an empty nest. With moving clinical examples, it illustrates how a couple's sex life can be altered on becoming parents and describes how parents can best help their children as they separate. *Couples as Parents* explains how couple therapy has a unique stance with which to help parents and describes clinical vignettes that demonstrate how parents have been helped in the past.

The book considers the historical context of couple relationships, utilises research and psychoanalytic ways of thinking to further understanding for psychotherapists and interested parents, as well as offering a variety of therapeutic approaches to the specific needs of parents, whether as a couple, separated or single.

**Kate Thompson** is a couple psychoanalytic psychotherapist and senior staff member at Tavistock Relationships (TR) with over 20 years' experience of therapy with couples and individuals. Currently heading up Couple Therapy for Depression Training of NHS practitioners, Kate is also clinical lead for TR's parenting services. Registered with BPC and BACP, Kate writes for a variety of publications; she co-edited *Engaging Couples: New Directions in Therapeutic Work with Families* (Routledge, 2018) and a special edition of *Couple and Family Psychoanalysis on Divorce and Separation* (2021). She is Co-Editor in Chief of *Journal of Couple and Family Psychoanalysis*.

**Damian McCann**, DSysPsych, is a psychoanalytic couple psychotherapist working at Tavistock Relationships, London; adjunct faculty member of the International Psychotherapy Institute (IPI) Washington, DC; an associate of Queen Anne Street Practice, London; and an editorial board member of *Couple and Family Psychoanalysis*. He is also a consultant systemic psychotherapist with many years of experience working with children, adolescents and their families. He has a particular interest in working with gender and sexual diversity in psychoanalytic practice and has published and taught widely on this topic. His edited book *Same-Sex Couples and Other Identities: Psychoanalytic Perspectives* was published by Routledge in 2021.

## The Library of Couple and Family Psychoanalysis
Series Editors
Susanna Abse, Christopher Clulow, Brett Kahr, and David Scharff

The library consolidates and extends the work of Tavistock Relationships, and offers the best of psychoanalytically informed writing on adult partnerships and couple psychotherapy.

Other titles in the series:

# Couples as Parents

## Explorations in Couple Therapy

Edited by Kate Thompson
and Damian McCann

Routledge
Taylor & Francis Group

LONDON AND NEW YORK

Cover created by © Rory MacLachlan

First published 2025
by Routledge
4 Park Square, Milton Park, Abingdon, Oxon OX14 4RN

and by Routledge
605 Third Avenue, New York, NY 10158

*Routledge is an imprint of the Taylor & Francis Group, an informa business*

© 2025 selection and editorial matter, Kate Thompson and Damian McCann; individual chapters, the contributors

*British Library Cataloguing-in-Publication Data*
A catalogue record for this book is available from the British Library

*Library of Congress Cataloging-in-Publication Data*
Names: Thompson, Kate, 1964– editor. | McCann, Damian, editor.
Title: Couples as parents : explorations in couple therapy / edited by Kate Thompson and Damian McCann.
Description: 1 Edition. | New York, NY : Routledge, 2024. | Series: The library of couple and family psychoanalysis | Includes bibliographical references and index.
Identifiers: LCCN 2023055680 (print) | LCCN 2023055681 (ebook) | ISBN 9781032482170 (hardback) | ISBN 9781032482163 (paperback) | ISBN 9781003387947 (ebook)
Subjects: LCSH: Marriage counseling. | Parenting—Psychological aspects. | Families—Psychological aspects.
Classification: LCC HQ734 .C86552 2024 (print) | LCC HQ734 (ebook) | DDC 646.7/8—dc23/eng/20240129
LC record available at https://lccn.loc.gov/2023055680
LC ebook record available at https://lccn.loc.gov/2023055681

ISBN: 978-1-032-48217-0 (hbk)
ISBN: 978-1-032-48216-3 (pbk)
ISBN: 978-1-003-38794-7 (ebk)

DOI: 10.4324/9781003387947

Typeset in Times New Roman
by Apex CoVantage, LLC

We would like to dedicate this book to our parents.

# Contents

# Contributors

**Linsey Blair** is a psychodynamic and psychosexual couple therapist. She is a graduate of Tavistock Relationships, where she also worked as a clinical lecturer and faculty staff. Since relocating to Ireland in 2018, she now works in private practice in Galway and continues to teach, supervise and write.

**Sophie Corke** is a psychodynamic couple and individual psychotherapist. Formerly a broadcast journalist working in international affairs, she trained as an adult psychotherapist at WPF Therapy and as a couple psychotherapist at the Tavistock and Portman NHS Trust. She has worked for over ten years in mental health settings, including the NHS and charities alongside her private practice. She has been involved in organising lectures on current issues in psychoanalytic thinking for the FPC (Foundation for Psychotherapy and Counselling). She is a visiting clinician in TR's parenting and perinatal services and has a special interest in working with couples at transitional stages of their lives such as starting a family and retirement.

**Simon Cregeen** is a child and adolescent psychotherapist and a couple psychoanalytic psychotherapist. Following a long career in NHS CAMHS, he now works in independent practice with adolescents, young adults and couples. He teaches and supervises and has published in the *Journal of Child Psychotherapy* and elsewhere. He is a co-author of *Short-Term Psychoanalytic Psychotherapy with Adolescents with Depression: A Treatment Manual* (Karnac, 2016) and co-editor of *Finding a Way to the Child: Selected Clinical Papers 1983–2021* by Margaret Rustin (Routledge, 2023). He is a trustee of Manchester Psychoanalytic Development Trust (mpdt.org.uk).

**Martha Doniach**, BSc MA, is a psychoanalytic psychotherapist trained to work with individuals and couples. She is a full member of the Foundation for Psychotherapy and Counselling (FPC-WPF) and of the graduate body of Tavistock Relationships, Tavistock Institute of Medical Psychology. She worked for several years in East London NHS Foundation trust in a tier-two specialist psychotherapy adult outpatient service, where she held the position of lead for specialist psychological therapies. At Tavistock Relationships, she is a visiting lecturer and was previously a visiting clinician and worked as a tutor on the MA in psychodynamic counselling and psychotherapy. She also teaches and supervises at the Tavistock and Portman NHS Foundation Trust. She works in full-time private practice in central London. Before qualifying as a psychotherapist, she was a social worker working within Children and Families, Child Protection and CAMHS. She is an accredited member of BPC and UKCP.

**Maria Franchini** has a background as a clinical psychologist and has worked in both statutory and charitable settings. She joined Tavistock Relationships as a group worker and clinical supervisor for the Parents as Partners Programme, a group intervention for couples, which she continues to teach and supervise. She has developed the model Mentalization-Based Therapy for Parenting under Pressure (MBT-PP) and was the clinical lead for implementing and delivering this model while funded by the DWP. She is currently involved in training MBT's skills and providing clinical supervision for MBT interventions within Reducing Parental Conflict projects, including randomised control trails.

**Krisztina Glausius** is a psychoanalytic psychotherapist and a couple psychoanalytic psychotherapist. She works as a visiting supervisor and lecturer at Tavistock Relationships, where she has formerly worked as Head of Clinical Services.

As well as her analytic work with couples and individuals, Krisztina has also developed several innovative approaches ranging from time-limited couple therapy to services providing therapeutic support to adopting parents or conflicted separating couples. She has co-authored papers resulting from these and other projects. She has published guides to support parents who separate as well as for professionals who are looking for ways to understand and work with couples.

She has worked as a senior research psychotherapist on TR's randomised controlled trial examining the effectiveness of its parents in conflict service and was part of the clinical team delivering the Parents in Dispute Project, a mentalization-based intervention aimed at helping high-conflict, separated parental couples to ensure better outcomes for their children. Both of these roles involve a creative application of analytically informed therapeutic work with couples, groups and individuals.

She sees couples and individuals in her private practice in South East London.

**Joanna Harrison** is a senior clinician at Tavistock Relationships, where she originally trained as a psychodynamic couple therapist. Prior to working as a couple therapist, she was a family law solicitor in central London. She has worked within the divorce and separation consultation service at Tavistock Relationships and within the parenting service, where she has a particular interest in working with couples who are separating, and she works with individuals and couples who are separating at the innovative family law firm Family Law in Partnership. She is interested in the potential conflict between couples can have for growth, and her book *5 Arguments All Couples (Need To) Have and Why the Washing Up Matters* was published in September 2022.

**Sarah Ingram** has a background in community development and has worked in both statutory and voluntary sector settings. Before joining Tavistock Relationships, Sarah was Head of Parenting with responsibility for the development and delivery of parenting support for hard-to-reach families. At Tavistock Relationships, Sarah leads the DWP-funded Reducing Parental Conflict Programme, a large programme with a remit to evaluate evidence-based interventions and their impact on reducing parental conflict.

**Sara Leon**, MPsych, MA psychoanalytic observational studies (Tavistock Clinic), MA psychoanalytic couple psychotherapy (Tavistock Relationships), is a psychoanalytic child, adolescent and couple psychotherapist and a psychoanalytic parent-infant psychotherapist (Anna Freud Centre). She worked for over 20 years in the NHS with children with disabilities and their parents, with a particular interest in neonates.

She has taught infant observations for many years. She is currently the clinical lead in the couple's perinatal service at the Tavistock Relationships.

**David Levy** is a family and systemic psychotherapist who worked for many years in the NHS as well as in private practice. Within the NHS, he specialised in community-based child and adolescent mental health, offering training and consultation within GP surgeries, schools and local authority social care. Since 2018, he has worked at Tavistock Relationships in projects developed for health and local authorities, as a trainer, supervisor and clinician.

**Damian McCann**, DSysPsych, is a psychoanalytic couple psychotherapist working at Tavistock Relationships, London; adjunct faculty member of the International Psychotherapy Institute (IPI) Washington, DC; an associate of Queen Anne Street Practice, London; and an editorial board member of Couple and Family Psychoanalysis. He is also a consultant systemic psychotherapist with many years of experience working with children, adolescents and their families. He has a particular interest in working with gender and sexual diversity in psychoanalytic practice and has published and taught widely on this topic. His edited book *Same-Sex Couples and Other Identities: Psychoanalytic Perspectives* was published by Routledge in 2021.

**Mary Morgan** is a psychoanalyst and couple psychoanalytic psychotherapist, fellow of the British Psychoanalytical Society, senior fellow of Tavistock Relationships, honorary member of the Polish Society for Psychoanalytic Psychotherapy and consultant member of the IPA Committee on Couple and Family Psychoanalysis. She worked for more than 30 years at Tavistock Relationships, London, during which time, she was the reader in couple psychoanalysis and head of the MA and professional doctorate in couple psychoanalytic psychotherapy. She has a private analytic practice with individuals and couples and supervises and teaches internationally. Her book *A Couple State of Mind: Psychoanalysis of Couples and the Tavistock Relationships Model* (2019) is available in English, Polish, Russian, Italian and Chinese.

**Marguerite Reid** is a consultant child and adolescent psychotherapist and couple psychoanalytic psychotherapist. She co-founded the perinatal service at Chelsea and Westminster Hospital, where she specialised in perinatal mental health problems. Her doctoral research was in the area of perinatal loss and the mother's experience when she gives birth to the next baby. This research interest followed her work as a child psychotherapist with replacement children. She has taught in the UK and abroad and co-founded the infant observation course in Izmir, Turkey, where she has taught for many years. She has published in the area of perinatal mental health and co-edited with Aleksandra Novakovic, *Couple Stories: Application of Psychoanalytic Ideas in Thinking about Couple Interaction* (2018). She now works in private practice in South Kensington, London.

**Honor Rhodes**, OBE, the strategic adviser and head of consultancy services at Tavistock Relationships, has spent nearly 40 years working with children and families. She is interested in families that live with complicated troubles and what we can do to help best. She worked with Graham Allen to set up the Early Intervention Foundation in 2013 and continues to write practice guides and blogs. These are designed to help frontline staff in local authorities and the NHS think about the importance of couple relationship quality and what they can do to help parents effectively so that every child can thrive, learn and fulfil their potential.

**Colleen M. Sandor** is a psychologist and psychoanalyst in Salt Lake City, Utah, where she is in private practice. She co-founded a master's in mental health counselling program at Westminster College, where she has taught for the last 18 years. Colleen is a faculty member of the International Psychotherapy Institute (IPI) and a teaching analyst for the International Institute for Psychoanalytic Training (IIPT). She is the former co-director of the Salt Lake City chapter of IPI and is currently the co-director of IIPT. Colleen's research and practice focuses on individuals and couples and on work within the LGBTQ community.

**Kate Thompson** is a couple psychoanalytic psychotherapist and senior staff member at Tavistock Relationships with over 20 years experience of therapy with couples and individuals. Currently heading up Couple Therapy for Depression (CTfD) Training of NHS practitioners, Kate leads TR's parenting services, along with Damian McCann. Kate has developed the model behavioural couple therapy for alcohol misuse and delivered the government-funded training to practitioners and adapted CTfD for a perinatal work. Registered with BPC and BACP, Kate writes for a variety of publications; she co-edited *Engaging Couples: New Directions in Therapeutic Work with Families* (Routledge, 2018) and a special edition of *Couple and Family Psychoanalysis on Divorce and*

*Separation* (2021). She is Co-editor in chief of *Journal of Couple and Family Psychoanalysis*. Kate also works in private practice in South West London.

**Sonja Vetter** is a senior psychodynamic couple and individual relationship therapist. She trained at Tavistock Relationships following an MA in social and organisational psychology and a career in research. She works in private practice as well as a visiting clinician across a number of clinical services at Tavistock Relationships, including parenting, mentalization-based couple therapy, divorce and separation and the international online service. Her interest in adolescence is based on personal experience.

**William Walker** is a psychodynamic couple and individual psychotherapist. He also has a background as a clinical social worker, with early experience working in local authorities and CAHMS settings. William has been an expert witness in Royal Courts of Justice Cafcass High Court Team, working on all matters dealing with international private law proceedings and highly conflicted divorce and separated parents. Currently, William is the clinical training lead and special projects manager and staff clinician at Tavistock Relationships. Some of the projects William leads are the Parents as Partners Programme, Mentalization-Based Therapy for Parenting under Pressure (MBT-PP) and the NHS Relationship Support Service.

# Acknowledgements

We would like to thank the editorial board of the Library of Couple and Family Psychoanalysis and, in particular, are grateful to Brett Kahr for his fulsome support and enthusiasm for this book.

We also extend our thanks to our publishers, Routledge, for the production of *Couples as Parents*. We particularly wish to thank Susannah Frearson for all the resource she provided to us and for her endless patience and understanding.

Throughout the process of producing this book, members of Tavistock Relationships' parenting workshop have been in our minds. We have continued to meet weekly to grapple with some of the complex cases the group carries, and we thank them for their unstinting commitment and skill in working with parents referred to the service. Eleanor Heavens, Sonja Vetter, Sara Leon, Sophie Corke, Wendy Meier and Charlotte Kondrup, working alongside us, have helped to clarify and illustrate many of the areas covered in the 14 chapters contained within this book.

Finally, we would like to thank our colleagues at Tavistock Relationships for the 'couple and relational thinking' that happens within the organisation, much of which is reflected within these pages. In particular, we wish to thank TR's CEO, Andrew Balfour, for his support and also Chris Clulow for agreeing to write the foreword which follows.

As co-editors, we have commissioned chapters from across the UK and the States and are eternally grateful to the contributors for their invaluable contribution to what we believe to be an essential resource for professionals and parents alike.

# Series editor's foreword

*Christopher Clulow*

It is a personal as well as professional pleasure for me to write the foreword to this important book about the many challenges associated with combining parenting and partnering roles. All change brings its challenges, but perhaps none so profound as the changes facing couples as they become parents. It is not only the rearrangement of relationship networks that must be accomplished to accommodate new arrivals in the family but also the internal reconfiguration of assumptions about what it means to be a parent, a partner and a child. Some of these assumptions only become evident as the experience of being a parent either conforms with or diverges from what was expected; others remain deeply unconscious yet powerfully influential in fashioning the course of family life.

For this reason, it is appropriate that all the contributors to this volume have an association with Tavistock Relationships, an organisation that throughout its 75-year history has focused attention on understanding and working with unconscious, as well as conscious processes in family relationships. I joined the organisation in 1974, the year in which I first became a parent. Shortly afterwards, I was given the responsibility of leading a team to carry out an action research project related to the impact of a first child on a couple's relationship. In conjunction with health visitors, we ran groups for expectant couples and conducted workshops for the health visitors who were supporting them in the early months after their babies had been delivered (Clulow, 1982). The challenge in both situations was to move beyond a dyadic mindset. For health visitors, and sometimes for new parents, the dyad was a mother and her baby; for couples, the dyad was their relationship, which had to make room for the new arrival. Either way, this new reality shifted the locus of intimacy within families, often creating emotional turbulence for parents when they registered that the changes taking place were not a temporary phenomenon and especially if they resurrected anxieties associated with their own childhood experiences (Clulow, 1991).

As all parents know (and, indeed, all couples who maintain their relationship without children), parenthood usually reconfigures relationships and activities to prioritise a focus on the newly created family unit. As with the personal, so with the professional. One of the unexpected and hugely rewarding consequences of conducting what we referred to as 'the first baby project' was meeting two university professors from the University of California, Berkeley. At that time, they were, like us, completing a programme of researched interventions aimed at supporting couples making the transition into parenthood. From their random controlled trials, they showed that programmes which focused on co-parenting relationships had better outcomes for young children and their parents than those focusing on parent-child relationships (Cowan & Pape Cowan, 2000). Their interventions were in stark contrast to the many parenting programmes that focus exclusively on a (usually) mother's relationship with her child. The Cowans research went on to show the effectiveness of interventions supporting co-parenting when children are older, and their work has received international recognition for demonstrating the value of involving fathers and supporting the parental couple in developing healthy family relationships. Their involvement with the work and staff of Tavistock Relationships has blossomed, and with their support, the organisation has rolled out programmes for parental couples based on their intervention model.

While my interest in the transition to parenthood continued, my attention in the 1980s turned towards investigating the significance of co-parenting for couples whose relationship was ending. While my previous employment had involved preparing welfare reports for judges tasked with deciding on residence and contact arrangements for the children of divorcing parents, I, like many others at the time, were enthusiastic about the emergence of services supporting parents in arriving at their own solutions to disagreements between them over post-divorce arrangements rather than having a judge decide for them. So Tavistock Relationships assembled a team to work as action researchers alongside a London team of family court welfare officers to explore ways of mediating between parents in conflict as part of the process of preparing enquiries for the courts (Clulow & Vincent, 1987). Findings from this and other projects consolidated a conviction long held by clinicians and researchers that what happens between partners has huge significance for the health and wellbeing of all family members.

At a time when family structures and processes have been undergoing radical change, it is easy to underestimate the value of the parental couple or to misunderstand its significance as being a relic from a marriage-obsessed past. What is clear from the contributions to this book is that couples come in many shapes and sizes: co-parenting is no longer (if it ever was) the sole province of women and men married to each other. An increasing number of same-sex partners are parents. When parents are on their own, they may form informal partnerships with family members or friends to manage the responsibilities that children bring. Moreover, the routes into parenthood can be as diverse as the people who have embarked on the journey: assisted conception, adoption and re-partnering are just some of the pathways that pose their own very particular challenges. Along with these variations on a common theme are, of course, children – the third parties whose gender, health, aptitudes and abilities can never be known about in advance. They are active players in the dramas of family life, confronting their parents with differences and similarities which can be at odds with the preconceptions held by their biological and social progenitors. As the years pass, they will test the capacity of their parents to adapt to their changing needs and will expose them not only to the joys associated with the enrichment they bring but also to vulnerability and loss.

It is with this affective dimension of family life that *Couples as Parents* is principally concerned. In accounting for the range of emotions children (and their absence) stir up in parents, the authors adopt developmental and phenomenological perspectives, combining historical and representational contexts with case examples to understand and illustrate central affective themes. What people think is happening to them is more important than any actuality: the meaning attributed to events is more important than the events themselves. Meanings are fashioned from experiences that have taken place during the earliest months and years of life, amended and elaborated upon with the passage of time. As many of these are formed before they can be shared and symbolised, they may remain buried in the dynamic unconscious, finding expression in later life through deeds rather than words. The capacity to reflect – to have the experience *and* understand its meaning – may be limited. Reflective capacities essentially involve having the resources and environment that encourage becoming one's own third party, sitting on one's own shoulder, so to speak, in order not only to perceive oneself as an outsider might but also to put oneself in the shoes of others to know what they might be thinking and feeling.

When the challenges of family life prove too much to bear, reflection can be difficult. Here, we circle back to the significance of the psychological function of the parental couple in containing – through the ability to talk about, respond to and reflect upon – what it is that seems 'too much to bear'. The hardest emotions to contain are those closest to home, and there can be few contenders for this position than the emotions generated by children for their parents. So it is to be expected that there will be times for all parents when things become just too much. The support of family and friends will then be very important. So, too, may be accessing professional help. Because conceptions of adult partnerships tend to be mired in privacy, it can be hard for parents to seek outside help as a couple. For them, it may be that this challenge can be mitigated by seeking help as co-parents rather than as a couple. As long as those offering help keep the couple firmly in mind, there need be no constraint on exploring how relationships may be generating difficult emotions that are contributing to the strain on families and considering ways of ameliorating these pressures.

The contributors to this book consider just this opportunity, providing valuable insights and illustrations that constitute an important resource for parents who are interested in learning from others about how parenthood can affect relationships between partners and the significance of the parental couple for their children, as well as for the many practitioners who work with parents and children in their different roles. Its publication is heralded by two previous publications in the *Library of Couple Psychoanalysis* (Balfour et al., 2012, 2019). As a trio, they encourage and support everyone working with families, however they are defined, to engage constructively with the emotional complexities and conflicts associated with being more than two and, by doing so, offer the possibility of infusing future relationships with the spirit of generosity. My co-editors join me in welcoming this book into the series.

Christopher Clulow, PhD
Series Editor, Library of Couple and Family Psychoanalysis
St Albans, 12th March 2024

## References

Balfour, A., Clulow, C. & Thompson, K. Eds. (2019) *Engaging Couples. New Directions in Therapeutic Work with Couples.* London: Routledge.

Balfour, A., Morgan, M. & Vincent, C. Eds. (2012) *How Couple Relationships Shape our World. Clinical Practice, Research and Policy Perspectives.* London: Routledge.

Clulow, C. (1982) *To Have and to Hold. Marriage, the First Baby and Preparing Couples for Parenthood.* Aberdeen: Aberdeen University Press.

Clulow, C. (1991) Partners becoming parents: A question of difference. *Infant Mental Health Journal* 12(3): 256–266.

Clulow, C. & Vincent, C. (1987) *In the Child's Best Interests. Divorce Court Welfare and the Search for a Settlement.* London: Tavistock Publications/Sweet and Maxwell.

Cowan, C. & Pape Cowan, P. (2000) *When Partners Become Parents. The Big Life Change for Couples.* Hoboken, NJ: Erlbaum (originally published by Basic Books in 1992).

# Introduction

## Kate Thompson and Damian McCann

### Editors

They fuck you up your mum and dad.
They may not mean to, but they do.
They fill you with the faults they had.
And add some extra, just for you.

(Philip Larkin, 2014, The Complete Poems, Faber & Faber)

All parents' couple relationship is at the heart of a child and young person's development. Whether parents live together or apart, their capacity to relate to each other will have far-reaching and profound effects on the children they care for.

This book is, therefore, concerned with understanding the challenges relating to the complex developmental tasks facing all couples as they transition to parenthood and beyond. The decision to create a family and have children is seismic and involves a plethora of emotion for the adults involved, much of which can be contradictory and complex to unravel. This book explores this multiplicity of meanings for parents as it examines the interrelationship between couple and parental functioning, which lies at the core of a fulfilling and well-functioning family life. What we believe is unique about this book is its focus on the specific obstacles facing couples in allowing these two roles, as parents and partners, to co-exist in distinct but related forms.

The chapters in *Couples as Parents* illustrate the key punctuation points for parents as they move towards, into and through parenthood and consider how these intersect with the key junctions in a couple's timeline together. The arrival of children often coincides with career ambitions becoming more achievable for one or both halves of a couple. Raising teenagers on the cusp of a more interdependent lifestyle hits couples as they are contemplating a slowing down and increased dependency on one another. Parents faced with an empty nest are often also confronting the approach of retirement or the fluctuations of menopause. Building on this premise, we have recruited an impressive array of couple psychotherapists and practitioners who provide insights into the ways

DOI: 10.4324/9781003387947-1

in which couples as parents attempt to manage these multiple challenges. The chapters map out the psychological hurdles some parents face, both conscious and unconscious, alongside the joys of raising their children. It also outlines how they must adapt their own intimate relationship alongside and within their role as parents: a developmental feat for which there is no instruction manual or guidebook.

For most couples, their experience of being parented, together with the exposure to their own parents' couple relationship, provide a highly influential template on which to build and shape their subsequent couple and parental relationships. In raising their children, many parents do so in reaction to their own experiences of being parented, whether it be repetition or over-compensation. For instance, for someone who has experienced trauma or abuse as a child, they may find themselves being overprotective, linked to deep-rooted anxieties about harm coming to their child. However, unconsciously, the anxiety references their own neglect, and for their children, this can lead to confusion and problems in their identity development. Understanding the nature of these intergenerational couple and parental dynamics helps couples and parents avoid the repetition and to arrive at their own healthier and bespoke version.

Throughout this book, the authors provide important insights and ideas that will help parents and couples navigate ways out of their problematic and destructive cycles. In this new 'good-enough' parenting landscape, it becomes more possible to reflect Adrian Mitchell's antidote to the bleakness of Larkin's verse.

> *They tuck you up, your mum and dad.*
> *They read you Peter Rabbit too.*
> *They give you all the treats they had*
> *And some extra, just for you.*
>
> (Adrian Mitchell, This Be The Worst in All Shook Up:
> Poems 1997–2000: Blondaxe, 2000)

All of the thinking outlined in this book is a culmination of our work with parents and couples conducted over many years at Tavistock Relationships (TR). During this time, we have been running a parenting service, alongside TR's 'Reducing Parental Conflict' programmes, its divorce and separation service and the clinical service for couples and individuals. The insights gained from our involvement in these different aspects of Tavistock Relationships' work inform much of what is outlined in the many chapters throughout the book. *Couples as Parents* is, therefore, intended to advance understanding and practice of clinical thinking when working with parents within counselling and psychotherapeutic communities, as well as support couples themselves as they gain a better understanding of their role as parents.

The book is divided into four sections. Section one is concerned with the preparation for parenthood and its impact on the couple relationship, whilst section two examines the developmental stages of the child. Section three explores challenges to parenting, and section four focuses on conflicted parents and their children.

The chapters are arranged across these four sections beginning with **Damian McCann** considering the motivation for parenthood and plotting the developmental challenges facing couples through pregnancy, birth and beyond. 'Nothing prepared me for this' provides a particular focus for the exploration of the range of emotions and challenges facing couples as they prepare for parenthood. He also considers the changing nature of intimate family relationships in the context of wider society. Through this expanded lens, he reflects on the importance of more diverse representations of family life, contrasting these with traditional notions of family constellations, with a specific emphasis on the heterosexual conjugal unit, rooted in marriage and co-residence. Challenging the idealisation of motherhood, he focuses attention on the role of the couple relationship and crucially, the importance of the co-parental relationship as they care for their vulnerable infant.

**Mary Morgan** describes the idea of an internal creative couple which she believes is pivotal in the capacity to parent. At the same time, she also acknowledges that children can challenge this internal capacity, as well as stimulate its development. She says that babies and children provoke strong feelings in the adults that care for them and that, at times, these involve intense love, hatred, anxiety, envy, narcissistic wounds, loss and disappointment. The hope is that these states of mind can be processed by finding a place inside in which their child's and their own feelings can be brought together. When this is possible, it can provide containment for the individual, the couple, for the parents and as a consequence, for their children.

**Martha Doniach** believes that assisted reproductive technology (ART) has revolutionised procreation and now offers wide-ranging possibilities for those unable to have children naturally, although she believes that it comes at a cost. Any difficulties are situated within a field shaped by many factors, including the interplay of social expectations and values; the constraints and opportunities created by advancing medical technology; and the psychological capacities of couples and individuals seeking help.

Doniach draws on four distinct themes in which she compares the experiences of same-sex and heterosexual couples, the importance of time as a factor in shaping couples' experience of ART and the impact of loss on the couple and, indeed, on the wider family. She argues for greater awareness and provision of services to help couples and families manage the parenting of children through ART.

**Colleen M. Sandor** suggests that parenting by lesbian and gay couples is still an underrepresented area and one that needs further examination, specifically concerning the challenges when moving into parenthood. While all parents must work out their differences to effectively parent their children, there are many unique factors the gay or lesbian couple faces. Becoming a parent recalls an individual's own experience of being parented, but for the gay and lesbian individual, their developing sexuality during their childhood and subsequent 'coming out' will also affect their parenting efforts.

Sandor also considers the different routes to parenthood for lesbian and gay couples and the outcomes for children raised in such households. Applying link theory, she plots ways in which links are formed and broken as same-sex couples approach parenthood within a heteronormative society.

**Sara Leon** reminds us that infants are exquisitely sensitive and, in their raw, chaotic, emotional states, can reflect and highlight problems inherent in the couple relationship which can present as postnatal depression in one or both partners. In view of this, she has developed a couple's perinatal service at Tavistock Relationships, involving the infant from the outset, from pregnancy until the end of the first year, as the baby's development and mental health take place within the context of the parental relationship.

Drawing on the work of the Anna Freud Parent-Infant Project, psychoanalytic theories and contemporary child development research, Leon outlines clinical approaches to working directly with parents and their infants in the consulting room, as the therapist attempts to secure the base during the perinatal period.

**Sonja Vetter** explores the impact of raising an adolescent on parents and couples. She suggests that a teenager's inevitable developmental pull towards adulthood and push away from it affects every aspect of family life. She plots the child's developmental trajectory from infancy through to adolescence and maps the ways in which it puts parents in touch with their own process of ageing, particularly relevant to the menopause and retirement, and intersects with their own navigation of adolescence well over a decade before. Vetter also describes, in clinical vignettes, the inevitable splits and pressures that occur within the parental couple relationship as they attempt to contain themselves and their children and face the inevitable losses inherent in launching their children out into the wider world.

**Linsey Blair** focuses attention on psychosexual aspects of parenting, emphasising the fundamental relationship between the emotional and sexual, as couples endeavour to accommodate a third into their dynamic. For all three protagonists, oedipal issues and possible struggles are likely to emerge, affecting the parental couple. Blair has this in mind when she explores the disruption caused by the arrival of a baby, as well as the joys. A couple may find themselves grappling with differences around routines, levels of tiredness, changes in libido and in role, all of which can lead to frustration and hurt. Utilising an integrated model, the couples presenting with difficulties are helped to overcome their differences.

**Krisztina Glausius** explores the empty nest syndrome, suggesting that children leaving the parental home ushers in considerable intrapsychic and interpersonal change for the parental couple. 'New fissures can open up and incomplete or botched psychic repairs might not hold when exposed to the sharp light of this new childless reality'. (p. 110). Using the metaphor of falling or flying, she describes couples confronted with new developmental challenges and draws attention to the central importance of reflective functioning within their relationship. The empty nest couple can confuse their newfound busyness with liveliness. The newly descending quiet can feel deadly and is often likened to a bereavement. Letting go ultimately requires considerable internal resource but can also represent opportunity for growth and development for the couple relationship.

**Marguerite Reid** examines the impact of perinatal loss on the couple and for the next generation. Reflecting on the layers of emotional experience in the context of the death of a baby, we learn that it is essential that couples have opportunities to discuss their losses. She describes couples unable to talk to one another as they come to terms with their grief and are unlikely to mourn at similar paces or in the same way. Reid describes how self-blame or blame of the other may need working through, as well as feelings of guilt and isolation. Attention is also focused on the birth of the next baby following the loss and the impact the shadow of unprocessed trauma can cast, leaving subsequent children feeling somehow wrong or haunted.

**Simon Cregeen** considers the nature of parenting in the context of adoption. He suggests that a common feature in work with adoptive parents is the presence of shame and guilt, leading to blame being projected into the other. This relates to the idea of persecutory guilt associated with a failure to repair the damage their adoptive children suffered in their original care settings. The pressure of getting it right may lead to conflict between the couple or their holding the adoptive child responsible for the disturbance. Adoptive couples need support to mourn an imagined 'ordinary' family experience with all its privileges and joys, linked to their determined efforts to conceive and possible miscarriages they have suffered, to enable more creative relating within the family.

**Kate Thompson,** in thinking about parents raising a child with a disability, suggests that it is the lifelong nature of loss that parents of disabled children need to process whilst living alongside its source, which creates the threat to their couple relationship. She also suggests that the reaction to their child of friends and family may cause a narcissistic injury from which it is hard to recover. Focusing for the most part on children with autistic spectrum disorder, it seems that parents of these children often lack confidence in their parenting and experience greater marital distress. For instance, splits may appear in which one parent becomes the expert in the care of the child, leaving their partner redundant or incompetent. Exploring the many facets of raising a disabled child, it seems that arriving at a place of acceptance can bring richness to families and secure the boundary around the couple relationship.

**Sophie Corke** addresses the all-too-familiar parental 'good cop – bad cop' phenomenon around the management of and relationship with children. These are parents, sometimes separated, who feel trapped in rigid roles with each angrily asserting their view of what is best for their children. These roles often hark back to the parent's own experience of being parented, and in the fight that ensues, there is a danger that they lose sight of their child's particular need. Corke maintains that couples who understand the role their own childhoods are playing in the setting up of one parent as right and the other wrong are able to relinquish their defensive roles embodied in the 'good cop – bad cop' split and recognise their own child's identity, separate to their own.

Authors **Rhodes, Walker, Franchini, Ingram and Levy** outline a home-based mentalisation approach to therapy for parents under pressure. Focusing on the story of Marie and Peter, it details the preliminaries of setting up the initial individual and joint meeting, describing how Marie and Peter's arguments had escalated from shouting to pushing and shaking each other. The authors illustrate how they engaged the parents by hearing their respective background histories, helping them understand the links between them, as well as thinking about how their conflictual couple dynamic impacts their children. Using this model, the worker taps into a seam where both parents agree that their children deserve parents who can agree to work together. A variety of techniques were subsequently utilised to support them in their wish to repair the damage and promote their children's wellbeing.

**Joanna Harrison** explores the challenges that couples face in the context of separation and divorce. She believes that although most parents wish to protect their children, they are unable to manage the emotional fallout of their split and lose sight of their children in the ensuing fight. She argues for time to process the end of their relationship at a deeper level in order to be freed up enough to work together. It is also suggested that financial aspects of divorce dwarf the emotional and psychological consequences, and professionals need help to think about the complex assault, in all areas of their lives, that separating couples face. Focus is placed on talking to children about separation, introducing a new partner and discussing matters with wider family and how separated parents might manage the practicalities of shared parenting.

# Part 1

# Preparation for parenthood

# Chapter 1

# *All Change, All Change!*
## Couples responding to the transition to parenthood

## Damian McCann

## Introduction

*"Nothing prepared me for this"*.

The aforementioned quotation relates to a mother's reflections after having her first child, a statement that not only reflected her own state of mind but also that of her partner, who also struggled with the transition to parenthood. It also reflects my interest in writing this opening chapter, relating to working with couples both before and during the transition to parenthood, as well as an appreciation of the extent to which this crucial developmental stage affects not only couple functioning but also the couple's capacity to parent a dependent infant.

I have been surprised by the number of couples whose long-standing difficulties within their couple relationship date to the birth of a baby. Some couples who present with a range of conflict or issues relating to intimacy and despair appear to have their roots in the birth of their first or subsequent children, some ten or even 20 years earlier. Therefore, understanding the nature of parenthood and its impact on the couple relationship is crucial if we are to support couples with the challenges they face during this period of change. This is especially so given the impact the decision to have a child, the pregnancy, the birth, and beyond can have on an otherwise happily functioning couple relationship.

In this chapter, I will examine aspects of the steps to parenthood, from conception through to the birth of a baby. Although for many the journey runs smoothly, for others, there may be hidden obstacles or challenges that threaten to derail the much-anticipated joyful event and which leave the parental couple in complete disarray. Understanding the nature of couple relating during the transition to parenthood provides a particular focus for this chapter, as does the impact of the child on the couple's own relationship. Observations from clinical and literary case examples will be used to highlight emerging themes and to provide a deeper understanding of the kinds of difficulties couples may encounter along the way.

DOI: 10.4324/9781003387947-3

## The desire to become a parent

For many couples, the decision to try for a baby is one that is both conscious and shared. For others, however, the decision is much less clear and may even be a source of serious conflict between partners. Carolyn Pape Cowan and Philip Cowan in their book entitled *When Partners Become Parents* (1992) outline what happens to couple relationships based on the accounts of 96 men and women recruited to their ten-year longitudinal study. As part of their study, they were interested in exploring the question "To Be or Not to Be a Parent", and whilst recognising that the decision to have a baby will be a positive experience, nevertheless, it may also put pressure on the intimate couple relationship and, for some, may even result in separation or divorce. That said, the Cowans believe that the seeds of new parents' marital problems are sown long before the birth of their first baby. Therefore, it appears that couples who can work together to manage the challenges that the transition to parenthood poses fare much better than those who are already experiencing strains within their relationships prior to the pregnancy. However, it is also the case that becoming parents increases their resourcefulness and capacity to manage together, although, according to Cowan et al. (1985), there is sufficient evidence to suggest that having a baby increases the likelihood of conflict and disagreement between partners. In other words, *"the prospect of children does not always have a unifying effect upon couples. It can be threatening and unsettling"* (Clulow, 2009, p. 4).

Returning to the question of the motivation for parenthood, the Cowans (1992) helpfully outline four distinct patterns comparing those regarded as *"planners"* with *"acceptance-to-fate couples"*, *"ambivalent couples"*, and *"yes-no couples"*. It is suggested that couples that can plan together are more able to actively consider the question of becoming parents and reach a joint agreement. *Acceptance-to-fate couples, on the other hand*, can accept and are pleasantly surprised by the news of their pregnancy, whereas *ambivalent couples* struggle with mixed feelings regarding parenthood, with one often being more disposed than the other, or both moving towards and then away from the decision. It is also suggested that the ambivalence these couples feel may well pervade other aspects of their relationship which is then played out in the decision to try for a baby. That said, when these couples can tolerate their own and their partner's mixed feelings, it seems to increase the possibility of them eventually coming to a joint resolution. For the *yes-no couples*, there is strong, unresolved conflict about becoming a family which can continue well into the pregnancy and which unsurprisingly creates further tensions within the couple's relationship as they strive to resolve their differences.

There is more than a suggestion in the Cowans' study that for many couples the motivation for parenthood is to a greater or lesser extent shaped by the quality of the parenting the partners themselves received. Whilst for some, the decision not to have children seemed to be directly related to what happened to them when young, others with similarly troubled background histories had a stronger desire to repair the damage by creating happier homes for their own children. They also found that the most frequent reason both men and women gave for becoming a parent was *"a desire for an intimate and special relationship with their children"* (p. 36). However, when that desire is frustrated by infertility or traumatic loss during pregnancy or conflict that arises in the context of parenting their child, these couples will inevitably experience distress which, if not properly processed, may lead to further difficulties within their relationship and will undoubtedly impact their capacity to parent.

A further consideration, and one that may also be influenced by the partners own experience of family life, is the question of how many children they wish to have. Although this may be dependent on available resources, it might also be influenced by the couple's own experience as siblings which then informs the size and shape of the family they wish to create together. In addition, the decision may also be based on the birth mother's experience of her first pregnancy as well as the stresses and strains that having a child exerts on the couple relationship itself.

## Pregnancy

*"She looked at him and smiled secretly. She was all secrets now she was pregnant, secrets and little silences that seemed to have meaning. She was pleased with herself, and she complained about things that didn't matter. And she demanded services of Connie that were silly, and both of them knew they were silly. Connie was pleased with her too, and filled with wonder that she was pregnant. He liked to think he was in on the secrets she had. When she smiled slyly, he smiled slyly too, and they exchanged confidences and whispers. The world had drawn close around them, and they were in the centre of it, or rather Rose of Sharon was in the centre of it with Connie making a small orbit about it. Everything they said was a kind of secret."*

(Steinbeck, 1939, p. 150)

Steinbeck's rich description of the centripetal pull of Connie and Rose of Sharon's shared experience of pregnancy seems to evoke Stern's (1985) ideas concerning attunement, which, according to Seigel (2017) occurs *"when we allow our own internal state to shift, to come to resonate with the inner world of another"*. The couple's preoccupation is a necessary part of the inner orientation that reflects the close bonding and cohesion that accompanies a pregnancy and their readiness for the new. It contrasts perfectly with the centrifugal force often associated with something more outward looking and disruptive, where, as Combrink-Graham (1985) suggests, the developmental focus is on tasks that emphasise personal identity and autonomy, as in adolescence, midlife, and retirement. As a consequence, the external family boundary is loosened, old family structures are dismantled, and distance between family members typically increases. The importance of these forces, for couples in the transition to parenthood, concerns the question of whether the two individuals are on similar or different trajectories. This is especially important since the disruption caused when they are not aligned may account for the stresses and strains that beset the couple relationship as they prepare for parenthood. In other words, whilst pregnancy has the potential to unite, it also has the potential to divide (Clulow, 2009).

## Case example

Daisy and Henry are an unmarried couple in their mid-20s who have been together for the past two years. They met on a 'singles' holiday and are both independently minded and ambitious. Their pregnancy wasn't planned; it was apparently a drunken mistake, and although they considered a termination, they decided to go ahead with the pregnancy. Three months later, Daisy was in great distress. She accused Henry of completely ignoring her and of tuning out. Daisy complained that Henry was out at least three nights a week. Defensively, he accused her of being unreasonable and that these were all business-related dinners that he couldn't avoid. The more Daisy complained, the more Henry seemed to distance himself.

Clearly, Daisy and Henry were confronted with the impact of their decision to have a baby and the demands that pregnancy has not just on the prospective mother but also on the couple relationship itself. Unlike Rose of Sharon and Connie, Daisy and Henry were struggling to hold their couple connection and appeared to be in completely different states of mind. Both were dismayed to find themselves in parallel universes, as Daisy began the process of preparing for motherhood whilst Henry's 'business-as-usual stance' protected him from the reality of the changes that were afoot. Although the couple appeared to be on very different trajectories, they seemed to share the psychological anxieties that pregnancy can evoke. For instance, Daisy was feeling overwhelmed with the changes to her body; nausea doesn't fit well with the demands of her high-powered job. She had also noticed a shift in her relationship with her friends who continued to party hard whilst she had stopped drinking alcohol altogether and was more concerned with preserving energy. From the day they discovered she was pregnant, Daisy had assumed that Henry would be alongside her but increasingly felt that he was in complete denial about what is happening. Henry furiously disputed Daisy's take on his position and instead purported to being there for her whilst accusing her of being unreasonable in her demands. He described how at weekends, he had let her lie in bed and had cooked breakfast, whilst Daisy complained that as soon as breakfast was over, Henry had rushed off to football with his mates and she would return to bed. The sense of Daisy's isolation and loneliness, compounded by the absence of sexual intimacy, contrasted with Henry's active lifestyle which afforded the couple very little shared excitement in the transition to parenthood. Instead, they appeared to be getting further and further apart.

As therapists, thinking with the couple about what was happening to them, whilst also attending to Daisy's obvious fear of how the baby would alter the life she had known and loved, and speaking to Henry's sense of being on the run, allowed for the possibility of attending to the couple's shared underlying anxieties. In that regard, they were both more able to connect with the questions and phantasies which the pregnancy had posed for them: fears that the pregnancy had come too soon and whether they could really make the necessary adjustments in their single independent lives to accommodate a baby. Would they be able to hold onto their couple relationship, which was still very much in the making when Daisy found herself pregnant? To a large extent, Daisy and Henry's presentation epitomises one of the central themes of this book, namely, the struggle that individuals have in becoming a couple and then finding the space within the couple relationship to accommodate an actual third in the form of a baby. In common with most couples, Daisy and Henry were embroiled in the hidden challenges that the decision to transition to parenthood poses for all couples. In many respects, for Daisy and Henry, the pregnancy represented the birth of a baby, but symbolically, it signified the birth of the couple relationship itself.

## The birth

Although the birth of a baby is indeed a cause for celebration and a time when extended family and friends may provide a supportive presence, it can also be a time of heightened conflict between partners and when both may be particularly vulnerable to depression. Furthermore, mothers who do not have a supportive partner or network may struggle to give the baby the best start in life. Winnicott (1964) believes that fathers (partners) provide *"elbow room"* for the mother, in that they protect the mother from having to turn outwards at a time when there is a need to turn inwards, towards the baby. Winnicott goes on to say:

> *"If human babies are to develop eventually into healthy, independent, and society-minded adult individuals, they absolutely depend on being given a good start, and this good start is assured in nature by the existence of the bond between the baby's mother and the baby, the thing called love."*

(Winnicott, ibid, p. 17)

Starting a family has the potential to revitalise the couple relationship since having a baby affords the couple new opportunities for shared insights and more collaborative ways for dealing with the associated challenges. This in turn may promote feelings of maturity and wellbeing (Cowan, 1988), possibly linked to the fulfilment of their common goal (Clulow, 2009). For some, however, the decision, either consciously or unconsciously, may be designed to save the couple relationship or marriage, although Cowan and Cowan (1992) suggest that *"When husbands give in reluctantly and resentfully to having a child in order to preserve the marriage, the child and marriage may be at risk"* (p. 47).

Continuing with the theme of starting a family, the quote at the beginning of the chapter, *"Nothing prepared me for this"* is best thought of as *"Nothing prepared us for this"*, and with that in mind, couples may experience difficulties regarding their individual and shared expectations. Examples of this are whether to and for how long to leave their baby to cry if there is no obvious cause for such distress, questions concerning where the baby sleeps, and ideas about the couple having a dedicated time for their own relationship. A further source of tension between couples following the birth of a baby concerns the issue of who does what around the home when one of the partners may be returning from a hard day's work away from the home only to then be faced with a demanding baby and an exhausted partner. Essentially, all these issues rely on the parental couple being able to collaborate. This distinguishes couples who can create the conditions for shared development from a more defensive and fractious coupling, which often leads to troubled parenting. It, therefore, comes as a surprise in the context of parenting when *"Men and women who were used to anticipating and mastering the complexities of demanding jobs and intimate relationships are overwhelmed by their unexpected and contradictory feelings"* (Cowan & Cowan, 1992, p. 76).

Another aspect of pregnancy and birth that may affect the parental couple relationship relates to the phantasies that one or either partner may have towards the baby. Here, I am thinking about the idealised child and the disappointment that ensues when that child doesn't meet parental expectations. Strout (2021) perfectly captures this unspoken truth when William and Lucy are out to dinner together. *"William, who had really said remarkably little since the baby had been born, said to me that night. You know, Lucy, I think I would have felt better if she had been a boy"*. And Lucy thinks, *"It was as though something dropped deep inside of me, and I did not say anything about it. But I have always remembered that. At the time I thought, Well, at least he is being honest"* (p. 56). Clearly, William's honesty was difficult for Lucy to hear and, whereas Connie and Rose of Sharon could share the secrets and mystery surrounding their pregnancy, William's secret wish to have a boy was potentially divisive and had not been shared between them.

When partners become parents, there is a requirement for a healthy balance between the individual needs of the partners, attention to the couple relationship itself, and the obvious need for parents as partners to provide the necessary care for their dependent infant. Slippage in any one of these domains often spells trouble for all concerned. I am reminded of a situation that happened some years ago whilst sitting outside a café quietly having a drink. Suddenly, a mother pushing her new-born arrived at the café and began loudly berating her partner, who was happily drinking with his mates and who clearly did not welcome the intrusion. As the mother forcefully communicated her outrage, which to me felt more like a call for help, the partner, perhaps embarrassed by the confrontation, turned to his mates, saying, *"You see what I have to put up with?"* Understandably, this response only served to increase his partner's rage towards him, especially as she demanded his return home. In this scenario, the parental couple were nowhere to be seen, as the only available response from each of the partners was to attack the other and to undermine or deny the reality of their situation. In circumstances like this, the ensuing dynamic often creates further conflict and distress which, in turn, negatively impacts the couple's ability to hold and contain the needs of the vulnerable baby. As that baby grows and continues to be caught in the crossfire of his parents ongoing conflict and disturbance, it is the child who suffers the consequence of this failure on the part of his parents to provide the necessary environment for his future development. Fisher (1999) reminds us that "*It is the children who are hostage to the destructive narcissism of their parents. It hovers in the background of our work with many couples*" (p. 5).

Another obvious challenge for the parental couple involves the management of the triangular dynamics between partners and their baby. Tensions concerning inclusion and exclusion are bound to emerge, often associated with Oedipal issues. However, it might also be possible that in the triangular dynamics of the parental couple's relationship with their new-born that the father's behaviour towards the mother may be a conscious or unconscious attack on the child, who is felt to be a threat to his position alongside his wife. Put simply, the mother and the baby couple-up, leaving the father feeling excluded. Taken to its extreme, as in Shakespeare's *A Winter Tale*, we see Leontes "*suffer a kind of jealousy and doubts*" (Fisher, ibid, p. 1), where, in his mind, he feels betrayed by the thought that the baby is not his but rather that of his best friend. The consequences of such states of mind regarding the position of the third in the couple's relationship may have equally disturbing consequences to that which befell Leontes and his wife, Hermione, who is imprisoned and subsequently dies from the shock and horror of the events that befell her. Afterall, the mother and baby have already coupled-up in the womb, and whilst forming the special bond, it is perhaps not inconceivable that the extruded other feels that a betrayal has already taken place and one that threatens his exclusive relationship with his wife and to that extent, the couple relationship itself. In this state of mind, the father may manage the betrayal through his rejection of the child.

## Case example

Harry and his wife, Eleanor, present for therapy three weeks after the birth of their son, Jamie. They were both in a terrible state, following the discovery that Harry had begun an affair six weeks into Eleanor's pregnancy. Eleanor could not believe that Harry would have done this to her and was understandably shocked and enraged. Harry was also understandably full of remorse and tried to reassure Eleanor that the affair was over. He said that he had no idea why he found himself turning to his co-worker (the other woman) other than to say that she was very attentive to his concerns relating to the change in Eleanor's moods and her relationship towards him. Eleanor admitted that she had become totally preoccupied with the longed-for pregnancy and felt that her mood swings and hostility towards Harry were the result of hormonal changes. Nevertheless, when asked why Harry had not discussed his concerns with Eleanor, he said that he was frightened of further upsetting her, whilst at the same time admitting that he was resentful of the way in which Eleanor was treating him, feeling rejected and pushed out.

Nathans (2012) in her paper *Infidelity as manic defence* locates the focus of the infidelity on the difficulty that partners may have with mourning past or impending losses, seeing the consequent infidelity as a manic attempt, for example, to replace anxiety or psychic pain with excitement. As previously stated, all couples in the throes of pregnancy and through the birth and beyond, there are developmental challenges that must be confronted as they attempt to make the necessary adjustments towards creating a space for the baby whilst also encountering disturbing thoughts, feelings, and behaviours. For Harry and Eleanor, changes were afoot which could not be thought about. As therapists, according to Fisher (ibid), we must try to help them to think about their experience. *"It is when you care – and I mean care deeply – about my truth, and I care – care deeply – about your truth, that we cannot simply ignore the consequences of our conflicting realities"* (Fisher, 1999, p. 41).

Fisher, in *The Uninvited Guest*, talks about the process of *"emerging from narcissism towards marriage"* (p. 1). With Harry and Eleanor, we might ask who or what exactly is the uninvited guest. Is it the pregnancy and the subsequent changes affecting Eleanor's body, mind, and behaviour? Is it Harry's struggle to tolerate the dynamic changes in the couple relationship? Or is it the actual introduction of the other woman? In thinking further about Fisher's ideas concerning narcissism and marriage, he says:

> *"By marriage, I mean to emphasise the passion for and dependence on the intimate other. By narcissism, on the other hand, I do not mean a preoccupation with the self, a kind of self-love. Rather, I mean to point to a kind of object relating in which there is an intolerance for the reality, the independent existence of the other, but a longing for another who is perfectly attuned and responsive, and thus not a genuine other at all."*
>
> (p. 1/2)

One could, therefore, suppose that the arrival of a baby constitutes a fundamental challenge for the couple in terms of maintaining their link and managing the tensions related to the longing for oneness alongside the need to escape, which relationally invokes feelings of abandonment in one or the other.

Ultimately, the significance of the triangular nature of the 'Oedipus complex' is the challenge for couples in sustaining a shared *"psychic space"* (Britton, 2004). This is related to one's capacity to understand another's point of view, whilst also holding onto one's own point of view and, through the interaction, creating the possibility of something shared. However, the capacity to achieve this level of functioning is believed to reside in the constant working through of Oedipal dynamics, from childhood and beyond. Therefore, how adults as children were helped to manage their own Oedipal longings, in terms of inclusion and exclusion regarding their own parent's couple relationship, informs the management of the Oedipal dynamics at play with their child. Nathans (ibid) suggests that *"If the child is able to accept the reality of the parental couple and tolerate being excluded from this dyad"* (p. 170), this creates the possibility of the child being able to manage inclusion, exclusion, and intimacy in an adult couple/parental relationship.

Unfortunately, with the arrival of the baby, the couple may struggle with the complexity of the needs of all three (i.e., the individual partners/parents, the couple, and the baby). Returning to Harry and Eleanor, and eight months into the therapy, baby Jamie remains in the couple's bed, a source of comfort for Eleanor and an irritation for Harry. In exploring this further with the couple, Eleanor explains that she cannot bear to hear Jamie cry when she is not close to him, whereas Harry is clear in his mind that Jamie needs to be in his own room "*so that we can get back to being a couple again*". The therapist framed their difference as a shared developmental challenge that they needed to resolve both for themselves and their son. After all, in common with many couples faced with transitioning their baby to his or her own room, Harry and Eleanor would be on hand and responsive to Jamie's distress in the night if he became unsettled. In essence, the couple may be depriving both themselves, as well as Jamie, of the reality of the couple as a separate but supportive presence in his life. To some extent, this touches on the much bigger question concerning the parent's confidence in knowing how to parent and the fears and phantasies that they may be getting it wrong.

## The idealisation of motherhood and unconscious hatred

Whilst accepting the obvious shifts in cross-gendered couple relationships and the increasing presence of fathers in their children's lives, according to Weldon (2004), "*Women are expected to carry out the difficult and responsible task of motherhood without having much, if any, emotional preparation for it*" (p. 17/18).

Weldon emphasises the mother's responsibility to raise healthy and stable babies with the capacity to adapt to external demands. Yet if we cast our minds back to the scene outside the café, the mother in that couple was literally left holding the baby while her partner sat, drinking with his mates, oblivious to her distress. In such a scenario, where the split between the parents is such that mothers are left shouldering the responsibility not only for the development of their baby but also for the parental couple relationship itself, it is hardly surprising that the tensions inherent in this situation can give way to conflict. In these moments, the idealisation of motherhood, as reflected in the iconic images of Duccio and da Vinci's *Madonna and Child*, is suddenly shattered.

Weldon's thesis is that mothers (and for that matter fathers) own experience of being parented play a crucial role in shaping their response to the demands of parenthood. For some, there will be an unconscious enactment of the trauma and hurt that blighted their own childhoods which, at worst, produces "*a terrible sense of despair, despondency and inadequacy* (which) *can easily turn into hatred and revenge directed at the new baby*" (Weldon, ibid, p. 18). In her foreword to Weldon's book, Juliet Mitchell reminds us that "*The source of both male and female perversion may lie in a disturbed infant/mother relationship*" (p. iii). However, for women, the internalisation and embodiment of the abused, neglectful, and depriving mother comes to life through the birth of the baby. This may arise because "*The hatred one is identified with and lies thus within or in the baby who extends the self as once the perverse woman was her own mother's extension*" (p. iii). This repeated pattern can create an undercurrent that threatens to pull the mother into a state of madness. Consequently, allowing ourselves to be drawn into these murky waters of hatred for the object, especially that of a vulnerable baby, is something unthinkable, something unbearable, yet we know that some mothers and, for that matter, fathers harbour such thoughts and feelings that threaten the whole basis of the conscious contract. To manage, couples must make space for the presence of hatred or intolerance towards their baby, without resorting to destructive acting out.

## Case example

Jenny and Richard, an unmarried couple, had both experienced trauma regarding their mothers. Jenny's mother, for some unexplained reason, was rejecting and cruel towards her. She had little or no tolerance for Jenny and would attach cruel attributions of meaning to things Jenny said or did at home. On one occasion, Jenny was a few minutes late for Sunday lunch, resulting in her mother accusing her of being ungrateful, ordering her out of the dining room, and binning her dinner. Jenny remained hungry for the rest of the day. Jenny's father was nowhere to be seen, and her mother's hatred reigned supreme. Richard, on the other hand, lost his mother when he was a baby, and her absence was felt acutely by him throughout his life. His father never remarried and used his sister's support to care for Richard and his older brother.

When Richard and Jenny met and fell in love, they both longed to have children. Essentially, they were determined to rewrite history and provide for their children in a way that they felt had not been possible for them as children. The pregnancy went well, and the couple had a beautiful, healthy daughter, whom they named Lottie. Although Richard had some paternity leave, he eventually had to return to work. At that point, Jenny was suddenly exposed to an anxious and uncomfortable feeling relating to their daughter. It seems that Lottie could not settle well, and Jenny experienced her daughter's persistent crying as both persecutory and infuriating. At one stage, Jenny shut Lottie in another room and tried to ignore her. Jenny's sense of isolation did little to disrupt the mounting and disturbing feelings she was experiencing towards Lottie. Although Jenny knew that she needed help, she was also ashamed of what she was feeling, and Richard remained unaware of what was really going on. In fact, Richard derived enormous contentment in knowing that his daughter had the doting and loving mother she needed, whereas Jenny's increasing hatred towards Lottie was beginning to drive her towards madness.

Things came to a head when Jenny could no longer endure Lottie's crying and found herself worrying that she might shake or throw Lottie into her cot. In floods of tears, she called Richard, saying that she would have to leave, as she feared harming Lottie. In that moment, Richard was faced with the shattering of his illusion of the idealised mother and the prospect of his own daughter being left as he had been, leaving him, like his father, to manage alone. Thankfully, after Jenny's admission, the local perinatal service stepped in and helped to stabilise the situation. Part of the therapeutic work with Jenny and Richard was helping them to think about the ways in which their past traumas had been activated through the birth of Lottie and how this was playing out between them. This included the necessary links to be made to their own childhood experiences to help them begin the process of grieving their respective losses. Through this work, they were able to use their couple resource, and Lottie began to settle and thrive.

## The gendered politics of family

In the spirit of *"All Change, All Change!"* it seems fitting to reflect more generally on the changing nature of intimate family relationships in the context of wider society. Whilst drawing on traditional notions of family that emphasise the heterosexual conjugal unit, rooted in marriage and co-residence (Silva & Smart, 1999) and whose purpose is *"to inculcate proper values in children"* (Morgan, 1995; Phillips, 1997, cited by Silva & Smart, p. 1), it seems imperative to also consider the diverse nature of parenting that has entered the public sphere. Changes concerning the nature of employment and the role of men within families constitutes an obvious reference point relating to developments in family life, but it is still the case that women continue to play a disproportionate role regarding childcare and the running of the family home. This appears to be in marked contrast to the parenting practices of some same-sex parental couples which reflect more egalitarian arrangements between lesbian mothers and their gay father counterparts. It might suggest that there is a greater commitment by same-sex parental couples towards the idea of 'doing family' rather than simply 'being family', involving a more overt and active participation in the creation of the family as a unit. According to Silva and Smart (ibid), these everyday experiments in family practices have thus begun to challenge the normative structures of family life.

Golombok (2015) reminds us:

> *"The traditional nuclear family of a heterosexual married couple with biologically related children is now in the minority. Instead, a growing number of children are raised by cohabiting, rather than married parents, by single parents, by stepparents and by same-sex parents, with many children moving in and out of these different family structures as they grow up."*

> (p. 1/2)

This shift, in terms of cohabiting, rather than marriage, could suggest that it is the child who sometimes replaces marriage as the symbol of commitment (Clulow, personal communication).

A further development relating to children and parenting is that referred to as *"Elective co-parenting families"* meaning two (or more parents) who are not or never have been in a romantic relationship having a child together, a phenomenon that is becoming more common amongst cisgender heterosexual parents (Bower-Brown et al., 2023). It seems that a key motivation for undertaking such an arrangement is that it ensures that the child will have both a mother and a father who are biologically related. *"Although co-parenting was generally considered a second-choice route to parenthood, participants aimed to approach co-parenting in a considered manner, choosing co-parents based upon shared values and managing their relationship with trust and respect*". However, although elective co-parenting appeared to offer participants the opportunity of liberating more traditional notions of parenthood, nevertheless, they experienced tensions in "*reproducing and modernising the traditional family*". For instance, participants seem to have replicated the gendered patterns of parenting seen in traditional heterosexual parental couple relationships, with mothers assuming primary responsibility for parental decisions, whilst the fathers represented a more symbolic presence with more limited involvement day to day. That said, it is the case that the more familiar parental couple relationship is being challenged and expanded.

In the context of these more radical developments in family life, one researcher asks the question, "*Who needs a father?*" (Donovan, 2000). In her paper, Donovan examines the negotiation of biological fatherhood in British lesbian families using self-insemination, which raises fundamental questions concerning the nature of parenthood in same-sex couple relationships using sperm from anonymous donor fathers. At issue is the question of the role of fathers in children's lives when the child already has a parental couple in the form of the biological mother and her female partner. Yet the privileging of heteronormativity raises questions concerning the apparent need of a cross-gendered parental couple to secure the child's development, despite convincing evidence that children raised in same-sex households are no different from children growing up with heterosexual parents in terms of psychological adjustment or gender development (Patterson, 2004). In many respects, this testifies to the reality of the family as a unit embedded in and influenced by other social institutions and public policy debates about what appropriately constitutes family. At the time of writing, Giuffrida (2023) highlights moves by Italy's conservative government to stop the registration of children born overseas to same-sex couples using surrogacy or IVF. Unsurprisingly, this move has been condemned by the European Parliament since it constitutes an obvious attempt to restrict LGBTQ+ rights.

Further developments in parenting regarding fluidity of gender and sexuality are embodied in a recent article by Hogan (2023), involving a heterosexual couple in Ireland who are challenging assumptions concerning the gender of their baby. Interestingly, the couple have decided not to gender their child, preferring instead to use the pronoun 'they'. The thinking behind this decision relates to a wish not to limit or direct their child's choices, preferring instead to create a space where the child in time will decide the gender that is right for them. However, in thinking about the contemporary issues confronting parental couples in what Smart and Silva refer to as 'everyday experiments in living', it seems important to recognise the tensions relating to the interiority of the family and its negotiation with the external world, consisting of the extended family, friends, institutions, and public policy. With that in mind, Hogan suggests that the couple recognise the need to negotiate their wish not to gender their baby with, for instance, childcare systems that rely on knowing the gender of the child. Progressive as this is, I would imagine many parents feeling uncomfortable with the radical stance this couple is taking. No doubt, it will also raise questions and anxieties about the potential impact of their decision on the baby's development. This all seems a far cry from Winnicott's cosy notion of the portrayal of the mother and baby in some sort of cocoon with the father providing a supportive presence in the form of *"elbow room"*. Here, we see two parents actively engaged in the construction of parenting and the redefinition of family in the context of gender.

## Conclusion

*Becoming a parent can be a time of extreme emotional turbulence. Couples can find themselves lost in familiar places, caught in the grip of feelings that sometimes renders them strangers to themselves and each other.*

(Clulow, 2009, p. 12)

In this chapter, I have examined the nature and impact of the transition to parenthood from the moment of conception and the pregnancy through to the birth and beyond. Although for many couples, the transition runs smoothly, for others, there may be unexpected obstacles and challenges that cut deep into the couple's resources and which expose vulnerabilities in their capacity to maintain their crucial link that will ultimately support their child's development.

Whilst there are obvious tensions within the family unit as partners become parents, this is also set against the backdrop of other narratives, some that emphasise traditional notions of family and more contemporary readings of becoming and performing family. Ultimately, babies need committed caregivers, as this will secure their wellbeing and development. In my view, there is no one right way of ensuring a positive outcome in that regard. Partners as parents come in many guises, such as those who are married and cohabiting; pairings across generations that include, for example, mothers and grandmothers; and reconstituted pairings as well as lesbian and gay parents, where the child may have any number of different parental couplings. Also, those parents we are beginning to see who are approaching the parenting task differently by, for instance, questioning the bedrock nature of gender and sexuality. Essentially, we all live in challenging but exciting times, and it will, therefore, be interesting to see how these new experiments in living and the myriad ways of doing family bear fruit for future generations.

## References

Bower-Brown, S., Foley, S., Jadva, V., & Golombok, S. (2023). *Grappling with tradition: The experiences of cisgender, heterosexual mothers, and fathers in elective co-parenting arrangements.* www.tandfonline.com/doi/full/10.1080/13229400.2023.2209060

Britton, R.S. (2004). Subjectivity, objectivity and triangular space. *Psychoanalytic Quarterly, 73*(1), 47–61.

Clulow, C. (2009). *Becoming parents together: Ten things to hold in mind when working with new parents (and then some . . .).* London: Tavistock Centre for Couple Relationships, Practitioner Pamphlets.

Combrink-Graham, L. (1985). A developmental model for family systems. *Family Process, 24*(2), 139–150.

Cowan, C.P. (1988). Working with men becoming fathers: The impact of a couples group intervention. In P. Bronstein & C. P. Cowan (Eds.), *Fatherhood today: Men's changing role in the family* (pp. 276–298). Hoboken, NJ: John Wiley & Sons.

Cowan, C.P., & Cowan, P.A. (1992). *When partners become parents: The big life change for couples.* New York: Basic Books.

Cowan, C.P., Cowan, P.A., Heming, G., Garrett, E., Coysh, W.S., Curtis-Boles, H., & Boles, A.J. (1985). Transitions to parenthood: His, hers and theirs. *Journal of Family Issues, 6*(4), 451–81.

Donovan, C. (2000). Who needs a father? Negotiating biological fatherhood in British lesbian families using self-insemination. *Sexualities, 3*(2), 149–164.

Fisher, J. (1999). *The uninvited guest: Emerging from narcissism towards marriage.* New York: Routledge.

Giuffrida, A. (2023). MEPs decry Italy's 'attack' on same-sex parents' rights. *The Guardian,* 1st April 2023, p. 38.

Golombok, S. (2015). *Modern families: Parents and children in new family form.* Cambridge, UK: Cambridge university Press.

Hogan, J. (2023). Paul Murphy: We don't want to limit our baby by saying you're a boy or you're a girl. Let them decide. *Irish Times,* 14th March 2023.

Morgan, P. (1995). *Farewell to the family?* London: Institute of Economic Affairs.

Nathans, S. (2012). Infidelity as manic defence. *Couple and Family Psychoanalysis, 2*(2), 165–180.

Patterson, C.J. (2004). Lesbian and gay parents and their children: Summary of research findings. In *Lesbian and gay parenting: A resource for psychologists* (pp. 5–22). Washington, DC: American Psychological Association.

Phillips. (1997). *The sex change state* (Memorandum no 30, October). London: Social Market Research.

Seigel, D. (2017). *What is attunement?* momentousinstitute.org

Silva, E.B., & Smart, C. (1999). Chapter 1: The 'new' practices and politics of family life. In E.B. Silva & C. Smart (Eds.), *The new family.* London, England: Sage.

Steinbeck, J. (1939). *The grapes of wrath.* New York: The Viking Press.

Stern, D. (1985). *The interpersonal world of the infant.* New York: Basic Books.

Strout, E. (2021). *Oh William.* New York: Penguin.

Weldon, E. (2004). *Mother, Madonna, whore: The idealization and denigration of motherhood.* Abingdon, OX: Routledge.

Winnicott, D. (1964). *The child, the family & the outside world.* London: Penguin Books.

# Chapter 2

# Being a couple and developing the capacity for creative parenting

## A psychoanalytic perspective

*Mary Morgan*

## Introduction

In this chapter, I describe the idea of an internal creative couple, which is developed as part of the process of psychic development. This supports creative relating in a couple relationship and is pivotal in the capacity to parent whether as parental couples, lone parents or in any other parenting configurations (Morgan, 2019). This internal capacity forms part of an individual's identity, though its development is not straightforward and without challenges. Many parents struggle because they have not been able to develop this capacity securely. Children can also challenge this internal capacity in parents but may also stimulate its development. Even when this development has occurred, external and internal pressures mean it is not always possible to maintain.

First, I will describe what I mean by an internal creative couple and the way it manifests in a couple relationship and in parenting. I will then outline my understanding of how an internal creative couple potentially develops as part of the process of psychic development. This outline does not do justice to the complex developmental trajectory of any one individual but signals key areas of psychic development for everybody. I will suggest some of the ways in which this capacity becomes impaired and affects parenting, illustrating this with therapeutic material from couples I have worked with. Finally, I will comment on the challenge of sustaining an internal creative couple state of mind.

## The creative couple development and parenting

Within creative couple development, there is a capacity to manage separateness and difference together with intimacy. The other's different thoughts and views can be taken inside the self without too much anxiety that one's own thoughts and views will be lost or annihilated. An internal mating can be allowed to take place. This capacity supports the individual and the couple in letting go of previous certainties, being able to not know and realising that while it may not be immediately apparent, an as-yet-unknown creative outcome to their difficulty might be possible. This makes it possible to allow previously held views to break down and be reconfigured

DOI: 10.4324/9781003387947-4

in an intercourse with another. This rests on a belief that out of this disintegration, further integration will occur, leading to new, previously unknown creative development. Over time, a couple can experience their relationship as an entity, a resource, something they have created and continue to create together, the whole being greater than the sum of the parts. When there is something difficult to manage, identifying with their internal creative couple helps the two come together in their different ways to try and think about the issue at hand. Such issues often centre around caring for children. Babies and children provoke strong feelings in the adults that care for them. These feelings will at times involve intense love, hatred, massive anxiety, envy, narcissistic wounds, loss and disappointment, to name a few.

In more reflective states of mind, a parent may be able to process these powerful feelings by finding a place inside him or herself in which their child's and their own feelings can be brought together to help understand what is happening. Even if one is not part of a couple, there is an internal sense of being part of a couple, which could lead to a better capacity to think, to talk to another adult and to engage with one's child. If one does not have inside oneself a creative couple state of mind, either because this development has not been possible or because it has stalled or is temporarily unavailable, a withdrawal into the self in the face of anxiety caused by a child is liable; we could call this an 'alone parent state of mind'. This prevents the engagement with the child that enables him or her to feel properly attended to by the parent. A worse scenario may occur when there is no 'good object' inside a parent, who will then experience the child as dangerous and may want to avoid or control them.

Parenting isn't only about a set of skills. Of course, knowledge and learning from experience, one's own and others', does exist. But to be able to fully utilise this kind of help, there needs to be a sense inside oneself of relationships being something in which help can be sought, in which it is all right not to know or understand, in which it is possible to get things wrong and acknowledge this and in which it is possible to share one's experiences, feelings and thoughts in reasonable safety. It is also an important experience for children to have a parent or parents who are able to function as a creative couple, rather than feel, in a non-thinking way, that they have to be 'on the same page', at all costs.

In whatever configuration parenting occurs, I am suggesting that what is important is that there is an internal creative couple capacity in the parent, and where there are two or more parents or parental figures, this capacity also exists within and between them. Awareness of what impairs this capacity can help us in our work with struggling couples and parents.

## Psychic development towards an internal creative couple

Psychic development, stimulated by physiological growth and the response of the environment, involves, in most cases, a natural trajectory towards the development of an internal creative couple. I am going to highlight three points in psychic development that are part of this process: first, the early relationship with the mother or primary object; second, the Oedipal situation; and third, adolescence. I will describe some of what can go wrong in this developmental process and how these difficulties might affect the individual when later in life, he or she becomes a parent.

For the purposes of this chapter, this presentation is in essence an overview. The development it depicts is, of course, not as linear as conveyed here, as in reality, it involves much returning to earlier stages or reworking them from later positions. This process continues throughout our life so that however 'adult' we become, we still struggle at times with primitive regressions, heightened Oedipal dynamics emerging in new forms, as well as anxieties about how independent we are or how dependent we can and want to be, as in the adolescent dilemma. It is also worth noting that during these different stages of psychic development, we are also working out what a couple is and can be.

## Early development: the first couple

From the beginning of life, there is a 'couple', as psychoanalysts among others have described. Winnicott, for example, writes: 'There is no such thing as an infant, meaning of course that whenever one finds an infant one finds maternal care' (Winnicott, 1958/1975). Others have stressed that along with the sociobiological drive to seek out an object, there is in the human infant the unconscious phantasy of there being an 'other' with whom the infant links or seeks attachment (Bion, 1962, 1963; Bowlby, 1969; Fairbairn, 1946/1952; Money-Kyrle, 1968, 1971). This can be thought of as something unconsciously 'known', an innate preconception of the existence of an object and, therefore, of 'coupling' or 'linking'.

It is through being in a relationship with an 'other' that the infant can process internal experiences and psychically grow. Following this, as Money-Kyrle has stated, it is also probable that the idea of a couple coming together sexually is derived from innate knowledge (Money-Kyrle, 1971). Thus, at the earliest stage of development, there is the beginning of a template for an adult sexual relationship. This differs from the adult couple relationship in several important ways, for example, the nature of dependency, separateness and infantile sexuality.

Later in life, when forming a couple, difficulties stemming from this early stage of development can manifest, in particular, states of mind where there is an overdependence of one partner on the other, a struggle of 'who is to be the baby' (Lyons & Mattinson, 1993, p. 108). Some adult couples find it difficult for the other to be separate, sometimes even physically separate in allowing the other to come and go, but more often, they may struggle with being psychically separate, accepting that the other has different thoughts and feelings. There may be a belief that the other should meet all of one's needs, just like a tiny baby will feel utterly dependent on the mother. If these needs aren't met, the other is felt to be failing. The unconscious recreation of the phantasised early mother-baby relationship may meet the needs of the couple, one directly and the other vicariously, as needs are projected into the 'baby' partner. Failure to maintain this unconscious arrangement is nearly always inevitable, leading to disappointment, blame and conflict. One partner feels completely justified in being angry with the other who has not been able or chosen not to meet his or her needs, whilst the other partner is left quite destabilised as the projective system breaks down.

There are other adult versions of this 'mother-baby couple' that could become disturbing in a different way. The partners in the couple can feel, on occasion, that the reverse of containment is happening; they may feel that the other is constantly projecting into them their difficult or unwanted feelings. Being part of a couple is then felt to be dangerous, and defences may be erected to protect the self from intrusion. There are also mother-baby couples in which the other is experienced as impenetrable and unable to take in any of their partner's communications (Fisher, 1993; Morgan, 2010/2017). This regressed kind of primitive mother-baby couple relationship can become stuck. Such couples would be likely to have difficulties when they become parents, with an actual baby entering into their lives. The child's needs may then be felt to usurp the position of the 'adult baby' and represent an attack on already limited resources. If the couple previously had a comfortable mother-baby union, the baby may be felt as an intrusion into their exclusive bond. The bond may then be disrupted, as the primary caregiver switches to an exclusive relationship with the baby, with the question of 'who is the baby' remaining open.

## The Oedipal situation: another couple

The Oedipal situation painfully presents us with another couple, as it dispels the phantasy that we have an exclusive relationship with the mother or primary caregiver, facing us with the reality of another couple that has been there all along. But also, as I hope to show, negotiating this is crucial in developing our own later capacity to become ourselves part of a creative couple. A different kind of space can then open up, with different possibilities, which Britton has described as 'triangular space'(Britton, 1989).

The capacity to take what has been described as a 'third position' is fundamental in psychic development – the ability to be oneself and reflect on oneself, opening up psychic space and developing thinking. This capacity to be in a relationship and simultaneously to observe oneself in that relationship is central to a couple state of mind (Morgan, 2019) and to becoming part of a creative couple. Although the child has been subjectively part of a couple with the mother, there is now, from the position of being outside a couple, the idea of a couple as an entity in the child's mind. This is important in being able to internalise a couple as an object, which will be part of the basis for the child's own couple relationship. While a parental couple may or may not exist in external reality, the child can become more aware of an internal creative couple inside the mother. This, Birksted-Breen argues, is part of the mother's containing capacity:

> "already combines both the maternal function of being with and the paternal function of observing and linking. In order to contain her infant, a mother (and

*an analyst) has to receive the projections empathically (the maternal function)
and also take a perspective on this (the paternal function)."*

(Birksted-Breen, 1996, p. 651)

So here we have, in the well-functioning primary caregiver, an internal creative couple with maternal and paternal aspects linked together.

The Oedipal situation is never completely resolved, but the adult couple relationship, once established, can provide the opportunity to continue reworking it, as the couple has to manage other 'thirds', which need to be included and excluded, most obviously the presence of children. If there has not been much working through of this Oedipal situation, then the couple may be quite challenged by the impact of children on their own sense of being a couple, as well as managing other 'thirds' – their own parents and each partner's separate interests and preoccupations, such as work. If there are difficulties in this area, a parent may turn to the child and may exclude the other parent, or in some cases, anxieties may lead to the couple preserving their coupledom by overly excluding the children.

At different stages in life, there may be different Oedipal challenges; for example, later in life, as Wrottesley points out, 'The grandparental couple, like the child, must stand outside of the procreative young couple's relationship, and look upon what they cannot have' (Wrottesley, 2017, p. 193).

In many cases, a couple relationship can be not only therapeutic and containing for the couple but also creative for them. In this way, in the creative couple development, the Oedipal triangle is reconfigured so that the third point on the triangle is the couple's relationship, a symbolic third to which the couple can turn to find a place in their minds from which each partner can observe him or herself in their relationship. Moving between their subjective experience of themselves and their relationship to a more objective reflection on it, the couple can then think together about what they are creating. They can observe that difficulties that arise from the dynamic between them but also can be creative in thinking together.

## Adolescence – separating from the parental couple

For many adolescents, changes in the body can be rapid and alarming, and powerful sexual feelings can be experienced as confusing and frightening. The triangular configuration of the Oedipal situation helps adolescents in their ambivalent state, caught between wanting to take ownership of their own body and mind, excluding themselves from the parental couple and developing their own identity but still feeling at times very dependent on their parents. For a while, this sense of independence can be idealised, and the parents rejected, in order for the adolescent to separate. The urges that the adolescent has been struggling with can clearly give rise to the illusion, based upon the infant's view of adults, that the outcome of being adult is to become somebody who is autonomous and independent. The older adolescent or young adult might also think of him or herself as available for occasional intimacy. Despite appearing to be the end of childhood, they have not really reached the state of a fully-grown adult. Some parents may misjudge the ostensible wish for independence in their adolescent by withdrawing support too early, thus impeding the young person's development.

At some point, in the trajectory towards and within adult life, there is usually an imperative, biological and psychological, to form a couple of some kind. This hopefully emerges from a position of having some psychological capacity to be an adult with a separate identity and mind, not from a position of wanting to return to a child-parent relationship; often, though, some regressive merging component still exists, at least initially.

The internal structuring which is achieved as an outcome of the early Oedipal situation helps the adolescent move between identifying with his or her internal objects, while also feeling separate from them, in the process of discovering who he or she is. In late adolescence, this experimentation can become very enjoyable, which is why some individuals resist taking the step of becoming part of a couple because of the fear of losing a sense of one's own separate identity, often represented by the new pleasures associated with the status of young adulthood. Once one is part of a couple, it can be challenging to create enough psychic space in the relationship for each partner to be their individual self as well as their couple self, thus successfully managing both separateness and intimacy.

## The creative couple stage of psychic development

Within the process of psychic development from infancy to adulthood, including being part of a creative couple and becoming parents, crucial developments can occur. From earliest infancy, the experience of dependence on an object, including experiences of intimacy, love, curiosity and interactions with the mind of another, provide the fulcrum for one's own development.

With early Oedipal development, we learn about and have to come to terms with the link between the parents, including their sexual relationship, from which we are excluded. As suggested earlier, this may take the form of an internal creative couple within a single parent or be manifested in a parenting configuration of two or more. This experience facilitates the development of triangular space and the awareness that the mother, or primary caregiver (the maternal), who initially contained us, was internally linked to a father or another partner too (the paternal). This helps in understanding a form of linked separateness and provides one with an arena in which later it is possible to experiment with being part of a couple, as well as being a separate individual within a couple.

In adolescence, there is typically a struggle with powerful feelings of dependence and independence, the adolescent identifying with important objects (including aspects of the parents) but also needing to be separate from them and have a mind of their own. In this way, if all goes well, the adolescent gradually takes ownership of their own separate identity and sexual body (Laufer, 1981).

Then for most individuals, at some point, there is a wish to build an adult sexual relationship of one's own and become a couple, though as Waddell points out, 'developing such a capacity may, for some, take many more years and possibly several different attempts' (Waddell, 1998/2002, p. 158). Psychic development can then continue in the context of being part of a couple.

## Psychic development and parenting difficulties

I suggest there are parenting difficulties that can be understood within the framework I have just described as areas of psychic development that have become stalled or need further working through.

## A parent's own need to be parented

One of the most common issues that can interfere with the capacity to parent involves one's own need to be parented. The adult couple relationship can sometimes have the same intensity, intimacy and dependency needs as that experienced in the primary mother-infant relationship. In fact, when we explore the unconscious beliefs (Britton, 1998; Morgan, 2010/2017) of couples coming for help, it is surprising how often they hold an idealised, unspoken belief involving the idea that their partner should provide total care. 'He is responsible for my happiness'; 'she should meet all of my needs'.

Such a relationship can be problematic both for the couple and for parenting in several ways. First of all, this is a 'two-person' relationship, similar to the primary mother-child relationship, in which there is only 'what you are doing to me or not doing for me'; there is no capacity in such a dyadic relationship to take a third position, a couple state of mind, thinking about the couple's relationship with each other, and separate to that, with their children: 'What is going on *between* us'?

Secondly, when parents feel so needy themselves, it is difficult to respond to the needs of their children. There may then be pressure on the children to meet the parents' needs, while the children may sometimes be excessively projected into. The children's needs may in some cases be seen as a threat to a parent's own baby needs being met. This is a complex situation, as inevitably, primitive needs are evoked in the adult while providing parenting for another. Being able to parent means being able to create a nurturing space for parenting, which is not too encumbered by the adult's primitive and unmet needs.

In order to preserve confidentiality, the following clinical examples are all composites, combining disguised material from various cases.

## Bill and Tanya

When Bill and Tanya started therapy, they presented a difficulty with boundaries. Bill could not bear for Tanya to have any boundaries whatsoever, as they left him feeling excluded and rejected. Conversely, Tanya felt that she had to have a 'force field' around her in order to keep Bill out and maintain her sense of self. Tanya felt that if she made herself available to Bill, he would be too demanding, especially when it came to sex, and then she would either feel obliged to engage in sex against her wishes or be left feeling guilty and bad in withholding it.

We had done a lot of work about their difficulty in being intimate and the dynamic in which Tanya felt as if in responding to Bill, she obliterated her own needs, just as her narcissistic mother had required of her. Bill was always clamouring for close contact with Tanya, something he had never had with his own mother; his need for this could take on a demanding childlike quality, which I came to know about directly, as any perceived failure on my part to meet Bill's needs led to angry outrage.

There was a turning point in the therapy when Bill behaved in such an invasive and aggressive way towards me that I felt I might terminate the therapy. This impulse to withdraw from this couple in response to feeling invaded was exactly what seemed to be going wrong between the two of them, and though difficult, this helped us all to see and experience this disturbing dynamic. We came to understand more about the disappointed rage Bill felt when his needs couldn't be met, by me, Tanya and earlier, by his mother. Moreover, we also came to see how Tanya felt so disturbed by the intrusive nature of his demands which was reminiscent of her experience with her own mother. It was because of this sense of Bill's trespass that Tanya created a force field around herself, acting as a shield. Unfortunately, this served to exacerbate their existing problems.

Gradually, in the therapy, Tanya was able to risk being more open with me, which Bill observed. When he could manage the difficult feelings this stirred up for him, he became a bit more interested in her, and his more infantile demands decreased. They were pleased to tell me they were now having consensual sex, an important experience for them in itself, as well as symbolising something more respectful of boundaries between them. That position ushered in the possibility of creative intercourse.

Around this time, they brought their concerns about one of their children, a son aged 10. They described to me how oppositional he could be; they said he often opposed them even when he lost out on something he wanted. They were devoted parents, but there was also a way in which they were completely over-involved in their children's lives, who consequently had very little space to develop. The work we had done on their couple relationship helped them to see that there was some confusion between their own needs and those of their 10-year-old son. They were able to consider that perhaps their son, through being oppositional, was trying to set some boundaries and protect himself from their unconscious neediness.

## A problem in being both a couple and parents

Another common difficulty, coming developmentally later than the one just described, is an Oedipal one, in which there is a problem in being able to both be a couple and be parents. Unresolved Oedipal development within earlier family experiences may mean that one is left with the unconscious belief that either there is only a parental couple from which one feels excluded or there is a denial of the parental couple and a belief that the sole relationship becomes that between parent and child.

## Lucy and Al

One couple I met with for several consultations did not have the chance to parent, as the realisation that they wanted children had come too late for them.

Al had grown up with a mother devoted to him and his brother, at the cost of his parents' relationship. When he, as the youngest child in the family, married, his mother had sunk into a severe depression. Lucy, on the other hand, had grown up with parents who seemed to adore one another, and she and her siblings had to tiptoe around them as best they could.

When this couple got together, they were both desperate for some space and freedom, and although they had passing thoughts about having children, they could never discuss this properly, leaving the issue unexplored and unresolved. The fact of Al's early life being overly child-centred while Lucy's had been overly parent-centred led to an unconscious belief that there wasn't room in their family for both a couple and children. There were no children that suffered in this family, but one can imagine from this example that while having children together might have been an opportunity for them to develop in this area, they may alternatively have had great difficulty in finding a way to be both a couple and parents.

Many couples struggle with the ordinary problem of finding it hard to hold onto their coupledom with the arrival of children. Sometimes, however, the anxiety about this is so strong that the couple's relationship is subsumed by family life; or alternatively, like Lucy's parents, they may become so anxious about preserving their coupledom that the children are overly excluded.

## Non-creative coupling or an alone parent state of mind

An alone parent state of mind can manifest in several different ways. Sometimes, as described by Hopkins (1996), the other parent is hardly felt to exist, while the 'too-good mother' develops a pleasurable, overly-attuned and vicarious exclusive relationship with her infant. As Hopkins shows, this untriangulated situation could potentially have serious consequences for the child. Sometimes the other parent is allowed more of a presence, but the primary caregiver may still have conflicted feelings towards needing or valuing him or her. They feel alone with their child, not in a pleasurable state but in an anxious and resentful state. These difficulties may link to unworked-through Oedipal anxieties, in which the third is experienced as disrupting the dyadic parent-child bond, or they may be connected to a later stage of development, in which dependence on another creates concern about a loss of autonomy – as in the adolescent dilemma.

With the creative couple development, mutual dependence within the couple follows the capacity for independence. There is an intercourse between two adults with a capacity to be separate and different inside them, which opens up psychic space and allows for more creative parenting. My last example is of a couple who had a difficulty with depending on each other and valuing the differences between them.

## Susan and Steven

Susan and Steven came for help because they felt continually let down by each other in ways that made them feel quite despairing about their relationship. The couple were married and had one child, Nina, aged 8. Both parents had busy professional working lives, but they were able to ensure between them quite a lot of time to look after Nina. They did try to work together as parents, but this tended to have a flat, uncreative quality. The sessions with them were very busy, too, with a lot of anxiety and little time for reflection.

The emotional quality of the therapy captured the feeling between the couple in their daily lives. The more I thought about them and my experience with them, the more I realised how little emotional contact they seemed to be making with each other; they were too busy just trying to manage. There was no sense of there being space for more than one emotional reality, let alone allowing for the idea that bringing their different realities together could be of value or could even be a creative experience. Nina, unsurprisingly, seemed to be a rather isolated child, with no particular friends at school and tended to be extremely clingy with Susan. Steven seemed to feel that this was normal, as 'a child needs her mother', but it was clear that he felt excluded from their relationship and blamed Susan for this.

The school also became concerned that Nina was not able to achieve her potential and seemed always to be quiet and withdrawn. I had the impression that she was a rather depressed little girl. On the other hand, I gathered that she could be quite a handful at home, in ways that amounted to her demanding constant direct contact from her mother. Steven would occasionally try to intervene in their dyadic relationship, but he felt that nothing he did was ever right, and he was sensitive to feeling that, quickly giving up and withdrawing. Susan was anxious and very organised and, in some ways, related to Steven as a junior work colleague, giving him lists of things that needed doing. He would try his best but was never able to succeed well enough. Unconsciously, his anger at being related to as an appendage to Susan led to him sabotaging various arrangements, which in turn infuriated Susan, resulting in her becoming even more controlling.

This is an example of a couple struggling in their relationship with each other and, consequently, struggling to parent their child. This left Nina distressed in this context and possibly depressed. For Susan and Steven, engaging with each other felt threatening. They were both aware that they needed help from their partner, but the only way they could conceive of help being helpful was for their partner to prop them up, not through having an intercourse. Each seemed to feel like a parent on their own. Susan felt she was the main parent, with an inadequate 'nanny/helper' in Steven, while he felt like a very inadequate father, with a severe and controlling superego in the form of Susan. While they were stuck in this position, there appeared to be no life in the adult couple relationship and no conception of the idea that they might be able to help each other, think together and find ways forward together.

I thought that the way to help these parents so that they could provide a truly dynamic container for their daughter was to help them see how deprived they made themselves of a shared position from which to think together. The experience of being in the room with them was essentially arid until, with considerable work, some fleeting emotional contact with them could be made. Only when this vital contact was achieved did it become possible to begin to understand their emotional experience and what might be leading to the difficulties between them and for Nina. They needed help to occupy a third position, but when they could, they gradually became more interested in what was happening between them and more able to think together about Nina. They were eventually able to recognise that the dynamic between them had deprived Nina of the help she needed to separate from her mother and to be supported by both parents in developing more interest in the outside world. Over time, Susan and Steven moved from simply trying to manage Nina to being curious about her experience, one outcome of which was to arrange some therapy for her.

## Conclusion

The development of an internal creative couple, both internally and as manifested in couple relating, is crucial in parenting. It is not a fixed state but one that is moved in and out of and, in optimal conditions, one that continues to develop internally and in relationships with friends, colleagues, intimate partners and children. I suggest that this comes about through the process of psychic development which is ongoing throughout life. Being a couple and being parents involve challenges, but it also offers opportunities for continued working through and for new psychic development within the couple and the two adults it comprises. Working closely with couples reveals that there are some difficult realities about the self, the other and a relationship that have to be engaged with, as they come alive at key points in psychic development and in roles as parents. These difficult to engage with realities can sometimes challenge the capacity to sustain an internal creative couple state of mind.

In my experience, the following points are important when thinking about these processes:

(1)  The acceptance of the fundamental difference, 'otherness' and unknowability of an other. This is not easy because a part of us all may long for that early experience of illusory attunement. We can get close to that experience sometimes, including, for example, in a good sexual relationship, but this cannot be a permanent or perfect state. This reality is not easy to accept, but if it can be, interest and curiosity about the other can be brought to life. Parents often disagree, but therapists can support them in engaging with each other's viewpoints, and the birth of a new, enlarged third perspective can be enabled,

through a process of psychological intercourse, to the benefit of the couple and of the child.

(2) We need others. Is it possible to feel a secure sense of independence while not being frightened of dependence on an 'other' or idealising either of these capacities (as in mother-baby fusion or adolescent independence)? In response to this reality, some parents enter into an 'alone parent state of mind' and find it hard to acknowledge they need help from another.

(3) In all relationships, there is hate as well as love, or perhaps I should say that there is hate in the context of love. Can the couple have room not to like aspects of each other, not to agree, without feeling that this could destroy them? This experience is also true in relation to children; we love them but sometimes hate them, too, as Winnicott pointed out (Winnicott, 1949). Children also love us but partly hate us too. Knowing this, rather than pushing it underground, makes it much less likely that hatred, in ourselves or those we love, will be acted out or reacted to in destructive ways.

(4) There is a need for a capacity for negative capability (Bion, 1970/1984; Keats, 1817/1958, pp. 477–478), being able to not know and, in the face of that, to avoid certainty. As I suggested earlier, parenting isn't about a set of rules; parents work it out as they go and try to learn from experience not only their own but also that of others.

(5) It is impossible to access the internal creative couple all the time and to always relate creatively to another. Parenting is a good example of how the pressures we experience can disable our capacity to function this way. The creative couple capacity may thus sometimes be lost, but it can be rediscovered and further developed with each new experience. When this can be achieved, it provides containment for the individual, for the couple, for the parents and, as a consequence, for the children in the family.

## Acknowledgements

My thanks to Simon Cregeen for suggesting that I could submit this paper to the *Journal of Child Psychotherapy* which is where an extended version of this paper was originally published.

## References

Bion, W. R. (1962). Learning from experience. Karnac.

Bion, W. R. (1963). Elements of psycho-analysis. Heinemann.

Bion, W. R. (1970). Attention and interpretation. Tavistock (Reprinted: Karnac Books, 1984).

Birksted-Breen, D. (1996). Phallus, penis and mental space. International Journal of Psycho-Analysis, 77, 649–657.

Bowlby, J. (1969). Attachment and loss: Volume I: Attachment. In The international psychoanalytical library, (Vol. 79). Hogarth Press and the Institute of Psycho-Analysis.

Britton, R. (1989). The missing link: Parental sexuality in the oedipus complex. In J. Steiner (Ed.), The oedipus complex today: Clinical implications (pp. 83–101). Karnac.

Britton, R. (1998). Belief and psychic reality. In R. Britton (Ed.), Belief and imagination: Explorations in psychoanalysis (pp. 8–18). Routledge.

Fairbairn, W. R. D. (Ed.). (1952). Chapter V: Object-relationships and dynamic structure. In Psychoanalytic studies of the personality (pp. 1–297). Tavistock Publications Limited (Chapter originally published 1946).

Fisher, J. (1993). The impenetrable other: Ambivalence and the Oedipal conflict in work with couples. In S. Ruszczynski (Ed.), Psychotherapy with couples: Theory and practice at the Tavistock Institute of marital studies (pp. 142–166). Karnac.

Hopkins, J. (1996). The dangers and deprivations of too-good mothering. Journal of Child Psychotherapy, 22(3), 407–422. https://doi.org/10.1080/00754179608254516

Keats, J. (1958). Letter to George and Thomas Keats 21st December 1817. In H. E. Hollins (Ed.), The letters of John Keats (pp. 477–478). Harvard University Press (Original work published 1817).

Laufer, M. (1981). The psychoanalyst and the adolescent's sexual development. The Psychoanalytic Study of the Child, 36(1), 181–191. https://doi.org/10.1080/00797308.1981.11823338

Lyons, A., & Mattinson, J. (1993). Individuation in marriage. In S. Ruszczynski (Ed.), Psychotherapy with couples: Theory and practice at the Tavistock Institute of marital studies (pp. 104–125). Karnac.

Money-Kyrle, R. (1968). Cognitive development. International Journal of Psycho-Analysis, 49, 691–698.

Money-Kyrle, R. (1971). The aim of psychoanalysis. International Journal of Psycho-Analysis, 51, 103–106.

Morgan, M. (2010). Unconscious beliefs about being a couple. fort da, 16 (1): 36–55. Reprinted (2017). In S. Nathans & M. Schaefer (Eds.), Couples on the couch. Psychoanalytic couple therapy and the Tavistock model (pp. 62–81). Routledge.

Morgan, M. (2019). A couple state of mind: Psychoanalysis of couples and the Tavistock relationship model. Routledge.

Waddell, M. (1998/2002). Inside lives: Psychoanalysis and the growth of the personality. Karnac. (Revised edition published in 2002 by H. Karnac [Books] Ltd.)

Winnicott, D. W. (1949). Hate in the counter-transference. International Journal of Psycho-Analysis, 30, 69–74.

Winnicott, D. W. (1958/1975). Through paediatrics to psychoanalysis: Collected papers. The Institute of Psychoanalysis. Karnac.

Wrottesley, C. (2017). Does Oedipus never die? The grandparental couple grapple with "Oedipus". Couple and Family Psychoanalysis, 7(2), 188–207. http:/mc.manuscriptcentral.com/rjcp

# Chapter 3

# Becoming parents through ART
## Infertility, loss, and the dilemmas of Assisted Reproductive Technology

*Martha Doniach*

\*

*A 38-year-old female has spent all her savings on freezing her eggs because she has not yet met a partner with whom to have children. Aware of the biological clock ticking, she is now considering sperm donation and single parenthood as an option.*

\*

*A lesbian couple is struggling to agree on whether they will use an anonymous sperm donor or friend. They are also arguing about whether they should both try to get pregnant at once or whether the elder of the two should go first.*

\*

*A heterosexual couple has suffered from years of infertility treatment; they are reaching the point of giving up and separating after 15 years of marriage.*

\*

*A gay couple has come to couples therapy because one wants to seek a surrogate to help them have a child while the other would prefer to adopt.*

These examples convey some of the possible dilemmas arising from infertility and Assisted Reproductive Technology (ART) that I have encountered in my work as a couple psychotherapist working in private practice and the National Health Service (NHS). These difficulties are situated within a field shaped by many factors, including the interplay of social expectations and values; the constraints and opportunities created by advancing medical technology; and the psychological capacities of couples and individuals seeking help.

Throughout the world, societies place enormous value on having a child (Roseneil et al., 2020), which contributes to the devastation most couples feel when unable to conceive a baby naturally. Many will spend years trying before deciding to use medical intervention, and even then, it is not a forgone conclusion that they will have a baby. Although starting from a different premise for same-sex couples, in

DOI: 10.4324/9781003387947-5

that they know from the beginning that they cannot biologically conceive a child, this does not preclude the emotional and psychological impact for some of not being able to create a child together.

Reproductive technology has revolutionised procreation. The Human Fertilisation Embryology Authority (HFEA, 2021) reports a tenfold increase in IVF cycles since 1991. Advancing technologies have transformed the shape and meaning of family in the same period. The age profile of contemporary families has changed because of a 30% increase in the live birth rates for women aged over 43 using donor eggs. The increase of both female same-sex parents and single parents by choice has been largely due to the threefold increase in the number of children born from donor sperm (HFEA, ibid).

ART now offers wide-ranging possibilities for those unable to have children naturally. However, this has come at a cost, literally, psychologically, and ethically. For example, as NHS funding for IVF treatments using egg or sperm donation has decreased, associated health care provisions such as surrogacy, gamete donation, and egg freezing have become big business, excluding those who are unable to afford treatment. ART also encourages an underground market of people wishing to make money. Some sell or rent their reproductive body parts, reinforcing the dehumanisation often felt by all parties involved in ART and perpetuating the denial of complex feelings involved in reproduction.

These market forces and the pressure arising from the female biological clock ticking can conspire to create circumstances where the psychological impact of ART on the individual, the couple, and the wider family is overlooked. This oversight is compounded by the routinisation of medical treatment and nursing practices which can function as professional defences against addressing patient vulnerability (Menzies Lyth, 1988). It is, therefore, unsurprising that, in a medical context, professionals may inadvertently avoid thinking about all that is psychologically involved in making a baby.

Important research has been conducted on the subject. Haynes and Miller (2003) explore the impact of ART on individuals and couples and attempt to bridge the destructive gap between psyche and soma, arising from the objectification of the body through the medicalisation of reproduction. Whilst previously, the analytic community tended to blame infertility on intrapsychic difficulties such as maternal ambivalence, this has been fiercely challenged, as these difficulties are often present in those who can conceive naturally (Apfel & Keylor, 2002). Mann (2014) and Fine (2015) continue the exploration of ART from a psychoanalytic perspective with both stressing the need for therapeutic help for those engaging in ART. They endorse avoiding secrecy around conception and having open conversations in families regarding identity and origins. Through her sociological research with families, Susan Golombok (2015, 2020a) demonstrates that what matters is the quality of the parent-child relationship as opposed to family composition or biological ties (McCann, 2021). New family structures and couple relationships that depart from conventional heteronormative ideas have necessitated long-needed changes in psychoanalytic theory (D'Ercole & Drescher, 2004; Lemma & Lynch, 2015; Giffney & Watson, 2017; Hertzmann & Newbigin, 2019, 2023; McCann, 2021).

From my clinical experience, in this chapter, I will draw on four distinct themes in connection to ART: comparing the experiences of same-sex couples and heterosexual couples, exploring the importance of time as a factor in shaping couples' experience, the impact of loss on the couple and working through mourning, and understanding the family perspective and how children and wider family members get caught up in the emotional turbulence couples experience.

I will exemplify my findings with short clinical vignettes and two composite extended case studies that explore in depth the complexities involved in using ART.

## Some comparisons between the experiences of same-sex couples and heterosexual couples using Assisted Reproductive Technology

In my work with heterosexual and same-sex couples, I have recognised some significant differences which may be helpful to keep in mind when supporting couples suffering from infertility and/or using assisted technology to have children. Perhaps the most blatant when working with LGBTQ+ couples is the impact on them of living in a heteronormative society. This reality and its conscious and unconscious influence on the therapist and her patients are keys. Colleen Sander highlights:

> *"while LGBTQ couples may look and act like heterosexual couples in terms of the issues they bring to the work, they also come with unique relational and intrapsychic challenges and stresses in familial and societal relationships having been raised in a predominantly heteronormative society."*
>
> (2021, p. 203)

While all kinds of couples may experience difficulty with conception, for heterosexual couples, gamete donation or surrogacy is often the last resort, whilst for same-sex couples (apart from fostering or adoption), it is the *only* way to have a child. This juxtaposition was aptly depicted by American psychoanalyst and author, Susan Vaughan (2007), who describes how she and her female partner appeared to be the only joyful ones in the IVF clinic while the heterosexual couples sitting alongside them were in states of angst and despair.

Significantly, lesbian couples and single female parents by choice can bypass infertility clinics and ART altogether and self-impregnate provided they have a willing sperm donor and no evident reproductive problems. Although this does not guarantee conception, it can be more straightforward and considerably less expensive. Furthermore, self-impregnation can be carried out in private as opposed to public exposure to institutionalised medical treatment. One lesbian couple I worked with felt relief that they could keep it 'all in the family'; they had choice about how and where they inseminated the sperm. In fact, the entire experience was intimate and ritualised and managed by the couple, giving them the feeling that they were creating the baby together.

Whilst same-sex couples *know* they are unable to jointly conceive, nonetheless, there may be deep feelings of loss, even if only in fantasy (Hertzmann, 2011). Although modern technology provides the opportunity for same-sex couples to create their own families, this means that for some, there may be real mourning involved in being unable to *biologically* create a child together.

There is increasing evidence that straight parents choose not to tell their children about gamete donation (Golombok, 2015; Freeman-Carroll, 2016). The non-disclosure of using gamete or uterus donation may function as a defence against acknowledging the loss of producing their own offspring. Donor insemination is more easily hidden from friends and family, but the reasons behind non-disclosure are complex. Infertility can be devastating to couples, knocking their confidence, and replacing it with shame which can, in turn, be projected onto the child (Freeman-Carroll, 2016). Their secrecy about conception can perhaps be compared to the former practice of adoptive parents being discouraged from being open about their children's biological parents. In these cases, where the truth about genetic identity has been hidden, it's now believed that these adopted children have an unconscious sense of something important connected to who they are being withheld, sometimes leading to developmental difficulties around identity in adolescence (Cudmore, 2005).

Research on straight parents' non-disclosure of donation highlights that the longer parents leave discussing their child's genetic origins, the harder it is to disclose (Freeman-Carroll, 2016). This emphasises the value of therapists helping parents to speak to their children about assisted conception from an early age.

So perhaps straight couples can learn from the LGBTQ+ community? Same-sex parents do not have any option but to be open with their children about their biological origins and incorporate 'where-I-come-from' stories into the family narrative from the outset. However, Ehrensaft (2007, 2008, 2014) reminds us that this does not prevent the desire of some LGBTQ+ couples to minimise the importance of donor egg or sperm and/or surrogacy, often rooted in fears and fantasies involving the donor. Ehrensaft makes the case that there needs to be space for all family members, parents, and children to sufficiently explore these fantasies. She created the phrase 'birth-other' to refer to those who have donated gamete or uterus and reminds us of Winnicott's famous idiom 'there is no such thing as a baby,' positing that "*in the context of assisted reproductive technology, there is no baby without a mother or mothers, father or fathers, and all the other individuals (donors or surrogates) who helped make that baby*" (Ehrensaft, 2008, p. 3).

For all couples using gamete donation or surrogacy, conscious or unconscious fantasies and fears regarding the birth-other or surrogate mother will influence the decision to choose an anonymous or known donor. For same-sex couples, this may be directly connected to internalised homophobia. One lesbian couple realised, when looking through the catalogue for anonymous donors, that they were unwittingly looking at men who would appeal to their own respective parents, as if to appease these parents' dismissal of them being lesbian.

## Sunita and Adrienne

*A lesbian couple, Sunita and Adrienne, chose an anonymous sperm donor believing it made things less complicated overall. They had several friends where the known donor had either "become overly possessive" and too involved in the relationship or had "not lived up to their agreement" of being involved at all.*

*Sunita, aged forty, a musician, and Adrienne, a management consultant aged forty-seven, came to couple therapy because of escalating arguments related to parenting. They had been married for one year and together for seven years. Sunita was the biological mother of both their children, a four-year-old son and a two-year-old daughter.*

*When deciding to have children, Adrienne didn't feel the desire to be pregnant so they agreed they would use Adrienne's eggs and Sunita's womb. Following three failed rounds of IVF, the couple opted for Sunita to become pregnant with her own eggs as the medical consultant advised that Adrienne's "were probably too old."*

*Sunita was exuberant in becoming and remaining pregnant both times relatively easily through IVF. On the face of it, Adrienne was also pleased. However, during the therapy it transpired that Adrienne had repressed her deep feelings of rivalry and loss in not being able to use her own eggs. This mourning had been sidestepped in the urgency to carry on trying and meant that there was no time to grieve having a child together. Adrienne maintained that "if my eggs had been used with Sunita gestating them, things would have felt more evenly balanced between us." She felt envious of Sunita's relationship with their children. That she wasn't genetically connected to them reinforced these feelings.*

*Throughout the therapy considerable work had to be done to help them come to terms with not creating a child together and recognising the loss that only one partner was genetically linked to their children. The "old eggs" comment by the consultant added to Adrienne's sense of inadequacy in becoming a mother. She had always believed her sexuality wasn't acceptable to her parents and their relationship was difficult as a result. "At least if my genes were involved, they would have felt they had a stake in it." Adrienne's fears were borne out when her parents seemed more interested in her older brother's children. She also found it painful when people commented that both their children resembled Sunita, feeding her sense of irrelevance. Sunita was aware of this and didn't know how to support her apart from making clear to Adrienne that the children "loved them both the same."*

*Whilst Adrienne derived much satisfaction from being a management consultant, she found herself increasingly resentful as the sole 'breadwinner' of the family. Sunita wondered if Adrienne managed her pain by working even harder and distancing herself from their marriage. She was indignant that Adrienne left all the domestic chores and childcare to her and bemoaned the lack of space for herself. Both felt alone and burdened by their respective roles, being aware of how delineated and exclusive their positions had become.*

*The final straw that led to their seeking help was when in the heat of a row, Sunita threatened to leave, shouting that the children "really belong to me as they are MY eggs and anyway, I have done all the hard work!"*

*How the children should refer to their two mothers had been a constant bone of contention between them and seemed to symbolise their acute difficulties in the relationship. This came to a head during one session. . . . When I referred to Adrienne's "loss of mothering" and forgot to include "genetics" in that phrase, she became agitated, "You're assuming that I am NOT their mother?" The shame I then felt seemed to convey the complexity of their inherent difficulties and feelings of unfairness; in heterosexual parenting, each parent's identity is taken for granted while lesbian couples often experience more explicit competition and rivalry, particularly when it comes to motherhood* (Vaughan, 2007).

*In becoming more conscious of their mutual distress, the couple became aware of their attempt to appease what they each imagined were the desires of their respective parents. Adrienne's feelings of inadequacy were underlined by her lack of genetic connection to their children and Sunita's desire to be "normal" partly lay behind her desperation to become a mother. Although they refuted my initial suggestion that they were perhaps "suffering the loss of not being able to create a child naturally together," the couple eventually recognised this sadness and their need to mourn their shared loss.*

*With hindsight, I recognised my tendency to generalise was avoiding the tension and anxiety regarding my unconscious bias, for example in being overly concerned about using the right language with this couple. Equally, I realised that too much self-scrutiny might inhibit my ability to address important difficulties which would then remain hidden. There is a delicate balance between being spontaneous and running the risk of making a verbal faux pas, while being sensitive to using non-biased language.*

## Time as a factor in shaping the experience of couples and families

The passing of time is often a determining factor in the decision to have a child. Associated questions are linked to age, partnership, and reproductive capability. Increasingly, we find ourselves in a culture that denies the limitations of ageing, and debatably, ART contributes to this denial by providing incredible opportunities for those unable to have children. It has been argued that the desire to have a child is linked to our own mortality and that the need to reproduce is a way of combating the inevitable limitations of time (Pawson, 2003), a possibility supported by a study identifying parents living longer than non-parents, although there may be explanations other than being parents for this difference (Modig et al., 2017).

Couples may spend many years trying to conceive a child, completing several cycles of IVF and/or experiencing multiple miscarriages. For those couples with infertility issues or those who have started the process in later life, a sense of urgency may result in not fully anticipating all that is entailed in gamete donation and/or surrogacy, perhaps in an effort to minimise the emotional significance of the entire process. Successful live birth rates following embryo implantation are still only 32% for women under 35 and 19% for women over 35 (HFEA, ibid). Multiple trauma and loss with no baby at the end may activate memories of unresolved losses from the past which will inevitably contribute to how couples manage together.

The resilience of couples will depend on their shared dynamics and will be significantly shaped by their respective histories. The impact of repeated losses, the invasive nature of medical treatment, and the temptation to project responsibility for infertility onto each other can place an overwhelming amount of stress on them. Without professional help, some relationships may be unable to contain the pressures of ART and will end as a result. As therapists, we know that a couple's capacity to reflect on their infertility is a key factor in determining positive outcomes in parenting (Cudmore, 2005), which may be in direct opposition to many infertility clinics invested in encouraging couples not to wait, using the urgency of time as a reason to move on.

Medical procedures for women undergoing IVF are emotionally, psychologically, and physically draining, and many women report the debilitating effects of egg collection or embryo implantation, often compounded by the devastating feelings following embryo loss. Couples describe the cycle of hope and despair that punctuates each cycle of IVF treatment – how the hopelessness is quickly replaced by a new impregnation. It is easy to see how this reinforces a manic defence (Klein, 1940) against trauma and loss. Many individuals and couples when looking back at their infertility history are aghast at the many years they spent trying with their own eggs or sperm before agreeing either to stop altogether or take the next step of gamete donation. Mali Mann (2014) links repeated failed IVF cycles to repetition compulsion and the desire to repeat with the unrealistic hope of changing their situation (Freud, 1920).

For some lesbian couples where both women desire pregnancy, the biological clock may suggest that whoever is older should try first. This can, even if unconsciously, set up competition between the pair. One couple I worked with had realised that there was stored-up anger and resentment because of the 18 months it had taken the older of the two to conceive. The younger partner felt she had missed precious time to try whilst her "eggs were still good." By the time she started trying for a baby, she was over 40 and then struggled to conceive. She was adamant that if they both tried at once, delays in her fertility would not have occurred.

Time may also be a factor in determining family size. It may contribute to disagreements about whether to have more children as, for example, when the prospect of being older parents is anticipated. Time may play a part in encouraging the implantation of multiple embryos even if more risks are involved. The elation following the successful delivery of twins after years of infertility treatment may then pose the ethical dilemma about what to do with unused embryos.

For those who can access ART, it provides the chance for children to be born to individuals and couples who are well beyond the normal child-bearing age. It has offered opportunities to be single parents by choice and has challenged the dominant ideal of the conventional nuclear family. Equally, and notwithstanding controversies regarding the commodification of reproduction, the lack of restriction concerning upper-age limitations introduces powerful ethical questions. For example, how old is too old to have a child? Should there be an age limit imposed? Should assisted reproduction be available for those prospective parents who can afford it and are over 60? What does this mean for children when they are faced with ageing parents before they are adults themselves? Is reproduction a human right to be pursued at all costs, or is it a physiological process that, if not possible to achieve, needs to be accepted as such? In a psychotherapeutic setting, will there be a point when clinicians need to encourage individuals or couples to stop trying? Therapists need to be aware of their own feelings towards ART, which may include personal experience, in order to distinguish their own responses from those of their clients (Siegal, 2017).

## Recognition of the impact of loss on the individual and the couple; managing and working through this loss as a key factor in helping couples to parent more effectively

Apfel and Keylor argue:

> *"The loss of parenthood is multifaceted and involves more than the loss of fertility; there is loss of spontaneous sexuality, of the pregnancy experience itself, of children and genetic continuity. There is stigma and isolation. Real-life and family situations are enormously variable and complex, necessitating the most open-ended, non-judgmental psychoanalytic treatment."*
>
> (2002, p. 93)

Infertility strikes at the heart of women's and men's sense of femininity and masculinity. Deeply shameful feelings may arise connected to their bodies not working 'normally.' However, the psychological and emotional loss of fertility is felt differently between men and women. Indeed, it is only recently that the impact of male infertility has been fully recognised in psychoanalytic literature despite low sperm count accounting for 45% of infertility (Keylor & Apfel, 2010). Whilst for women, there may be feelings of incompetence and correlated sadness, for men, a sense of shame is often related to a lack of potency and consequent sexual problems. Egg donation allows women to still gain the experience of bearing the child even if not genetically theirs, whilst men do not have a parallel physiological experience if a sperm donor is used.

One male partner I worked with felt a deep sense of humiliation at having a low sperm count, and this triggered anxiety-related erectile dysfunction. Although the couple had two healthy daughters through IVF, the man described constantly feeling like a fraud, causing difficulties in both his relationship with his wife and his two daughters. Through couple therapy, it transpired that a troubled relationship with his father was at the heart of his profound sense of impotence, and he came to understand a hitherto unconscious fantasy that he had been unmanned by his critical father.

Intense feelings of guilt may be felt by women who have waited to try for a child.

Many older women unable to conceive believe they are getting their comeuppance for pursuing a career first. Equally, if women have chosen to terminate when they were younger, fertility difficulties in later life are experienced as a punishment. These feelings may dovetail with unconscious aspects that relate to their individual family histories.

Couples undergoing ART often report their sense of exclusion from society, describing feelings of isolation and humiliation. This prohibition can become entangled with competition and rivalry with others; childless couples may avoid contact with expectant friends and family, who, in turn, may be uncomfortable with their 'success' in becoming pregnant in the face of their friends' seeming failure. This culture of avoiding complicated realities and difficult feelings can sometimes reinforce the decision to use an anonymous donor and keep this fact from any children, friends, or family. As stated earlier, it is still more likely for heterosexual couples to keep anonymous sperm or egg donation a secret (Golombok, 2015; Freeman-Carroll, 2016), and secrets can cause tensions that can be more detrimental than the contents of the secret itself.

An important way of understanding 'couple resilience' in the face of infertility is to consider their capacity for containment, *"the couple feels they have something to which they both relate, something they can turn to. . . . It is something they have in mind, and they can imagine the relationship as something that has them in mind"* (Morgan, 2005, p. 29). From a developmental perspective, containment is the consequence of good-enough, early, object-relating and successful resolution of oedipal challenges. It allows an individual to identify with the feelings of others and not be consumed by angry and destructive impulses when faced with loss. Kremen (2012) suggests that creative coupling is threatened following and during years of infertility, and he proposes that therapeutic work is necessary to mourn not being able to produce a child and in being able to rediscover creative couple functioning.

## Jean and Will

*Jean, fifty-five, and Will, forty-nine, were referred for couple psychotherapy due to difficulties with their only son, thirteen-year-old Adam, who was abusing drugs and refusing school. A successful professional couple, they spent two years trying to conceive naturally, eventually opting for IVF. . . . Following several cycles of IVF and four miscarriages, Adam was born through egg donation via an unknown donor eleven years later.*

*At the point of attending therapy, the couple was on the brink of separation. Will was furious with Jean who he felt held poor boundaries and low expectations for their son. Jean resented Will's general lack of support, especially throughout their years of trying for a child. She described him as being emotionally absent, with little empathy for all the treatment she went through, yet "he got all the glory." When I clarified this, Jean retorted, "at least genetically, Adam belonged to Will" whilst she had to live with knowing that Adam "was not naturally connected to her." The couple soon revealed that they agreed to keep Adam's egg donor secret believing that revealing it would cause unnecessary difficulty.*

*They were surprised at my concern and curiosity in their son not knowing about the egg donor; I had to be careful not to become the critical parent who was scolding them for "doing the wrong thing."*

*During the early phase of our work together the tension in the room was palpable and, in my countertransference, I had a sense of having to hold things together; that expressing feelings might result in everything falling to pieces. Jean welled up when I put this to the couple, saying she was furious with Will. Despite early menopause causing the difficulties in conceiving, she held her husband and his ambivalence about having a child responsible for their eventual need for egg-donation. Precious time had been lost through his indecision.*

*Will argued there had been a conflict about the egg donor as he would have preferred to use a relative. Jean worried that this overcomplicated things and believed anonymity was best as "that way there would be no threat to our family and Adam would not have the additional worry of being different."*

*Both Will and Jean grew up in emotionally avoidant families and suffered childhood trauma and loss. From an early age they learned to push away unhappy feelings and protected themselves through academic achievement and, later, success in their professional lives. Jean described her shock at not being able to "achieve" pregnancy. . . . Her answer was to try everything she possibly could in her determination to make a child, including IVF and eventually an anonymous egg donor. Understandably their once "great sex life," suffered. Will hated the mechanistic way in which Jean was determined to have intercourse even when neither of them felt desire. They had not had sex since Adam's birth. Both felt resigned to this although it had never been discussed over the thirteen years.*

*We came to understand it was as if these difficulties, including their lack of sexual intercourse, were kept in a locked box. If this box was opened, everything would fall apart. As concerns about their son escalated, the couple felt even more compelled to "hold the box tightly closed." Until attending therapy, neither had been aware of the tension around keeping the egg-donor's identity a secret. It soon became evident that the anger they felt towards each other in how they had each managed the miscarriages, IVF and egg donor treatment, and their disavowed feelings of guilt and self-loathing, had been unconsciously projected into their son, who seemed to be acting it out.*

*The irony was that they "had avoided telling Adam the truth about egg-donation so he felt normal." Suffused by their own failure, Will and Jean agreed that they had wanted to "turn a blind eye" to the whole egg donor experience but Adam's presence constantly triggered feelings of shame, sadness, and anger.*

*During their three years of therapy, there was a growing realisation that while they needed to talk to Adam about his genetic history, they held back for fear that revealing the secret might tip him over the edge. Between a rock and a hard place, they knew that if they didn't disclose how he had been conceived, there was a danger his struggles would continue but they dreaded his expected anger and hurt at not being told the truth before. Ultimately the couple opted to tell Adam, convinced that sharing the truth was the only healthy way forward and would release the pressure-cooker of tension they had all been living with.*

This case conveys some of the manifest intricacies and dilemmas resulting from ART. Those born in the UK from anonymous gamete donation since 2005 are legally entitled to trace their donors at the age of 18. Many adult children of anonymous gamete donation believe it is their right to know about their biological and medical history, and there is growing consensus that donor anonymity should be abolished (Byrne, 2022). In her recent *The Guardian* article, Dorothy Byrne (ibid), a single parent by choice, describes changing her mind about anonymous sperm donation, recognising the importance for her daughter's sense of identity. In the article, her adult daughter is quoted as saying that "*The benefits (of knowing your donor) outweigh any downside. I don't think it's right to stop someone knowing who they are.*"

### The importance of taking a 'new' family perspective and understanding how children and wider family members get caught up in the emotional turbulence couples endure with ART

Whether built on convention or not, the family is an 'open system,' the experience of which is shaped by intra-family dynamics but also by its interaction with the extended family and the wider community. Within this nexus, becoming a parent is usually challenging for all individuals and couples (Clulow, 1996), and this is made more so when children are conceived using ART.

The dominance of the traditional nuclear family of two heterosexual parents with biologically related children is something psychotherapy and psychoanalysis has not sufficiently addressed (McCann, 2021; Hertzmann & Newbigin, 2019). It is structurally embedded in different religions and cultures. Any deviation from this 'gold standard' is likely to be discriminated against, producing strains within the family and in relationships with the wider community. This is despite research consistently showing "*children growing up within LGBTQ and single-parent by choice families, turn out just as well as – and sometimes better than – kids from traditional families with two heterosexual parents*" (Golombok, 2020b).

Within the family itself, key stresses may include the following:

- Isolation for single parents using anonymous donation who may not have a partner or co-parent to share in the experience of the birth.
- Feelings of loss through not being genetically connected; one partner commented that every time she saw her baby, she was reminded of her lack of biological connection. Freeman-Carroll (2016, p. 43) highlights:

*A potential pitfall of dissociating from (this) loss and ambivalence moving forward can be a mother's tendency to equate motherhood and genetics, a complicated experience that can create a sense of inadequacy in the mother that is often difficult to repair. Motherhood is much more complex than a biological link through DNA.*

- Resentment for a variety of reasons, for example, inequality in carrying the financial cost of ART. If these feelings are not worked through, they may impact parenting of a baby who becomes the recipient of parental projections.
- Avoidance of processing confusing feelings and fantasies regarding the birth-other. These feelings and fantasies may be denigratory or idealised; birth-others can be regarded as anything from kidnappers to saviours (Ehrensaft, 2008, 2014). They may also be denied in favour of perpetuating the idealised euphoria often felt following childbirth. Ehrensaft emphasises the need for all of these fantasies, whether wanted or not, to be thought about and processed:

*"The stark reality that the birth-other is no stranger to the baby but rather someone who either is genetically related to the child through sperm or egg donation or housed the child in her womb for nine months and, furthermore, may be a family member or friend, only fuels the fearful fantasy."*

(Ehrensaft, 2008, p. 6)

Within the context of the wider family and community, stresses may include the following:

- Stigmatisation and discrimination from relatives and others who struggle to understand new family forms. For example, a gay couple described how, following the birth of their daughter through surrogacy, the midwife did not know how to refer to them and so just called them 'parent.' Similarly, a single parent by choice described how her grandmother referred to her (known) sperm donor as her husband.

One partner of a lesbian couple described how it was obvious that each of their mothers was more invested in the grandchild that was biologically related to them, questioning whether it was unconscious bias or biological determinism. This perpetuated competition between the couple.

- Misrecognition when family members may insensitively state whom a child resembles, failing to realise that this may reinforce the anxieties and competitiveness between partners where one or both are not genetically connected.

Freeman-Carroll (2016) contends the importance of recognising the unconscious bias towards 'resemblance-culture' that society endorses. From a psychoanalytic perspective, arguably, the importance of generativity and the need for children to look like their parents may be connected to narcissism.

These points are by no means exhaustive but highlight some key aspects to be aware of concerning those undergoing ART. They also reflect the fundamental importance of being aware of wider social paradigms that will inevitably impact all involved with ART.

## Final thoughts

The field of infertility and ART is dominated by complexity and change – psychologically, politically, and sociologically. On a personal level, it is characterised by uncertainty and loss. While there has been a huge increase in live births born through IVF over the past three decades, approximately two-thirds of all embryo implantations are still unsuccessful, conveying the tremendous amount of risk involved with fertility treatment (HFEA, ibid). Furthermore, LGBTQ+ couples and single parents by choice are still likely to face widespread societal discrimination and prejudice in spite of the opportunities ART has provided (McCann & Sandor, 2021). All these aspects challenge individuals and couples to make coherent meaning out of their experiences. In the absence of this, there may be many 'unthought' and unresolved narratives resulting in stress and symptoms which bring individuals and couples into the consulting room.

The recommendation for therapeutic support may feel counterintuitive when undertaking ART treatment. Treatment itself is demanding enough on a couple's time and, for many, very costly. However, there is a well-established link between couples functioning well together, ensuring successful parenting of children born through ART, thus creating the case for increasing services that support these crucial connections.

In drawing on my experience of providing therapy to couples struggling with infertility issues and those using ART to become parents, I hope that my account will help alert all professionals and would-be parents to the challenges these individuals and couples face whether these are encountered in treatment clinics or the therapist's consulting room.

## References

Apfel, R., & Keylor, R. (2002) Psychoanalysis and infertility: Myths and realities. *The International Journal of Psychoanalysis*, 83: 85–104.

Byrne, D. (2022) I agreed to my sperm donor's anonymity, now I see that my daughter has a right to know who she is. *Guardian Newspaper*, 31st May 2022.

Clulow, C. (1996) *Partners Becoming Parents*. London: Sheldon Press.

Cudmore, L. (2005) Becoming parents in the context of loss. *Sexual and Relationship Therapy*, 20: 299–308.

D'Ercole, A., & Drescher J. (Eds.) (2004) *Uncoupling Convention: Psychoanalytic Approaches to Same-sex Couples and Families*. New York: Routledge.

Ehrensaft, D. (2007) The stork didn't bring me, I came from a dish: Psychological experiences of children conceived through assisted reproductive technology. *Journal of Infant, Child, and Adolescent Psychotherapy*, 6: 124–140.

Ehrensaft, D. (2008) When baby makes three or four or more attachment, individuation, and identity in assisted-conception families. *Psychoanalysis Study Child*, 63: 3–23.

Ehrensaft, D. (2014) *Family Complexes and Oedipal Circles: Mothers, Fathers, Babies, Donors, and Surrogates*. London: Psychoanalytic Aspects of Assisted Reproductive Technology.

Fine, K. (Ed.) (2015) *Donor Conception for Life: Psychoanalytic Reflections on New Ways of Conceiving the Family*. London: Karnac.

Freeman-Carroll, C. (2016) The possibilities and pitfalls of talking about conception with donor egg: Why parents struggle and how clinicians can help. *Journal of Infant, Child, and Adolescent Psychotherapy*, 15(1): 40–50.

Freud, S. (1920) 'Beyond the pleasure principal group psychology' and other works. In *The Standard Edition of the Complete Psychological Works of Freud. 1955*. London: Hogarth Press.

Giffney, A. N., & Watson, E. (Eds.) (2017) *Clinical Encounters in Sexuality*. Earth, Milky Way: Punctum Books.

Golombok, S. (2015) *Modern Families*. Cambridge, UK: Cambridge University Press.

Golombok, S. (2020a) *We are family what really matters for parents and children*. Melbourne: Scribe Publications.

Golombok, S. (2020b) 'Children flourish in new forms of family, but some still suffer outsiders' stigmatization. *Child and Family Blog*. https://childandfamily blog.com

Haynes, C., & Miller, J. (Eds.) (2003) *Inconceivable Conceptions: Psychological Aspects of Infertility and Reproductive Technology*. East Sussex: Brunner-Routledge.

Hertzmann, L. (2011) Lesbian and gay couple relationships: When internalized homophobia gets in the way of couple creativity. *Psychoanalytic Psychotherapy*, 25(4): 346–360.

Hertzmann, L., & Newbigin, J. (2023) *Psychoanalysis and Homosexuality*. London and New York: Routledge.

Hertzmann, L., & Newbigin, J. (Eds.) (2019) *Sexuality and Gender Now: Moving Beyond Heteronormativity*. London and New York: The Tavistock Clinic Series, Routledge.

Keylor, R., & Apfel, R. M. (2010) Infertility: Integrating an old psychoanalytic story with the research literature. *Studies in Gender and Sexuality*, 11: 60–77.

Klein, M. (1940) Mourning and its relation to manic-depressive states. *International Journal of Psychoanalysis*, 21: 125–153.

Kremen, A. (2012) Beyond conception: Recovering the creative couple after infertility. *Couple and Family Psychoanalysis*, 2(1): 80–92.

Lemma, A., & Lynch, P. E. (2015) *Sexualities: Contemporary Psychoanalytic Perspectives*. East Sussex: Routledge.

Mann, M. (Ed.) (2014) *Psychoanalytic Aspects of Assisted Reproductive Technology*. London: Karnac.

McCann, D. (Ed.) (2021) *Same-sex Couples and Other Identities; Psychoanalytic Perspectives*. London and New York: Routledge.

McCann, D., & Sandor, C. (2021) Responding to the challenge that same-sex parents pose for psychoanalytic couple and family psychotherapists. In *Same-Sex Couples and Other Identities: Psychoanalytic Perspectives*. London and New York: Routledge.

Menzies-Lyth, I. M. (1988) *Containing Anxiety in Institutions: Selected Essays*, Vol. 1. London: Free Association Books.

Modig, K., Talbäck, M., Torssander, J., & Ahlbom, A. (2017) Payback time? Influence of having children on mortality in old age. *The Journal of Epidemiology and Community Health*, 71(5): 424–430 (Published online 2017 Apr 10).

Morgan, M. (2005) On being able to be a couple: The importance of a creative couple in psychic life. In *Oedipus and the Couple*. London: Karnac.

Pawson, M. (2003) The battle with mortality and the urge to procreate. In Haynes and Miller (2003). Inconceivable conceptions: psychological aspects of infertility and reproductive technology. East Sussex: Brunner-Routledge.

Roseneil, et al. (2020) *The Tenacity of the Couple-Norm Intimate citizenship regimes in a changing Europe*. London: UCL Press.

Sander, C. (2021) The LGBTQ couple choice of therapist he/she/they, straight or gay. In *Same-Sex Couples and Other Identities: Psychoanalytic Perspectives*. London and New York: Routledge.

Siegal, R. (2017) "Where did I come from?" The impact of ART on families and psychotherapists. *Psychoanalytic Inquiry*, 37(8): 512–524.

The Human Fertilisation and Embryology Authority (2021) www.hfea.gov.uk

Vaughan, S. C. (2007) Scrambled eggs psychological meanings of new reproductive choices for lesbians. *Journal of Infant, Child, and Adolescent Psychotherapy*, 6(2): 141–155.

## Chapter 4

# Gay and lesbian parenting

## Choices, choices and more choices

*Colleen M. Sandor*

### Introduction

One of the most fundamental decisions in the life of a couple is whether to become parents. A successful pregnancy or adoption is typically a cause for celebration for the heterosexual couple and their extended family, and this is no different for the same-sex couple. While all parents must work out their differences to effectively parent their children, there are many unique factors the gay or lesbian couple faces. The prospect of becoming a parent will give rise to an individual's own experience of being parented, often evoking strong feelings and defenses. For the gay and lesbian individual, the experience of their developing sexuality and subsequent "coming out" will also affect their parenting efforts.

Parenting by lesbian and gay couples is still an underrepresented area of the psychodynamic couple's treatment literature. This chapter will examine several factors gay and lesbian couples moving into parenthood face and consider them from a psychoanalytic perspective. It will also apply link theory, which will be described later, to further our understanding of this transition and show how gay or lesbian couples may enjoy supportive links or suffer breaks in links as they strive to be a successful parenting couple. Several short clinical vignettes will be offered to illustrate the concepts being discussed. The scope of this chapter will be gay and lesbian parents only – as parenting from the perspective of bi or trans individuals deserves chapters unto themselves. This chapter will also only consider gay and lesbian couples that choose to become parents using biological methods. Blended families, adopting families or families where the individual has children from a previous heterosexual coupling will not be considered, though they are important areas of study in their own right.

### The kids are all right

Increasingly, same-sex couples are choosing to raise children, as marriage rights have been extended to the gay and lesbian community and assisted reproductive technology (ART) and adoption have become more widely accessible. According to Goldberg and Conron (2018), US household counts indicated that approximately

DOI: 10.4324/9781003387947-6

114,000 same-sex couples were raising children, including 28,000 male couples and 86,000 female couples. The majority (68%) of couples were raising biological children, while 21.4% were raising adopted children and 2.9% foster children.

One of the major questions same-sex couples as parents have endured since they became more visible is whether their children fare as well as children raised in heterosexual families. Thanks to the pioneering work of Golombok (2020), it is well established that children raised in same-sex families are indeed as well-adjusted as those raised by more conventional families. According to Golombok's research, children were shown to flourish in all kinds of families. Indeed, those raised by lesbians or gay fathers or born through ART (assisted reproductive technology), including donor egg, sperm, embryos and surrogacy, failed to show any evidence of psychological distress. Outcome of the research conducted by Golombok and colleagues in the States (Patterson, 2004) conclude that "lesbian mothers were just as warm, involved and committed to their children as heterosexual mothers. Their children were no more likely to show emotional and behavioral problems, and the boys were no less masculine and girls no less feminine" (p. 21). With regard to gay fathers, Golombok notes that stereotypes around parenting still abound. Gay fathers face prejudice and judgement because the idea that children need mothers is ingrained in many societies. However, the researchers found that when compared to lesbian parents, gay fathers were shown to have just as positive a relationship with their children.

While it has been established that children in same-sex families are well adjusted, Golombok states that these children still face a great deal of prejudice, including in some of the most progressive societies. Gay and lesbian couples also find themselves either discriminated against or having to navigate a heteronormative world, where their unique needs are either overlooked or ignored. Golombok's work has been instrumental in establishing the legitimacy of gay and lesbian parenting.

In this chapter, I intend to move beyond a descriptive understanding of gay and lesbian parenting so as to deepen our understanding of the dynamics unique to these families. It is important to appreciate the choices gay and lesbian couples face in becoming parents, the subsequent impact on their children and the unconscious forces at work societally and within the family. Analytic theories will assist in understanding what is at work at the more profound level.

## The couple's choice to become parents

Therapists working with gay and lesbian couples seeking to become parents need to keep in mind a number of areas for exploration. When a gay and lesbian couple decide to start a family, there are many choices they must make. First, the couple must decide if they will adopt, foster or bring a biological child into the family. For the purposes of this chapter, I will focus on the couple bringing a biological child into the family and the issues surrounding choices regarding pregnancy and the use of assisted reproductive technology.

For gay and lesbian couples, choices relating to the way they actually become pregnant are many. Lesbian and gay couples may choose sperm and egg donors, either from a known donor or a sperm or egg bank. The banks will give the couple information about a donor's race, ethnicity, facial features, temperament and other basic details. Gay couples must also select a surrogate who will carry their baby. When choosing donors, lesbian and gay couples need to decide whether to use an anonymous donor or one the couple knows who may or may not agree to be known at a designated time in the child's life. If the couple chooses a known donor, they must decide whether that person will be a part of the family and potentially part of the parenting process, someone who will agree to meet the child when the child is a certain age or one who is simply there to donate their egg or sperm. Although, to a large extent, these decisions remain conscious, we must also accept that the choice may embody fantasy and imaginings on the part of the couple and, eventually, the child, as we will see.

Another area to explore with the couple is the complexity of feelings that may arise as the couple choose to become parents. Gay and lesbian couples may have many feelings relating to the process of donor choice and around birthing a child. In many instances, there is a great deal of gratitude for a donor who is helping the couple realize their dream of becoming parents. But there is also a fair amount of mourning that takes place and for which space must be made. Firstly, couples may mourn the fact that they are unable to conceive a baby on their own and must turn to someone outside the relationship for assistance. They do not have the opportunity for at least one partner to share a biological heritage with their offspring. This can set up the non-biological parent to feel like an outsider in the process because they do not share DNA with the child. Additionally, gay and lesbian couples may face legal hurdles and scrutiny from their families that straight couples do not as they try to conceive.

Another area of mourning may come with the choice of sperm or egg donor. For example, lesbian couples in this situation may spend a great deal of time pouring over profiles, screening for traits they prefer in a sperm donor and choosing their "perfect match" only to find that donor has no sperm available when they attempt to purchase his vials. Or they may use several vials from the chosen donor and then move on to their second choice if their first donor is no longer available. Couples in this situation may mourn their "ideal" donor and feel like they are "settling" by using their next choice. Couples must be ready to explore these complex feelings and leave space for the grief that accompanies them. The same would also apply for gay couples using an egg donor and surrogate.

Unsurprisingly, negative emotions may also come up during the process related to the donor themselves. Ehrensaft (2005) coins the term "birth other" to describe the person, or people, who helps the gay or lesbian couple become pregnant. She says the couple may have many complicated feelings about this person. In addition to gratitude, she says, "negative or uncomfortable parental feelings run the gamut from sexual threat or desire to envy or hatred of the 'birth other' as a potential kidnapper of the baby's love and affection" (Ehrensaft, 2015, p. 131). The couple may envy the "birth other's" ability to render life, a capacity not available to them.

Amidst the many feelings associated with the process of getting pregnant, we must consider what happens to the couple in the process. One area of focus is the introduction of one or more people into the couple relationship by virtue of the donor or birth other. Ehrensaft (2005) not only refers to individuals who help the couple create their family as "birth others" but also the resulting families as "birth other families." This is an apt description which captures the idea that there are many people involved in the couple becoming pregnant, not just the two individuals. "Others" could also include doctors and fertility specialists if that is the route the couple needs to go to become pregnant.

When the couple is choosing a sperm or egg donor, they may do so within a fantasy of an ideal partner and ideal family. They may rely, unconsciously, on a heteronormative ideal, concluding that this type of family is better or more acceptable than a gay or lesbian family. This may be so profound that it may, in part, influence donor choice. Mamo (2004) tells us that "affinity ties provide legitimacy in everyday interactions with heteronormative society. Looking like and being like someone accomplishes 'true' familyhood" (p. 133). For the lesbian or gay family, a child with a donor poses the risk of not looking like the biological offspring of the couple. The task, therefore, of looking for a donor who is, in appearance and temperament, like the non-biological partner may, in part, be embedded in the desire to birth a child that can make the family look a little more like the heteronormative ideal. As comfortable as the couple is, as a gay couple, surprising heteronormative strivings get enacted as they begin the task of forming a family.

Whenever individuals are added to the couple, like donors and medical professionals, what gets stirred up by the presence of another must be considered. As Vaughan (2015) tells us, the donor is very much a presence within the couple. The couple must struggle with this presence but also must come to terms with what the absence of this presence might mean for them. Each individual in the gay or lesbian couple may project their hopes, fears and anxieties onto the donor. In the triangular nature of the oedipal, the two partners form a bond and the baby looks on, learning to be on the outside, looking in without panic. If all goes well, the triangular configuration is resolved. If not, there is much anxiety and many feelings of expulsion and favour. In the gay and lesbian couple, the addition of a third in the form of a donor may lead to one partner feeling left out of both the birth couple, biological partner and donor and the resulting parenting tasks. Consequently, unresolved oedipal conflicts may get stirred up. In the following composite example, we see how each partner feels left out of the parental couple as they come together to start a family.

## Case example

Both Marsha and Felicia, a lesbian couple, brought unresolved oedipal longings from their childhoods, which influenced their parenting. They had been married for ten years when they decided to start a family. Because of her advanced age, they agreed that Marsha would become pregnant first and Felicia would follow. They each gave birth to a son three years apart with the same anonymous donor. The couple came to treatment because they were having difficulty with their second son's behavior, Felicia's biological son.

Marsha herself was raised by a single mother, while Felicia was the "apple of her father's eye" and had a strained relationship with her mother, who was competitive with her. While they seemed to have a strong couple identity prior to starting a family (I had seen Marsha for many years in individual therapy), that connection broke down once the children were born. When talking about their children, Marsha and Felicia left the impression that they were two single mothers caring for each of their children alone, rather than as a couple. Each biological mother formed a couple with her own biological son. Marsha was very bonded with her son, almost fused, while she had a hard time bonding with Felicia's son. Felicia had a hard time forming a close relationship with either child and struggled setting limits, which led to substantial acting out on the part of both children. As a response, Felicia immersed herself in her work and spent significant amounts of time away from the home, focused on her career advancement.

In our work together, Marsha expressed how excluded she felt by Felicia's pregnancy because she was not biologically connected to the conception and, in so doing, turned to and fused with her son. She excluded Felicia, just like Marsha's mother excluded her father from the parenting of her as Marsha never saw her father after her parents divorced. For her part, Felicia talked about how she felt on the outside of Marsha's bond with her son and turned away from the family and toward her work, where she felt competent, acknowledged and praised, much like she felt with her father. The couple therapy focused on strengthening the couple bond and helping Marsha and Felicia establish appropriate bonds with each child as a parental couple, not single mothers. As they began to come together, Marsha accepted Felicia's influence as a parent, to the benefit of their couple relationship. Subsequently, their son began to settle down, and many of his more difficult behaviors began to abate.

## Link theory and the gay and lesbian couple as parents

As the gay and lesbian couple becomes a family, we must look at the ways in which family of origin history and the sociocultural environment impact the individuals and their relationships to each other and to the wider community. Link theory provides us with a comprehensive lens through which to view these dynamics. Argentinian psychoanalyst Pichon Riviere was influential in developing link theory beginning in the 1940s (Scharff et al., 2017). He took Klein's work and expanded on it by examining internal and external links. As Scharff et al. (2017) say, "He saw internal links as being in constant interaction with the external world through external links – that is actual internal interactions with others" (p. 130). The individual will be in a continual interaction with her inner world, the familiar external world and their community and larger society. Riviere proposed two axes, a vertical and a horizontal axis. Through the vertical axis, the individual is connected to their parents, ancestors, children and the history of the society in which he lives. Through the horizontal axis, the individual is connected to life partners, family, extended family, their community, current society and current culture. This results in a web of interactions that forms and holds the couple and family.

When the gay and lesbian couple is beginning to consider donor choice, link theory can help us understand a number of issues they may face. When a heterosexual couple becomes pregnant, the ancestorial and familial links are already cemented through the partner choice. However, when gay and lesbian couples are choosing egg or sperm donors, they will introduce a third link, likely to trigger their imagination and fantasy. In some cases, the vertical and horizontal links may be stronger with the donor in fantasy than with the partner in the couple in reality. Mamo (2004) discusses potential social relationships formed between lesbians and the donors they choose. She used the phrase "affinity ties" to describe what emerges when lesbians translate donor listings into potential relationships. She says, "Through their interactions with donor catalogs, lesbians envision social connections with potential children as formed by shared social, cultural, and ancestral histories" (p. 128). Thus, the horizontal and vertical links may be made up, in part, of fantasy. Left to the imagination are all of the cultural, social and ancestral links. The couple may attempt to "match" the donor egg or sperm history to the other partner by their choice of donor. Mamo says that women choose donors based on racial and ethnic qualities as a form of "matching" with qualities of the non-biological mother and as a form of sharing cultural and ancestral roots. Is this choice of donor a way for some couples to strengthen the vertical link? There will be a non-biological vertical link with the non-biological mother or father in the case of donor egg and a biological vertical link with the donor. This biological vertical link is one made mostly of information on paper and of ancestral and societal dreams and musings. So with sperm and egg donation, we see the complexity of the links in the lesbian couple in a way we do not see in a heterosexual couple who can conceive with both partners' DNA. The web is cast much further and deeper with all of the ways the couple may imagine that the donor contributes to the child. There is a third other, the birth other, and possibly a fourth in the case of surrogacy, that needs to be considered in the network of links.

The presence of another can have many effects on the gay and lesbian couple. And as Palacios says (2022), participating in links and being a part of them demands psychic work. The idea of more links can either be used playfully by the couple in their imagination, dream and fantasy life or can cause difficulties and disruptions. Many gay and lesbian couples can incorporate the donor in novel ways, giving him a fictitious name and life based on their imagination. Mamo (2004) describes a lesbian couple who gave their donor a fictitious name, imagining what his life was like. They would think of him as a character out of a novel. So the question becomes, can the couple use the presence of the donor creatively, incorporate the donor's presence and maintain a creative couple state of mind, or does the donor's presence cause difficulty for the couple? Morgan (2019), in discussing link theory, describes how the presence of an other is "an 'interference' for the subject, and on their previously held conceptions. This can lead to instabilities in a relationship or also development" (p. 137). In the previous example from Mamo, we see how the couple uses the presence of the donor in a playful way, incorporating him into the couple. The interference the donor provides leads to the couple coming together in a more creative manner.

Rather than creativity, interference can occur in the gay or lesbian couple when the non-biological partner is excluded from the consideration of the link by either the biological partner or the extended family. In the next example, the extended family caused a disruption in the couple's relationship based on their feelings of disruption, provoked by the presence of the donor.

### Case example

Mark and Nathan are a couple who, after five years of marriage, decided to start a family. They chose to use Mark's sperm, an anonymous egg donor and a separate surrogate. Mark and Nathan spent many hours pouring over egg donor catalogues and decided to use a donor who matched Nathan's racial and ethnic characteristics. They had baby pictures of the donor that resembled Nathan when he was young, and the donor matched many of his interests and educational achievements. Nathan and Mark were very happy to find such a donor and even made up a story about her and why she would be happy to create a family for the couple. When their baby was born, Nathan and Mark began to spend a lot more time with Mark's family who lived close by. They were a conservative Christian family who had hated Mark's sexuality at first but who came to accept his life and Nathan as his partner. They would now visit often and tend Mark and Nathan's son.

Soon after the baby was born, Mark's mother and sisters began to say how much the baby looked like Mark and how he had all of his physical characteristics and mannerisms, as if there was no donor and the baby was conceived with Mark's sperm only, like an immaculate conception. There was no place for "another;" Nathan or the donor. Nathan began to feel increasingly excluded from the conversation and from consideration of being the other father in the couple that brought the baby into the world. As time went on, Nathan began to say that their baby looked like pictures of his brother as a baby and that the baby also resembled the donor. He did this as a way to establish himself as the other father.

While Mark always acknowledged Nathan as the baby's father, he failed to say anything when his family did not. This caused numerous arguments and a great deal of disruption in the couple relationship. Mark's family could not tolerate the idea of an other, and Mark had a hard time understanding Nathan's hurt. Over time, Mark came to realize the pain Nathan was feeling and why he felt his parents' actions were a microaggression toward the couple's relationship and their family. He moved from defending his family to empathizing with Nathan to defending him when his family made subtle gestures to exclude him. The couple was able to use the "interference" of the donor creatively by making up stories about her. However, Mark's family was disturbed by the interference, which disrupted the couple, threatening the horizontal link. Only because the couple had such a strong relationship, were they eventually able to overcome this difficulty and form an even stronger bond as a family.

Another complicated area for the gay or lesbian couple that link theory can help us understand is that of raising this type of family in a heteronormative environment. Pichon Riviere developed an idea he called "ecological internalization," which refers to the subject's internalization of the environment in which they develop. This underscores the importance of the social environment in the constitution and preservation of the individual's identity (Scharff et al., 2017). Individuals in a gay or lesbian couple relationship, who have had a long history of being out of the closet and living an affirmative life, may find themselves faced with coming out over and over again in their role as parents in a heteronormative culture. When an individual is with their child, it is often assumed they are part of a heterosexual couple, a belief the gay or lesbian individual must constantly correct. This happens daily and in many settings, including at doctor's and other health care providers' offices, the school gates, with coaches and leaders of sports or club activities, and with the parents of their child's school friends. Often, gay and lesbian parents must make the choice of providers, schools and other activities not only based on the best options but also based on how affirming specific individuals and each environment is.

Here, the horizontal link is important since we might ask whether a disruption in the link stresses the couple or alternatively will a strong link provide a holding place for the family. The manner and degree to which a disruption in this link will affect the couple may depend on how much internalized homophobia each member of the couple still has. While pre-children, each individual may report that they have resolved their homophobia for the most part, what is stirred up once they have children may surprise them. As Vaughan (2015) says for the LGBTQ couple and individuals, "Parenting . . . pushes one to be as out and as comfortable as possible with one's identity. If you are not, your children will be only too happy to out you, usually in an elevator in a conservative midwestern city" (p. 51).

In the earlier example of Marsha and Felicia, Marsha's internalized homophobia came up in a way that was surprising to all three of us. While single and also early on in their relationship, Marsha was a strong leader in the LGBTQ community through her professional work and advocacy. She was fully out in a conservative, male-dominated profession and often gave talks about how to work with the LGBTQ community. When she became a mother, she ran into a level of internalized homophobia that startled her. One day in session, she was talking about dropping her kids off at school and said, "There I am in line with all of the normal parents." We all paused, surprised by this statement. She subsequently talked about how she felt she wasn't like all the other parents and that her family probably would have been happier if she were. She also expressed her fears that her children may be treated differently, especially since they lived in a conservative neighbourhood dominated by predominantly religious heterosexual families. Marsha displayed an ecological internalization and the horizontal links provided difficulty for her. Fortunately, she was able to examine this homophobia, rather than shut it down, and open herself to a deep exploration of how it was affecting her, subsequently freeing her from some of the fears she was holding. As a result, the bond with her children and partner became much stronger.

Marsha's experience illustrates what can happen when another (in this case, the child) is introduced into the space of a lesbian relationship. The presence of her children changes Marsha and helps her understand herself in ways that surprise her and cast her into a space of uncertainty. This is an important point when we consider that we all are embedded in a social context when starting families and raising kids. Gay and lesbian families are embedded in a heteronormative culture that in some ways is accepting and in others still vilifies the lesbian and gay individual and family. Link theory helps us understand concepts of difference, representation, uncertainty and interference. When an other is introduced into the couple – a donor or birth other and, eventually, a child – many new configurations and links emerge in the couple and family, and if change does not take place, then strife will emerge. Berenstein (2012), speaking about the therapeutic relationship, says that interference occurs when the presence of two or more subjects produces something new and unknown. It is as follows:

*"about making room for the other as a different subject. It is about the couple members' ability to produce something new and different, instead of reproducing what each carry from childhood and what he or she has brought to the couple."*
(p. 576)

Each of the individuals in a gay or lesbian couple will bring many experiences of homophobia and their experiences in the heteronormative world into their couple relationship. While many of these issues may be resolved, the couple transitioning to parents will encounter parts of themselves they had not anticipated. The couple and family are a part of a society or culture which may or may not see them as belonging. The greater the degree of difference or not belonging, the greater difficulty the couple may face.

Palacios and Monserrat (2017) underscores the importance of social culture in discussing three psychic spaces, the intrasubjective, intersubjective and the transubjective. The intrasubjective considers drives and fantasy, the intersubjective is where two or more subjects meet and the transubjective is where individuals "participate in a specific culture and are a part of a society that gives a sense of belonging" (p. 9). For many gay and lesbian couples and families, the transubjective space is not a space of belonging, and they must face the challenges of this in bringing a child into the couple and the larger world. However, for others, the family and the society they find themselves in may be more accepting and affirming. It will depend in large measure on how their family of origin embraces them, how their close community (extended family and neighbourhood) receives them and how larger society treats them. Our minds are built in the society we are in (Palacios, personal communication). The strength and the affirmative quality of the links will be significant to the development of the individual, couple and family.

## Implications for the children

As Golombok has established already, kids in gay or lesbian families fare just as well as kids in heterosexual families. But how can we understand some of the unique qualities these kids and families possess and some of the challenges they may face? I begin by looking at the oedipal situation and its resulting configurations in the mind of the baby. Morgan (2019) informs us that, for the child, the early oedipal situation "requires the relinquishment of the exclusive relationship with the early primary object, facing and being able to tolerate the special link between the parents" (p. 130). What triggers the early oedipal is the baby's awareness of the absence of the primary caregiver. With her absence, the baby conceives of her in a relationship with somebody else. This absence opens the possibility of a "triangular space," and the baby's identity takes on the form described as the "oedipal triangle." Morgan (2019) continues:

> "The baby begins to experience himself as loved by a loving couple. With this development the child can also experiment with being at different points in the triangle – in a relationship with either parent, observed by the other, or witnessing the parents' relationship as the excluded other."
>
> (p. 131)

Also with this development comes the idea of an internal creative couple in the mind of the mother. The child will internalize this internal creative couple, resulting in her being able to begin to form such a couple later in life.

Morgan helps us see how the mind of the baby develops in the presence of the loving other and loving couple. One of the unique factors for gay and lesbian families is, as stated earlier, the presence of the birth other. As the child continues to develop and understand his relationship to others and the coupling of his parents, he will have to account for the fact that there were more than two people that made him. He may be left with confusion about who the creative couple is, mom and mom or mom and donor, for example. Or whether there is one couple or two. How the couple speaks of the donor will have far-reaching implications for the child. The child is also likely to project many attributes onto the donor and even fantasize about his relationship with the donor, especially if the donor is unknown.

## Case example

Sara Jane was in therapy, along with her wife, when she became pregnant by an anonymous donor and gave birth to a daughter, Penny. From early on in Penny's life, Sara Jane and her wife would talk with her daughter about being in a different kind of family. They would tell her how lucky she was to have two moms and that most kids weren't so lucky. While they focused on the positive, the couple was aware of leaving the space open for any feelings Penny might have about being from a different kind of family, knowing the importance of the need for the expression of negative feelings if they existed. One day when Penny was four, she was eating her breakfast and looked up and off into space and said, "Wow I have two moms. . . . I'm really, really lucky." Sara Jane overheard her daughter say this and commented that she was indeed very lucky. Three years later, when Penny was 7, she was talking to Sara Jane about a television show they were watching where competitors who did not do well were asked to leave the competition. Penny and Sara Jane liked to choose a competitor and follow them through the show to see if their person won. Penny would choose two people, one her primary contestant and the second her backup contestant in case her primary one was eliminated. She called the backup contestant her "ID." Sara Jane was confused about this term and asked Penny about it. Penny laughed and said, "Oh, it means 'invisible dad.'" Sara Jane asked Penny if she had an invisible dad, and she just laughed and started talking about something else. Sara Jane was startled by this interaction and held it in mind for a later discussion, well aware it would come up at another point in Penny's development.

In couple therapy, I was curious, along with her parents, about what was happening in the mind of Penny. How was she considering an invisible father in a family with two mothers, and what would she do when she learned more about the birth other? Penny wasn't consciously aware of a donor but clearly had some idea that there was more than just her two moms. How was this affecting the triangular space and the couple configuration in Penny's mind? As she learns about the birth other, how will this change how she envisions her internal couple? Who will the couple be in her mind, Sara Jane and her wife or Sara Jane and the donor? Gay and lesbian couples will do well to leave the space open for many complicated feelings on the part of their child regarding learning about their family configuration. Fluidity, in terms of allowing the child to create many couplings in his mind, will be essential to his developing a sense of a creative internal couple. While gratitude for the donor is important, foreclosing space for the negative can have many important ramifications for the child and the family.

Ehrensaft (2015) tells us that children conceived through ART face certain developmental tasks specific to their birth other origins. These tasks are grappling with their sense of difference, establishing a sense of belonging and confirming their identity. I would add that children born into gay and lesbian families will face these tasks in a unique way from children in straight families who use ART.

The first task Ehrensaft (2015) proposes is grappling with a sense of difference. She says that children in families that use ART were not conceived of a sexual union. Instead:

*"Each of us is conceived out of the desire of one or two people and possibly the assistance of one or more people who participated in our conception or gestation not out of sexual desire but as a result of providing use of their uterus or donating their gametes so that we could be born."*

(p. 140)

What is critical here, she says, is that science replaces sex, and there is an outsider who is participating in the process who never intended to be a parent to this child. This potentially leaves the child without the knowledge of half of their genetic heritage, depending on how much information is known about the donor.

This lack of knowledge about their genetic heritage, coupled with what both intimate others and society reflect back to these children about their conception, may create strong feelings of uniqueness and difference that emerge in the child's psyche. Some of these may be positive, as we see in the case of young Penny, and some negative. I believe children in gay and lesbian families will experience this to a greater degree. They face a double uniqueness, that of being conceived through ART and donor material and living in a non-heterosexual family. Each of these facts may give rise to many fantasies and imaginings. For example, how will the child understand their situation? It appears that Penny relishes her uniqueness as a young child, but will she retain such positive feelings as she gains a greater understanding of her family composition compared to others? Will she be content to have an invisible dad, or will she long for a "real dad" like many of her peers and schoolmates? What hopes and anxieties will she project into the birth other and birth other's imagined family over time?

The second developmental task of children conceived with a birth other is that of establishing a sense of belonging. As Ehrensaft (2015) describes, the child's family matrix includes the couple who had them, the person or people who donated sperm or eggs or the use of their uterus, their siblings and their half siblings if there are siblings from the donor.

If we think of this in terms of link theory, we see many links for the child, some present and some much more invisible. Ehrensaft also says if the child is in a two-parent family, they may experience genetic asymmetry, as only one of the parents is biologically related to the child. Speaking of the child, she says, "If the donor or surrogate remains anonymous, they may suffer from 'genealogical bewilderment,' a blocked access to half their genetic heritage, which may affect not only their feeling of difference but also their sense of belonging" (p. 142). The child may suffer a disruption in the vertical link, as part of that link is broken. The child may have some sense of the biological and psychological attributes of the donor but will not understand the fullness of half of their ancestral heritage. This may be more difficult for children in gay or lesbian families who may already struggle with a sense of belonging in a heteronormative world. They also may experience a lack of belonging to their extended families based on the families' attitudes toward same-sex relationships and these couples having children. Genetic asymmetry in these families may affect the vertical links, while lack of recognition or support from the immediate family or society may affect the horizontal links, thus compromising the child's sense of belonging.

Finally, the third area of developmental task is that of forming one's identity. As Ehrensaft (2015) says, the child must weave in their birth other origins as they begin to develop their own sense of self. It is assumed knowing one's genetic roots is an important part of one's identity and that children who do not know this will have a difficult time forming their identity. A child may have a sense of a "missing piece."

Children in gay and lesbian families will have a sense of a missing piece in many ways. First of all, as established, they may know little to nothing about their donor. This will leave them to fill in the blanks about half of their genetic material as they strive to form their identity. Also, if the gay and lesbian couple uses a donor who has had other successful pregnancies with other people, the child will, over time, become aware that they have half siblings in the world. In some cases, there may be many half siblings. The child may seek to connect with these siblings who themselves may become interferences in the links and an extension of the child's family. The donor and these siblings are absent, but they are also present in the inner world of the child as he begins to form who he is.

The way the couple and family address these issues will affect the child's sense of development and identity formation. If the couple disavows the "other" and the "other family" in the form of the half siblings, they run the risk of shutting down an extensive exploration of who the individual is. Finally, if the child chooses to meet either the donor, if this is a possibility, or the half siblings, the child will face a "coming out" process of his own given that he is from a gay or lesbian family. There is no guarantee how the "others" will accept him and his identity as a child of same-sex parents.

## Conclusion

In this chapter, I have attempted to highlight the many challenges and choices gay and lesbian couples face as they move toward parenthood. I have done so using a psychodynamic theoretical lens to explore how both conscious and unconscious factors are at play in donor and surrogate choice. I also describe link theory and use it to deepen our understanding of how a heteronormative society and bias in the extended family may cause stress in the couple relationship. While I chose to focus on gay and lesbian couples, much more work must be done to explore the unique challenges facing bi and trans couples.

## References

Berenstein, I. (2012), Vinculo as a relationship between others. *The Psychoanalytic Quarterly*, 81 (3): 565–577.

Ehrensaft, D. (2005). *Mommies, Daddies, Donors, Surrogates*. New York: Guilford.

Ehrensaft, D. (2015), Chapter 6: When baby makes three or four or more: Attachment, individuation, and identity in assisted conception families. In K. Fine (ed.) *Donor Conception for Life: Psychoanalytic Reflections on New Ways of Conceiving the Family*, 129–150. New York: Routledge.

Goldberg, S. K., & Conron, K. J. (2018, July), How many same sex couples in the US are raising children? *UCLA School of Law Williams Institute*. https://williamsinstitute.law.ucla.edu/wp-content/uploads/Same-Sex-Parents-Jul-2018.pdf

Golombok, S. (2020), *We Are Family*. New York: Public Affairs.

Mamo, L. (2004), Chapter 7: The lesbian "Great American Sperm Hunt": A sociological analysis of selecting donors and constructing relatedness. In A. D'Eracole, & J. Drescher (eds.) *Uncoupling Convention: Psychoanalytic Approaches to Same Sex Couples and Families*, 113–140. New York: Routledge.

Morgan, M. (2019), *A couple State of Mind: Psychoanalysis of Couples and the Tavistock Relationships Model*. New York: Routledge.

Palacios, E. (2022), Editorial. *Couple and Family Psychoanalysis*, 12 (2): 7–10.

Palacios, E., & Monserrat, A. (2017), Chapter 5: Contributions to the link perspective in interventions with families: Theoretical and technical aspects, and clinical application. In D. Scharff, & E. Palacios (eds.) *Family and Couple Psychoanalysis: A Global Perspective*, 63–88. New York: Routledge.

Patterson, C. J. (2004), Lesbian and gay parents and their children: Summary of research findings. In *Lesbian and Gay Parenting: A Resource for Psychologists*, 5–22. Washington, DC: American Psychological Association.

Scharff, D. E., Losso, R., & Setton, L. (2017), Pichon Riviere's psychoanalytic contributions: Some comparisons with object relations and modern developments in psychoanalysis. *International Journal of Psychoanalysis*, 98: 129–143.

Vaughan, S. (2015), Chapter 3: Scrambled eggs: Psychological meanings of new reproductive choices for lesbians. In K. Fine (ed.) *Donor Conception for Life: Psychoanalytic Reflections on New Ways of Conceiving the Family*, 49–65. New York: Routledge.

# Part 2

# Developmental stages of the child

# Chapter 5

# Perinatal couple psychotherapy and the role of the infant

*Sara Leon*

## Introduction

For many couples, having a baby is central to their relationship, and although bringing new life into the world is often a momentous and joyous moment, the transition to parenthood can also be fraught with many unforeseen challenges which throw parents into turmoil. Infants are exquisitely sensitive and often in their raw chaotic emotional states can reflect and highlight the problems inherent in the couple relationship. For example, unresolved Oedipal conflicts that have remained dormant in the couple relationship can emerge with the introduction of a third. The parents' own unprocessed infantile feelings of being parented can be stirred up, leaving them despairing and disorientated. Such challenges often start in pregnancy and, if not addressed, may create for the infant complex and disturbing relational patterns that may become one of her/his most violent grievances.

Tavistock Relationships (TR) has, therefore, developed a couple's perinatal service to support parents. This involves the infant from the outset, as the infant's development and mental health takes place within the context of the parental relationship. Within this service, the parameters of the perinatal phase are defined as starting from pregnancy up until the infant is 1 year old.

Drawing on the work of the Anna Freud Parent Infant Project (Baradon et al., 2005, 2010), psychoanalytic theories, together with contemporary child development research, as well as a composite case study, I will attempt to demonstrate the importance of working with couples and their infant in the perinatal phase. Although the case material focuses primarily on postnatal depression, it is worth noting that this is not the only issue that can arise for and between couples.

## The importance of the parenting couple

Classic psychoanalytic theories offer rich and profound insights into early infantile developmental processes. The focus of these has predominantly been the infant's relationship to the mother as the main carer, with the father having little consequence other than protecting the mother infant dyad, that is, until Oedipal dynamics commence. Freud claims this occurs when the toddler is 3 to 5 years of age

DOI: 10.4324/9781003387947-8

(Laplanche & Pontalis, 1973), whilst Klein suggests Oedipal feelings emerge when the infant experiences frustrations around weaning and starts to turn towards the father (Klein, 1928). Winnicott famously observed that 'there is no such thing as a baby' and thought that the infant's relationship with the father begins when the mother thinks the infant might be interested in him (1960).

Contemporary psychoanalytic and child development research theories have expanded the role of the father, starting when the foetus is in utero, placing him alongside the mother in a central position in the infant's development. Schoppe and Sullivan (cited in von Klitzing, 2019) claim that the father's prenatal beliefs about himself as a significant object to his baby contributes to the infant's higher capacity to relate to two objects at the same time. von Klitzing (2019) also found that when the father has the capacity to anticipate his own relationship with the baby without excluding the mother, the infant's capacity to actively engage with both parents is greatly increased.

Mahler and Abelin (cited in von Klitzing, 2019) acknowledged the specific role the father plays in the symbiotic phase, and their research claims that the father's role stands for a '*distant non mother space*' (p. 15) which enables the infant to playfully engage and explore with the father, who is not as yet, an object of frustration. Abelin (1971) (cited in von Klitzing, 2019) developed the concept of early triangulation which claims to help the infant's mental organisation move from the level of relationships to the symbolic, so the infant, in her/his mind, can experience the father as enabling instead of a threat. von Klitzing (2019) also evidences that the infant's experience of triadic relationships from the birth strongly influences the infant's development and her/his pre-Oedipal complex, as the father is already known and, therefore, less frightening.

Fonagy and Target (2002) argue that the father's role is more than just to sever the symbiotic ties with the mother and that the presence of a third from the beginning helps to open the representational mentalizing world for the infant. They suggest that classic psychoanalysis can overlook idiosyncratic characteristics of the father-infant relationship and that the literature does not attribute much importance to the father's personality in his role as a father. They suggest that attachment theory indicates that the child's attachment to the mother only slightly corresponds with his pattern of attachment to the father and that father's own attachment history has as much influence on the child's security of attachment as that of the mother (Steele et al., 1996).

von Klitzing (2019) stresses that attachment theory does not attribute essential significance to the gender difference between the father and the mother position for early development. He claims that the gender differences between mothers and fathers do not matter for the infant and states, '*Taking any gender specific aspect out of the paternal function makes the concept more applicable for the varied living conditions of the modern world, such as same sex parents, patchwork families and gender fluid parenting*' (p. 25).

Harold et al. (2007) longitudinal study reveals that parental conflicts can adversely affect the infant's psychological and cognitive development in negative ways. In the perinatal service at TR, we have found that having parents in the session, alongside the infant, enables the therapist to give equal weight to both parents in their relationship with the baby, something that can be overlooked in daily life as, for example, one of them may have to work full time.

## Postnatal depression

TR clinicians and theorists have recognised over the years that in their work with couples that the focus is on the couple's relationship and extends beyond that of the individual. Morgan (2019) states that the relationship is what the couple create between them both consciously and unconsciously.

> *"The relationship becomes a psychic object in its own right which the couple relates to symbolically and can feel contained by . . . and embedded in concepts such as 'shared unconscious phantasy'. . . and the 'creative couple'."*

(p. xxi)

In couples where the projective system is strong, each partner might hold a particular state of mind for the couple. For example, one partner might carry the optimism whilst the other might carry more pessimistic feelings. This can also apply to postnatal depression, that is, I think more often than is recognised by the couple or the therapist since the couple's postnatal depression is a *shared couple experience*, which can manifest very differently in each partner, something which I will illustrate in the case material.

Much has been written about maternal mental health, including postnatal depression (PND) – (Parker (2012), Raphael-Leff (2003) and Beebe et al. (2012) to name but a few. Such writing underlines how PND can significantly adversely affect a child's emotional, cognitive and social development (Emanual, 2008). If the mother has postnatal depression, her relationship to the father is important, provided she can allow the father into the mother-infant dyad since the father's readiness to parent the infant is crucial (von Klitzing, 2019). The father's involvement is necessary, particularly if the mother is over-invested in the infant, since he may be obliged to carry the burden of the mother's depression and internal conflicts. Fain (1981, cited in Fonagy & Target, 2002) describes one mother who was still breastfeeding her 3-year-old several times during the night, had turned away from the father and was getting her needs met through her child. The father was unable to find a way into the dyad, leaving him feeling impotent and depressed at the loss of his adult relationship with his wife and the inability to develop a relationship with his child. The child, in turn, deeply resented the father's intrusion whilst at the same time needing him to help disentangle her/his merged relationship with the mother. The mother who desires her partner is likely to have less problems separating from her infant and will stimulate the infant's interest in the third.

Postnatal depression in fathers has become more widely recognised over the past approximately seven years (Hanley & Williams, 2020; Baradon, 2019), though support for them is not so commonly available.

This neglect of postnatal depression in fathers is perhaps, in part, because if it was not severe and did not lead to some sort of mental breakdown, it often went unnoticed, even to the father himself. Bevington (2019) describes how on his journey into fatherhood, and feeling at a loss, he found himself rebuilding an old fireplace. It was only after much reflection that he realised that he had been suffering from postnatal depressive feelings which were not identified at the time. One mother I worked with recalled how in the first six months of their baby's life, her husband always seemed to be covered in grouting. What is interesting with these two particular fathers is that both engaged in a repair activity, as if perhaps unconsciously, they sensed that with the birth of their new-born, something had been 'broken', whether this was internally or intrapsychically or both and that some kind of repair or reorganisation was needed.

### The infant at 0–6 months

For the infant, the first months of life are crucial in the development of its internal world which is shaped and structured by internalised object relationships (Rustin, 1989). In the first weeks of her/his life, the infant is still in the watery world of the womb and undifferentiated from her/his mother. At around two months, s/he starts to emerge and is ready to slowly and incrementally begin her/his journey of distinguishing between inner and outer spaces – that is, 'what is me and what is not me'.

It is at approximately six months, when the baby manages to separate from the mother enough and begins to be able to differentiate her/himself from the outside world, that s/he has made an important step in personality development; s/he has discovered a self (Fraiberg, 1959). Although s/he still has much to achieve developmentally, this is a time for exploration and enormous discovery. It can also be a perilous time in which the infant is in danger of slipping out of control. S/he will have all kinds of intense emotions, such as fear, helplessness and terror, without having the language to express them or the ability to process them. Her/his ego is not yet fully formed, her/his defences not organised and the lack of an internal structure renders the baby very vulnerable and dependent upon her/his parents to offer containment by noticing her/his feeling states, putting them into perspective and giving words to these experiences.

If this parental containment fails, the infant can be overwhelmed by unbearable feeling states, described by Bion (1962a) as nameless dread. Bion developed Klein's (1946) view that the infant's early anxieties are psychotic and need to be worked through and modified. He viewed projective identification as the means by which the infant communicates primal and violent emotions to the mother. If the infant cannot find a container in her, a primal disaster ensues in which the container has been destroyed and the infant's anxiety turns into psychotic pain, that is, a nameless dread. In addition to Freud's and Klein's focus on love and hate as central components to development, Bion (1962b) added another component which he described as knowledge. He claimed the frequent failure, often in early life, to have these unbearable feelings thought about and contained, take on more of a quality of fragments of feelings which can give rise to the feeling of fragmentation of the ego.

## Case study – Miriam and James

Miriam and James met at university and came for help in their early 30s because there was no intimacy between them – emotionally, physically or sexually. They believed their sexual relationship broke down following the birth of their first child, Tom, who was almost 5 years old at the time of the assessment, and the couple's second child was expected imminently. Miriam, who was on maternity leave, reported that she found motherhood difficult and did not think that their couple relationship would survive another child. She felt criticised, undesirable and unloved by James.

James was a medical researcher, and although he excelled at his work, he was seen by his colleagues as a lone wolf. They were both Dutch and had lived in the UK for eight years.

The therapy was carried out online, and although I began seeing Miriam, James and baby Andy together, when Andy was 6 months old, I then worked with the couple only and they remained with me for a further two years. Paradoxically, their child's existence was the cause of the broken connection between them, and at the same time, his presence was also instrumental in the reparation.

## First session

Immediately, James told me not to worry about him, as he was all right, and to help his wife. James made it clear that he was very committed to Miriam and only attended because they had problems with sex, although what later emerged was that the couple had a shared a fear of intimacy. Miriam agreed with James but spoke more of her fears about their second child, as she had so many difficulties with their first born, Tom.

She had suffered postnatal depression after Tom's birth and felt very isolated and abandoned by James, who had not helped at all. She felt ashamed and humiliated at having to seek help. Her son now had a problem with eating, and they had constant battles, as he rejected most of the food Miriam offered him. She was furious at James, who gave Tom sweets. She feared how Tom was going to manage when the baby arrived. Who would watch over him? James, looking helpless and in the voice of a child, said, '*You let him have sweets too*'. This dilemma caused frequent tensions between them and arguments that left Miriam desperate, and James frozen and unable to respond.

I was struck by several things. The couple dynamic seemed to suggest they functioned more like a parent-child dyad than an adult couple, or a parental couple. With another baby due, they conveyed a sense of profound desperation and helplessness. Would their relationship survive? Would Tom survive having a sibling? And lastly, would the baby survive? If so, the question was how as they had so painfully struggled with the arrival of Tom and had not as a couple fully recovered their connection. Miriam seemed to be suffering from both prenatal and postnatal depression and was pleased when I said that the baby could attend sessions at least for the first three months after which we could review the situation. James was less enthusiastic, so I agreed that we could negotiate when they needed a session for themselves as a couple. Miriam was on a low dose of antidepressant medication to help with her prenatal and possible postnatal depression.

They used the three sessions before the baby was due to speak of Miriam's anxieties about the birth and how, as a couple, they would manage it together. For instance, what would be the sleeping arrangements and what might Tom need from James. I had a sense of them feeling more contained and that they were more able to think together, but James was not happy about sleeping in the spare room, despite acknowledging that it might help him at work.

### Meeting baby Andy

When they first introduced Andy, he was 4 weeks old. I detected a sense of pleasure and pride in both parents as they presented their baby boy. In turn, they both held him gently and lovingly and seemed to be in tune with his needs, that is, his need to suckle and sleep. Interestingly, although James held Andy tenderly and touched him with what seemed to be enormous sensitivity that poured out from his fingertips, when I asked him how he felt towards Andy, he responded by saying that he did not have any feelings for him whatsoever. I wondered about the split between his mind and his body, in which his hands seemed full of feeling which his mind could not access.

As Andy nuzzled into his father, I welcomed him to the sessions. By speaking to him directly, I wanted to let him know that I considered him to be a person in his own right and part of the therapeutic process. Baradon and Joyce (2005) suggest that the baby's innate capacity for attachment can be inhibited if there is a lack of appropriate parental interaction: '*Met by a withdrawn or intrusive parent, a baby may himself withdraw or give up any attempts to engage*' (p. 26). I think this can also apply to the therapist.

The birth had been quick and easy, and Andy seemed to have entered the world with some ease. The parents told me how James was attending to Tom, frequently taking him out, whilst Miriam remained with Andy. In the sessions, Andy slept on either one of his parents. Interestingly, as he was passed from one parent to another, there was no scaffolding, that is, talking to him and letting him know what was going on as he was passed from one parent to the other or from one activity to another. The parental voice can 'hold' the baby and help him negotiate the transition by giving meaning to it, rather than it feeling like a random act. Some parents have an intuitive sense that the baby has some kind of mind to receive the words or be sensitive to the parent's voice. I tentatively commented to Andy on how cosy he seemed, being held first by his mummy and then by his daddy. Andy responded by looking at me with some curiosity, as if perhaps sensing that I was also there for him and that he was included into the sessions.

All seemed well for the first two or three sessions, then suddenly, Miriam started to become unsettled, criticising James for not supporting her enough. James responded by saying he valued all she did and he was happy and open to doing more but felt he needed to be told what to do. He described how all he remembered from his childhood was being told what to do, and these were mainly chores. Miriam seemed gratified that James could acknowledge how much effort she was making, but in the following session, James turned up on his own. Miriam requested that the sessions be postponed for a month, as Andy was being a nightmare. I emailed her, encouraging her to attend the next session, to think about what was happening, which she did.

Miriam said that Andy was being a nightmare at night, crying, refusing the breast and not going to sleep. It was unbearable for Miriam, and she had to call James to try to calm the baby down. James walked him around the house, holding him close to his body with his head on his shoulder so he was unable to see his face. He did get Andy to sleep, but when I asked him what was going on in his mind as he walked with his son, he replied, 'Nothing'. he just thought about work.

As Miriam spoke, Andy was sitting on James' right arm, nestled as far as he could into his body. He looked very still, perhaps dissociated, certainly cut off from his surroundings and his parents. Dissociation is an internal mental process that disrupts object relations and body relations. Trauma survivors are often in some state of dissociation which may vary depending on the perceived threat and the level of anxiety. When the ego is formed and there is enough ego strength, dissociation may serve as a loss against the object or the self. In Andy's case, in the primal position, that is, when the ego is not fully formed, there is a diffusion of self that results in a loss of both self and other (Eekhoff, 2022). Andy's emotional state was fragile, and he needed containing and very gentle handling. My fear was that if I did not help him out of this state, he might become traumatised, while at the same time, I was aware that the parents themselves were in various states of excitation and may have been stirred up my contact with him, perhaps even seeing me as being on Andy's side. Therefore, so that my contact with Andy was gentle and unintrusive, I made eye contact and smiled, occasionally greeting him. By doing this, my gaze and voice held him enough to prevent him from further withdrawal.

It went like this. I said hello to Andy and looked at him as I acknowledged what a hard time they were all having, nobody sleeping or feeding, everyone feeling very sad and lonely, including him. James let out a manic laugh, telling me that Andy could not understand me. I was startled by the strength of his rage which made me feel very stupid to think Andy had a mind. Instinctively, like Andy, I, too, wanted to withdraw but realised that painful memories and unprocessed traumas from the dark ages of their infancy were being stirred up, putting them in conflict with the reality of their relationship to Andy. Neither seemed to have the presence of mind to see Andy for who he was, a vulnerable, developing baby. So the question '*How was Andy experiencing his parents?'* was very much to the fore in my mind, as his withdrawal seemed to suggest he was in the grip of frightening states of mind.

### Hidden traumas and lost parental objects

The next few sessions were crucial. The therapeutic task was to find a balance between helping both parents separate out their own infantile experiences and the actual needs of Andy. Rustin (2002) claims that *'the growth of the personality is rooted in the introjective identifications with the parental objects which form the unconscious substrate of the self'* (p. 19). With the birth of a baby, parents have to renegotiate a new relationship to the internal parents which involves both *identification* with them and *differentiation* from them.

I was concerned about Andy's emotional state and thought he was at risk of introjecting the same traumas as his parents had experienced as infants, resulting in what is termed *'intergenerational trauma'*, that is, unprocessed traumas which can be passed down through the generations (Fraiberg et al., 1980). Intergenerational trauma is less likely to be repeated when the infant is in the room. For example, Andy's presence created an opportunity for him to bond with his parents and for them to bond with him, which contributed to preventing the repetition of the trauma.

Miriam spoke about her overwhelming feelings of shame for feeling unable to manage her own baby. It had been so hard for her even to admit she needed help. What really got under her skin was how in the evenings, alone in the marital bedroom, she could not get Andy to take her breast milk or to go to sleep. Andy just cried and cried. I explored what this did to Miriam. She felt very persecuted by Andy and felt that she could get nothing right for him, just as she had not been able to get anything right for her parents. She described her father as a bully with a violent temper and criticised her constantly. Miriam feared being like him but worried she was. This thought was extremely painful for her and gave rise to excruciating levels of shame. Parker (2012) emphasises the significance of shame in magnifying anxiety and fear mobilised by maternal ambivalence. She also suggests that *'shame powerfully institutes concealment'* which seemed to account for why it was so difficult for Miriam to attend sessions with me, as in her mind, I represented the critical eye of her internalised father. At other times, when Andy would not feed or sleep, he became the persecuting, critical eye.

I was curious about Miriam's mother. Where was she when Miriam's father was shouting at her? It sounded as if her mother would tend to be with her younger brother, her favourite child to this day. I began to wonder if the jealous feelings she felt towards her brother might now be located in Andy, especially when he was offered breast milk. Perhaps such jealous feelings of resentment were sensed by Andy and felt to be too toxic for him to take in and to sleep. Miriam's own experiences of being fed were not easy. Her mother was very strict around feeding and could not tolerate any mess, so everything was cleaned up immediately. I thought the physical mess also stood for messy feelings, particularly raw infantile feelings, and that Miriam may have been left alone to manage them, as they were too intolerable for her mother. So when Miriam herself became a mother, she was thrown back into that preverbal state of being on her own to manage terrifying anxieties.

James had started to feel depressed, for the first time as far as he could remember, and suggested it was because of work and feeling under-stimulated. He said he felt empty. Since he was able to feel an empathy towards Miriam and her early experiences, I enquired about his. He described a rather bleak experience and could not remember much. His father worked away a lot. His younger twin siblings occupied a lot of his mother's time. He remembers his mother as being needy and demanding. James spent his life yearning to be old enough to leave home, which he did as soon as he could. I thought with him about how he conveyed a sense of loneliness, of nobody being around to think about him and his emotional experiences and how he told me that he has no feelings, not even for baby Andy. He agreed, saying that he thought that people who had feelings had something wrong with them and he felt sorry for them. Now he was beginning to realise that having feelings is normal. He was the abnormal one.

I suggested that not being held in mind as an infant had left him with no expectations to be thought about and understood, as he felt he did not exist in relation to others. This included with me, and I reminded him how in the first session he told me to help Miriam and forget about him, as if I would not be interested in him, or perhaps even more, that his existence did not matter. I suggested these feelings had haunted him all his life and might explain why he did not feel or expect to be part of a group, such as his colleagues, Miriam's family or even with his wife and children. He still felt like an outsider who really does not matter. I think the same applied to Miriam, who had felt so excluded by her mother and brother.

I suggested that James did have feelings for Andy which were partly expressed in the way he touched him with such gentleness. Also, he had other feelings towards him, such as anger – anger that he had taken his place in the marital bed and with me for thinking he might have a mind. When I spoke to Andy as if he had a theory of mind, I thought that perhaps it stirred up for him unconscious memories of being little and not being held in mind or treated as if he had no mind. James was taken aback but said this resonated with him. He had never ever realised that his childhood had had any impact on him, and this was his first experience of being thought about in such a way.

Making such links helped lessen the divide between the couple. James began to reflect on himself, and although he did not understand the concept of projection, he took back a significant projection into Miriam that she was the mad one in need of help. He started to realise that he had a problem by not being in touch with his feelings. As a consequence, Miriam felt less angry and depressed, as she felt no longer so alone with her unbearable feelings. As a couple, they both had postnatal depression. It was for them a *shared couple experience* which manifested in their relationship in very different ways. Interestingly for both, their postnatal depression had its roots in their disturbing early experiences, leaving them both mistrustful of intimate relationships. This demonstrates why it was important to have both parents in the session so that postnatal feelings can be explored in each partner.

Although these particular sessions seemed to be focused on the parents, I included Andy in the dialogue, as I did not want to risk him being alone in anxious states and becoming depressed. By holding his gaze and talking to him, I wanted him to feel held in mind by me, and this contributed to him beginning to feel safer and less withdrawn. When the material lent itself, I spoke to him directly as I made interventions that embodied all three of them. I would respond in a way that contained the parent's infantile anxieties whilst encouraging a new parental identity as the parents that I thought both Miriam and James longed to be and had the capacity to be. Interpretations based on the observed behaviour in the here and now of the session are more powerful than those made by the parents on the infant's 'reported' behaviour.

These sessions were not wasted on Andy, and as the work progressed, he responded by communicating non-verbally that he appeared less disturbed and much happier. At first, his gaze was serious, and he looked at me intensely as I spoke, but within a few weeks, Andy joined the sessions, conveying a sense of enjoying them. For instance, he would often greet me by bouncing up and down, smiling and waving his arms in the air. His sense of liberation from his parent's projected past traumas was apparent and delighted both Miriam and James, enabling them to start developing a new confidence in themselves as parents. Andy's relationship to both parents changed, particularly to Miriam, who reworked a healthy attachment to her baby. This was reflected in Andy's feeding and sleeping problems which were resolved, as both mother and infant were able to be *in identification* with Miriam as a good maternal object. This was a result of Miriam being able to differentiate within herself from her early experiences with her own parents and thus develop her own confident parental self. James felt this work had changed his life. Miriam's only regret was that she did not receive this support with Tom.

After six months, James returned to the marital bed and Andy moved in with Tom to a bed made by his father. The success of the work with Andy provided them with a renewed sense of confidence to explore more bravely and honestly their relationship. They also told me that their relationship with Tom had improved. Tom also benefitted. Although he had not received couple perinatal work as an infant, he was very much affected by his more open and thoughtful parents.

## Discussion

### The role of the infant in perinatal couple psychotherapy

The perinatal service for couples at TR aims to facilitate parents to establish a supportive couple in which both can form a bond with the infant which is inclusive of the other – a bond that is sensitive to the age-appropriate communication and needs of the infant. In other words, a triangular relationship is created in which each individual has a place and the couple can form a parental bond and rediscover and hold onto their couple relationship. The infant's involvement is seen as an integral part of the process. For example, in the sessions, after the initial crisis, I found I was able to couple with Andy, or Miriam, or James, or Miriam and Andy, or James and Andy, or Miriam and James and sometimes with all three of them together. My aim was that the constant repetition of these interactions would contribute to what Abelin (1971, cited in von Klitzing, 2019) and von Klitzing (2019) claim is the capacity to form a solid but fluid pre-Oedipal triad in which all can explore and interact. For Andy, this would hopefully form the blueprint for his future relationships.

One of the most important questions for therapists to hold in mind is this: *How is the baby experiencing the parents?* For example, when parents have postnatal depression, as in the case of Miriam and James, they tend to see the infant through the lens of their own early experiences. By allowing Andy into the sessions, he became more alive to me, and I was able observe and experience him directly and not just as he was 'talked about'. This is particularly important if the couple share a picture of an impossible baby. I was able to observe Miriam's '*nightmare baby*' and James' '*baby with no mind*' and the projections which were located in him. At the same time, I was able to witness the strengths in the parents as they gazed at, held and fed him in the sessions. This enabled me to gently help the parents separate from their own early and unprocessed infantile feelings and find new dimensions to themselves and to their development as parents (Rustin, 2002). For example, when James claimed to '*feel nothing at all*' towards Andy, I was able to explore with him how his fingertips told another story and how soundly and safely Andy slept in his arms. When Miriam raged about how 'crazy' Andy was making her by refusing her breast milk, I could also think with her about how Andy seemed hungry for her milk in the sessions. This highlights how some very important non-verbal communications may have been missed had Andy not have been present.

Miriam's and James' early hidden traumas were unknown to them until the birth of Tom and then Andy. Not having received help with Tom, Miriam had feared that as a family, they would not survive a second child. Understanding and putting words to their disturbing experiences and feelings in the presence of Andy and myself proved to be powerful and beneficial. Andy appeared to feel contained, as reflected in his developing ability to drink his mother's milk and sleep in his father's arms. Experiencing Andy as able to feed and sleep while they spoke openly also seemed to helped both partners, especially Miriam, to develop more confidence in themselves as parents. They found that expressing their ambivalence and avoidance did not destroy their baby son. They all survived.

Perinatal work with the couple and infant requires a leap from seeing the patient as the relationship between the couple to the patient being the relationship between all three. A perinatal couple therapist is required to observe and hold in mind the infant as well as the parents and not be drawn into the couple relationship so much that the infant gets lost from the therapist's mind. This involves enabling the parents to reflect upon states of mind in themselves, in the relationship between them and in the infant as their interactions impact her/him. If all three patients in the session dysregulate, or if one is particularly vulnerable, the question will arise for the therapist of when to attend to the infant, or to the couple, or to one of the parents (Baradon & Joyce, 2005). However, when partners are preoccupied with their issues as a couple, work might first be needed to create a safe relational and physical environment for them to explore the meaning of their interactions as they unfold.

Andy's presence facilitated my observations of the non-verbal communications within the family. Understanding these helped me to comprehend and address the unconscious dynamics, thus interrupting the development of difficult relational patterns. Andy was a passive baby with a tendency to withdraw and possibly dissociate when distressed. This meant it was easier for me to observe him and monitor his emotional states, as he did not demand an instant response. I could make observational comments and ask the parents what they thought might be happening without them feeling overly persecuted. At the same time, I could talk to Andy about his feelings and enable him to connect to my voice, preventing further withdrawal.

Viewing an infant in her/his own right as a person may, even in a small way, contribute to the infant's sense of self as a psychological being who possesses a theory of mind (Thomson-Salo, 2018). If an infant's behaviour becomes meaningful to the parents, for example, by the therapist making an observational comment such as '*I notice that baby smiles when you stroke her/his head*', they can develop an idea that the infant has a mind, is active and their behaviour has meaning. Such simple interventions may lead to parents becoming more reflective about the infant and open to her/his ever-changing and raw emotional states. There may be times when the parents have different views or react differently to the infant's behaviour, and when this happens in the session, the therapist can validate each parent's view and perhaps promote dialogue and the idea that there is not a right or wrong way.

How Andy experienced his parents at the beginning and then end of the work is an interesting question. His withdrawal in an atmosphere of significant parental conflict would suggest he felt anxious and uncontained and at times not able to trust what he was being offered as reflected in his early refusal of breast milk. As the sessions progressed and his parent's internal and relational struggles eased, it appeared that he became safe enough to come into the world and form secure links with both parents. This could help prevent the repetition of the intergenerational traumas which Fraiberg et al. (1980) describes so vividly in their seminal paper, *Ghosts in the Nursery*.

The arrival of a baby will inevitably impact the couple relationship. When the disturbance is significant, toxic relational patterns can develop, and in worst cases, families can break down. The infant's emotional states can often reflect what is happening in the couple relationship. I believe that by including the infant in the therapeutic work, reparation can take place which enables the three to form a robust triangular relationship as a secure base for future development.

## References

Abelin, E. (1971). The role of the father in separation individuation processes. In: *Separation – Individuation 229–52*. Eds. Devitt, J., & Settlage, C. New York: International Universities Press.

Baradon, T. Ed. (2010). *Relational Trauma in Infancy*. East Sussex: Routledge.

Baradon, T. Ed. (2019). *Working with Fathers in Psychoanalytic Parent-Infant Psychotherapy*. London: Routledge.

Baradon, T., Broughton, C., Gibbs, I., James, J., Joyce, A., & Woodhead, J. (2005). *The Practice for Psychoanalytic Parent-Infant Psychotherapy*. East Sussex: Routledge.

Baradon, T., & Joyce, A. (2005). The theory of psychoanalytic parent-infant psychotherapy. In: *The Practice of Psychoanalytic Parent-Infant Psychotherapy: Claiming the Baby*. Eds. Baradon, T., Broughton, C., Gibbs, I., James, J., Joyce, A., & Woodhead, J. East Sussex: Routledge.

Beebe, B., Lachmann, F., Jaffe, J., Markese, S., Buck, K. A., Cohen, P., Feldstein, S., Andrews, H., & Chen, H., (2012). Maternal post-partum depressive symptoms and a 4-month mother-infant interaction. *Psychoanalytic Psychology*, 29(4), 383–407.

Bevington, D. (2019). A journey into fatherhood. In: *Working with Father in Psychoanalytic Parent-Infant Psychotherapy*. Ed. Baradon, T. London: Routledge.

Bion, W. R. (1962a). *Second Thoughts*. London: H. Karnac (Books) Ltd.

Bion, W. R. (1962b). *Learning from Experience*. London and New York: Heinemann; Basic.

Eekhoff, J. K. (2022). *Bion and Primitive Mental States Trauma and the Symbiotic Link*. Oxon: Routledge.

Emanual, L. (2008). *Disruptive and Distressed Toddlers: The Impact of Undetected Maternal Depression on Infants and Young Children*. London: Tavistock Clinic.

Fain, M. (1981). Diachrome, structure, conflict, oedipian. *Revue Francais, Psychanalise*, 45, 985–997.

Fonagy, P., & Target, M. (2002). Fathers in modern psychoanalysis and in society: The role of the father and child development. In: *The Importance of Fathers*. Eds. Trowell, J., & Etchegogen, A. East Sussex: Routledge.

Fraiberg, S. H. (1959). The new born. In: *The Magic Years*. New York: Fireside.

Fraiberg, S. H., Adelson, E., & Shapiro, V. (1980). Ghosts in the nursery: A psychoanalytic approach to impaired infant-mother relationships. In: *Clinical Studies in Infant Mental Health* (pp. 164–193). London: Tavistock.

Hanley, J., & Williams, M. (2020). *Fathers and Perinatal Mental Health: A Guide for Recognition, Treatment and Management*. Oxon: Routledge.

Harold, G. T., Aitken, J., & Shelton, K. H. (2007). Inter-parental conflict and children's academic attainment: A longitudinal analysis. *Journal of Child Psychology and Psychiatry*, 48(12), 1223–1232.

Klein, M. (1928). Early stages of the oedipus conflict. *Internal Journal of Psycho-Analysis*, 9, 167 (IJP).

Klein, M. (1946). Notes on some Schizoid mechanisms. In: *Envy and Gratitude and Other Works*. London: Virago Press.

Laplanche, J., & Pontalis, J.-B. (1973). *The Language of Psychoanalysis*. London: H. Karnac (books) Ltd.

Morgan, M. (2019). *A Couple State of Mind: Psychoanalysis of Couples and the Tavistock Relationships Model*. Oxon: Routledge.

Parker, R. (2012). Shame and maternal ambivalence. In: *The Maternal Lineage Identification, Desire and Transgenerational Issues*. Ed. Paola, M. London: Routledge.

Raphael-Leff, J. (2003). Ed. Where the wild things are. In: *Parent-Infant Psychodynamics: Wild Things, Mirrors & Ghosts*. London: Whurr Publishers Ltd.

Rustin, M. (1989). Encountering primitive anxieties. In: *Closely Observed Infants*. Eds. Miller, L., Rustin, M., Rustin, M., & Shuttleworth, J. London: Duckworth & Co.

Rustin, M. (2002). Struggles in becoming a mother: Reflections from a clinical and observational standpoint. *The International Journal of Infant Observation and its Applications*, 5(1).

Steele, H., Steele, M., & Fonagy, P. (1996). Associations among attachment classifications of mothers, fathers, and their infants. *Child Development*, 67, 541–555.

Thomson-Salo. (2018). *Engaging Infants*. London: Karnac Books Ltd.
von Klitzing, K. (2019). The role of fathers in early child development. In: *Working with Fathers in Psychoanalytic Parent-Infant Psychotherapy*. Ed. Baradon, T. London: Routledge.
Winnicott, D. W. (1960). The theory of the parent-infant relationship. In: *The Maturational Processes to Psychoanalysis in the Theory of Emotional Development*. Madison, WI: International Universities Press.

# Chapter 6

# Back to the future, together

*Sonja Vetter*

*A thing which has not been understood inevitably re-appears, like an unlaid ghost, it cannot rest until the mystery has been solved and the spell broken.*

(Freud, 1909)

This chapter explores the possible impact on parents and couples when their children reach adolescence. Whilst the adolescent is grappling with their own search for autonomy, this often conflicts with their dependency needs towards their parents. The inevitable developmental pull towards adulthood and push away from it, fearing the uncertainty this change inevitably stirs up, tends to affect every aspect of family life. To further the progress towards maturity, development cannot be limited to the adolescent only; it also requires growth on the side of parents too.

The question of what this process of a child's individuation means and potentially activates in parents provides a particular focus for this chapter. Does this new and intense phase stir up a developmental hope not only in adolescents but in parents, too, allowing them to work through unresolved, newly evoked or re-evoked complex emotions such as loss, exclusion, dependence, uncertainty and ambivalence?

Adolescence can be a time that is full of promise, excitement and opportunity. Engaging with a teenager, whose leap into a more intellectual being with an increased ability of abstract thought can be enormously rewarding and fun. Their passion and energy can be invigorating and infectious. However, this period of change and growth can also bring emotional pain, and the doubts this developmental stage stirs may be painful for the parents alike.

Throughout this chapter, attention is given to the parental requirement and capacity to be available enough so as to contain their adolescent son or daughter, with a particular focus on the challenges that parental couples themselves face during the process. Inevitably, parents' own adolescent experiences are evoked when parenting teenagers, and these together with possible strains within the couple relationship itself may create further tensions for all concerned. Additionally, challenges relating to life cycle considerations, such as a mother going through the

DOI: 10.4324/9781003387947-9

menopause whilst her adolescent daughter is beginning to embrace her own sexuality, will be examined.

## Defining adolescence

I was struck when listening to Kate Bush's recently revived classic "Running Up That Hill", how much her lyrics resonated. She imagined that striking a deal with God was the only way to understand what it's like to be her partner and to be understood by him so greater harmony can be achieved in the relationship.

These lyrics put me in touch with my own feelings, not about my partner but around raising my teenager, where similar gaps had opened up between us, the parent and the teenager, as well as between the parents, and the idea of swapping places for increased understanding felt longingly empowering and comforting.

Researching this chapter revealed a striking abundance of literature on adolescence and how it is experienced by the young people in contrast to the relative paucity of written material on the effects of adolescence on the parental couple relationship. This left me wondering whether the absence of focus on the parental couple's own experience of parenting an adolescent may be linked to the pain caused by their adolescent son or daughter's individuation.

In searching for a definition of adolescence, there appeared to be a shared core understanding across all classifications, relating to the 'transformation' that occurs during adolescence, with a particular emphasis on the complexity of the process. Few, if any, definitions touched on the duality of the transformation of the adolescent and the parental or couple relationship.

Margot Waddell, a fellow of the Institute of Psychoanalysis and a child analyst, writes:

> *"Adolescence can be described, in narrow terms, as a complex adjustment on the child's part to major physical and emotional changes. This adjustment entails finding a new, and often hard-won, sense of oneself-in-the-world, in the wake of the disturbing latency attitudes and ways of functioning."*
>
> (Waddell, 2002, p. 140)

She goes on to describe adolescence as "character formation, finding and solidifying the self and sexual development", "a process, often painful, of becoming independent and separating from parents and/or carers" and "a period of restructure, particularly personality" (Waddell, 2002). Stokoe (2023) quotes Mo and Egle Lauder's suggestion that "The adolescent task is to take possession of the adult sexual body". In his paper, he explores the deceptive simplicity of this statement, a process which is in fact deeply complex. Adolescence requires throwing out the previous "owners", namely, the parents, and grappling with and growing into the owner of a new identity and body, as created by oneself. The task is additionally demanding since the adolescent brain undergoes reconfiguration towards increasing maturation, and there are challenges represented by the upset of the hormone balance.

Dr Judith Smetana (2011) sees adolescence as an ongoing concern with autonomy, personal choices and agency, whilst Novik and Jack Novik (2013) believe that the major developmental tasks for both parents and adolescents as involving transformation of the self and the relationship, in the context of separateness rather than separation. Developing the point further, if the goal of adolescence is transformation, it is harder for adolescents to progress into adulthood without the accompanying change in their parents. The necessary shedding of the supportive parental structure on the part of the adolescent concurrently requires the parents and the parental couple to step back and gradually let go, creating space for new ways of relating to emerge.

## Adolescence as a developmental phase

### A brief excursion to infancy

In order to understand the adolescent and parental interplay, it is important to realise that adolescence represents a developmentally crucial period and is seen as a repetition of the formative infantile phase.

When an infant has an experience of a 'consistently enough' available parent or carer, not only will the experience be one of containment but also, the blueprint of a model of how experience can be contained. Where a child has not experienced this kind of containment, it may be more difficult in later life to contextualise experience. The means to draw on the ability to step back, observe and think about experience, in short, to keep perspective.

Trowell (2008) writes:

> "How carers manage negative feelings in the child and demonstrate their own capacity to manage their own rage and destructiveness is crucial. Parents find themselves very distressed at times by the strength of their feelings of anger, rage, and resentment towards their child; it can be very frightening to realise that this small person provokes such fury. When the child is being difficult and defiant or when parents are under pressure, these strong feelings can erupt. Then the parents have to bear being hated by the child, which can be very upsetting, and also bear the fact that at that moment they also hate the child."

She further elaborates the parents' responsibility to keep control of their own powerful feelings of rage and hatred whilst accepting the child also hates them. Being confronted with a child that hits and kicks requires a parent who, despite an urge to retaliate, can keep control of these powerful feelings with the aim of protecting their child and themselves.

## Adolescents' experience of adolescence

Fast forward to adolescence, a phase of profound change and development inside a growing child's body and mind. This stage can feel like a lively tornado tearing through life, for both the adolescent and parents alike.

The young person is grappling with the twinned and intertwined task of psychic development and physically growing into an adult body, which they are likely to experience as having no control over. The task is confusing and taxing.

The necessary separation between adolescent and parent that occurs during adolescence can be felt as a great loss to both. Transformation implies loss of one and development into a new phase. Caught up in an internally conflictual stage, the adolescent is pulled towards growing up on the one hand while often fearing and grieving the loss of childhood on the other. Confusing for the young person experiencing these contrasting forces, this is likely mirrored in a sense of disorientation for the parents, not used to the lack of control and helplessness that dealing with their teenager can evoke in them.

Young people, awash with hormonal, physical and psychological change, look to their peers as a new stronghold for identification, safety and security. Letting go of parents as the centre of the world is a prerequisite: in order to experiment and explore freely, parents must be kept at arms' length to help discover their own ways, views and ideas. Identification with a peer group is an important first step, as is turning away from their immediate family. This rejection of all that was known and familiar stirs up intense feelings of pain and anxiety, of loss and also of uncertainty – a veritable rollercoaster.

As the adolescent grows towards adulthood, internal turbulence can be too great to be contained within. Instead, teenagers tend to 'act out' and project their intense emotions, often depending on their parents to be able to contain these split-off feelings, just as the infant projects unmanageable feelings into the mother.

Waddell suggests:

> *"Teenagers may get rid of their inner tension and discomfort by enlisting projective forces, evacuating unwanted and bad parts unconsciously into someone else who then, in their eyes, becomes the problem. Conversely, by projecting their good parts, an other can become idealised."*
>
> (Waddell, 2002, p. 146)

She further suggests that adolescents can exhibit a tendency to avoid emotional reality, in acting out rather than thinking. She points to the adolescent experiencing the world in extremes, polarised into good and bad. Engaging in drugs and alcohol may feel helpful to numb the mind and the experience.

## Parental experience of adolescence

Living alongside the internal and external turbulence of adolescence is disturbing, added to which, adolescents and their parents are thrown into this new developmental phase together with varying contact points and remarkable intensity.

For the parent, this new developmental stage can represent hope for working through unresolved feelings, which they may now be in touch with. Parents, whether on a conscious or unconscious level, relive their own experiences of adolescence, including the hopes and fears this developmental stage stirred up in them. Their own experience of individuation, as well as any other experiences of separation throughout life, can make it more difficult to retain perspective and not feel overwhelmed alongside their teenage child. Experiencing a withdrawn teen may remind the parents of their own painful struggles during adolescence and lead them to project their own difficulty, for example, awkwardness among peers or lack of peer acceptance, into their children. Teenagers need to negotiate new relationships, which can be thrilling but this phase also includes the inevitable letdowns and possible betrayals this stage brings. These difficult feelings may return and hurt the parents again, thereby making it more difficult to be available for their teenage children's concerns.

The process of separation that parents now get in touch with can lead to deep psychic pain. If finding themselves on the more defensive end of the scale, parents may avoid the psychic pain and 'act out', which means their ability to remain thoughtful and keep perspective will be more difficult to access, and instead, they act on their powerful feelings. This could lead to a delay or missed opportunity for a different way of relating between the parent and the young person but also between the parents. One parental couple with a teenage daughter I have worked with in the past found it too difficult to allow themselves to make use of their couple to think about jarring feelings aroused through their child's adolescence. Instead, the mother acted out by getting increasingly angry with her daughter, whom she considered withdrawn and disinterested in family life. This led to prolonged parental conflict over their parenting styles. What was not possible to safely explore in their couple was their shared fear of their daughter suffering from depression since both parents had had experiences of low mood throughout their own respective teenage years. These parents felt bewildered, overwhelmed and unable to contain the tumultuous inner life of their adolescent alongside the turmoil within their own inner selves. This led to the loss of previously stable relationships within the family. The parents themselves felt helpless and out of control.

Parents who themselves feel overwhelmed with unresolved anxieties have a more challenging job at providing containment for their adolescents. "The denied, rationalised or 'forgotten' pains and abjection of aspects of our own adolescence" (Jacobs, 1990) "is felt to be threatening and may stir up fears of losing control of a more rational and balanced approach" (Diem-Wille, 2020).

Anderson (1998, p. 166) writes "it may feel as though all the unwanted feelings, hopelessness, incompetence, and fear on the one hand, and responsibility and worry without the power to go with it on the other, are left with the parents".

Andrew Soloman (2012) suggests that "Parenthood abruptly catapults us into a permanent relationship with a stranger, and the more alien the stranger, the stronger the whiff of negativity" (p. 1). Perhaps adolescence represents yet another level of being catapulted into a relationship with a stranger since not only the body but also the personality of the child starts changing and solidifying. This can lead to feelings of joy and surprise but also puzzlement and deep feelings of disappointment in the parent, raising uncomfortable questions over their own inadequacies and their role in their child's personality formation.

A previously sweet-smelling and cuddly child is now on their way to growing into a sexual adult, often smelly and awkward looking, with limbs all out of proportion. With it comes a loss of childhood and a loss of childhood ways of relating. One adult male friend once shared with me that when he started to become a teenager, he really wanted to remain a playful child, but hormones got in the way, which made him focus on his sexual self. He was painfully aware of the confusion around relating as a child, which he at times naturally retained and at other times rejected. This was as confusing to his mother as it was to him, leading to some conflict between the two since he remembered how disappointed his mother could be with him.

Parents raise or hope to raise their children to conform to their own parental standards. In adolescence, perhaps something that feels a closer fit is sought and identified with, and so the adolescent distances themselves from their parents, en route to defining themselves as adults. Previously at the centre of a child's life, the often idealised parent can now feel or in fact become irrelevant and denigrated.

The adolescent's ascent to maturity, physically and psychologically, can put parents in touch with their own process of ageing, including sexual decline, and may coincide with the maternal loss of fertility, namely, the menopause. The hormonally flooded teenager may be in juxtaposition with the menopausal mother, who is experiencing a decline in hormones and all this entails for her. This threat and perceived provocation may be too painful to tolerate and can result in envy or hatred being stirred up unconsciously. Work situations may also be unhelpful reminders of parents' waning powers, particularly when feeling overlooked or contemplating retirement. The ascent of the new generation inevitably leads to questions of decline and relevance in the parental generation. It may also lead to questions and feelings over one's own missed opportunities.

My previous point about loss of youth is beautifully brought to life in the US series *Better Things* (FX) – funny, heartwarming and unafraid of the less palatable aspects of the challenges of raising adolescent children. The series first aired in 2016 and ran for five seasons. Sam, single mother, ageing and working actor, is an example of a parent who can, by and large, contain her brood of three daughters. She reliably enough manages the emotional turmoil and projections of her teenage daughters, able to retain her capacity to think when confronted with teenagers who act out. In one scene, however, emotions between Sam's eldest teenage daughter, Max, and her mum are already running high, with Max being particularly self-absorbed and anxious. Insults fly at astonishing speed, which Sam counters with a singular level-headedness, but Max then finally gets her mum to react with her comment that "Sam no longer knows what it's like to be a woman". This bombshell of a comment collides with Sam's anxieties about her life stage – her relevance, her potency, her loss of youth. Sam is peri-menopausal and aware her reproductive life is coming to an end. Her daughter's comment most likely tapped into feelings of loss and raked up envy of opportunities missed or no longer available to her but opening up for her daughters.

This comment proved too overwhelming for Sam, and she retaliated. Their exchange reaches a new high, with Max then coolly observing how her provocation unsettled her mum. She had managed to safely project her own worry into Sam, who retaliated when coming face-to-face with her own anxieties.

It may feel very provocative for a parent to see and experience their teenage daughters and sons with their nascent beauty and youthful energy and power growing into sexual adults. Likely to have outgrown their parents physically, this metamorphosis may be experienced as a recognition of living through a process of being outgrown on all levels.

This may be particularly relevant if parents were risk-takers in their own adolescence, such as sexual promiscuity or use of drugs and alcohol, evoking anxiety about their teens' welfare and trust in their decision-making ability. These concerns, which may get projected into their teens, make understanding and containment more challenging and difficult to disentangle whose anxiety is being grappled with in the family.

Adolescence is not only a physical and sexual maturation but is a period of personality restructure. It can leave the parent having to engage once again with a stranger and negotiate a new relationship. Some parents, whose adolescent children develop fundamentally different beliefs and interests, or engage with entirely different ideas and people, may hold themselves responsible for their children turning away from them. So not only is there anxiety in the fact that the child is separating, this can be augmented by inner unrest, believing themselves to be responsible by not being good enough to create a child in their own image.

## Some further considerations of the impact of adolescence on the parental couple

In a parental couple, whether together or separated, emotions triggered through raising an adolescent can render them too helpless. Sometimes leading to 'splitting', one parent becomes overwhelmed with their own emotions, as well as their teen's projections, while the other parent withdraws and becomes unavailable. Containing parental anxieties, providing space to think about what is stirred up between themselves, as well as their teenager, can be provided by couple or parental psychotherapy.

Parental couples may recognise that they have grown apart from one another while raising their young children with insufficient investment in their couple relationship. Their sexual, intimate life may have waned or stopped altogether. Coming face-to-face with their children's aliveness and sexual potency can be challenging and leave them feeling redundant or excluded not only as parents but also as potent members of society. This can bring to the fore unresolved aspects of the Oedipal situation. If the couple cannot recreate a safe space within their relationship to process and think about this emotional upheaval and 'midlife crisis', their relationship can suffer, sometimes irrevocably.

A further consequence of the couple 'splitting' is that it can result in one parent siding with their adolescent, unable to grapple with their own ambivalent feelings, leaving their partner excluded and unsupported. The ensuing Oedipal split results in being unable to contain each other with blame and criticism becoming the dominant mode of couple relating, often accompanied by shame at not being able to cope.

### Clinical illustrations

The following three case studies aim to enliven some of the challenges parents and couples with adolescent children may experience. All my illustrations are a composite of clinical material, with all significant details changed or disguised, and fiction.

### Case study one: Anita and George

Anita and George are a couple in their early 40s. Both came to live in the UK in their late teenage years, seeking independence from their families of origin and opportunity abroad. They met and fell in love in their early 20s. Both agreed they were ready to start a family two years into their relationship, and by the time they came into couple psychotherapy, their teenage daughters, Salma and Sarah, were aged 17 and 13 respectively. Faith and religion were taken seriously in their family, driven largely by Anita, to whom spirituality was key. Anita was Muslim while George was agnostic. Over the course of their long relationship, their religious difference was largely managed by making Anita's faith dominant. George was accepting of this imbalance, mainly for the sake of their children, who were raised as Muslims. The couple came into therapy because of escalating rows and days of sullen silence between them which worried them both.

Clouds had started forming on the horizon when Salma hit adolescence, straining the relationship between child and parents. Distance started to appear between the generations and arguments were frequent. Both George and Anita experienced their daughter turning away from them, but both managed it very differently. George became very accommodating, acquiescing to Salma's demands for more freedom, while Anita was at loggerheads with what she considered an unnecessary and subversive teenage rebellion. Over the months of therapy, their therapist observed that it became noticeably more difficult for both her and the couple to think about what may be going on for Salma, both individually and as a couple. Alongside their emerging couple difficulties, Salma started to question her own religious beliefs and spirituality, finally threatening to leave the Muslim faith altogether. This was understandably threatening to Anita, as a refusal to follow her rules and boundaries. She accused her daughter of severing their bond and directly attacking her and her culture.

Anita longed and strove for a deep connection with her daughters, often by engaging them in long conversations, which was contrary to what the young people were interested in. For Anita, religion formed an important part in how she could connect to her children. Her first born, however, was beginning to spend time on her own, either in her room or with friends, and perhaps more importantly, started to solidify her personality. She was going through significant developments internally as well as externally. She was experimenting and wanted to engage with her parents strictly on her own terms. The relationship between the elder daughter and the mother strained even further since Anita struggled with the loss she felt around her daughter's individuation. Her own anxieties could feel overwhelming, which made thinking about her children more challenging. George tended to withdraw when faced with anxieties, and Anita felt excruciatingly alone. Their couple relationship now started to strain and feel uncomfortable, with little or no space for either of them to think about their experiences.

Unable to engage and think in a safe way about the deep anxieties their daughter's push for independence was stirring up in Anita, religion became her mouthpiece and hope to connect. The young people started to experience their mother as increasingly demanding and controlling, which added to the growing tension. Anita demanded her eldest daughter's attention and attendance at religious rituals. Unable to fully break free, the daughter rebelled by subverting the process, either by disregarding a punctual arrival at ceremonies or by eating foods not allowed by her religion. Her eldest daughter's first romantic relationship, particularly her choice of a non-Muslim boyfriend, catapulted her mother into a crisis of rejection. She struggled to engage with Salma, her eldest, over her choice of boyfriend, seeing only a threat to the mother-daughter relationship. She felt a profound and growing disturbance around how different her daughter was to herself and experienced this as a colossal loss of connection. This was, of course, interesting in the context of how similar Anita's own relationship with George had developed, given that they came from very different backgrounds and different religious beliefs. Perhaps the parents were in touch again with unresolved anxieties from their own youth and individuation, brought on by their daughter's choices.

The glue through which Anita could safely connect had become brittle and unreliable, often causing her enormous pain since it put her in touch with feelings of abandonment, separation and difference.

Anita's need for connection used to be met in the family through her children and her faith. Needs perhaps not fully met in the couple could be safely masked this way. Now that the children were individuating and developing into young adults with their own personalities, choices and tastes, a space had opened that was often painful and at times unbearable.

It appeared, in a parallel movement, that George had become more assertive in his own choices and wishes, previously masked by the collective of the family. He tended to withdraw, leaving all the pain associated with the children's individuation located in Anita. He started to feel restricted by Anita and resented her demands for closeness with him. The children's growing sense of independence refocused her need for connection to her husband, which he experienced as a demand, and he responded by moving away from her. Both Anita and George were left with a void and an unsettling sense of loneliness.

The couple struggled to make use of their relationship as a resource, where the very fact of being different can lead to the recognition of new possibilities.

Both George and Anita had experienced difficulties in their own respective teenage years, which led them to leave home young. Neither had a strong and anchored sense of being important in their families of origin, and they felt disconnected as a result. This couple were put in touch with their own anxieties, aroused through their children entering adolescence, which made containment of their adolescents' anxieties harder and more challenging, and caused cracks in their couple relationship.

## Case study two: Karen and Bernd

Australian couple Karen and Bernd sought couple psychotherapy after feeling increasingly separate and lonely in their relationship, which made them concerned about the future of their couple and the family. Bernd was the more vocal of the two in expressing his commitment to improving the relationship for the sake of their children. They have been married for over 25 years and have two teenage children together. Alice, their daughter, was aged 17 and Ollie, their son, was aged 16 when they sought therapy. The couple would often sit in silence, unsure how to start and how to express their thoughts and feelings, and there was a real lack of clarity at the beginning of therapeutic process.

Karen thought their couple had started to change when Ollie, their son, became a teenager. Ollie was indeed very present in the consulting room. He had started moving away from his parents and actively sought out his friends and peers. This had happened suddenly and unexpectedly, which had put Karen and Bernd in touch with unsettling feelings. Their daughter had not evoked the same discomfort in them since she was very focused on her schoolwork and enjoyed spending time at home with the family.

The locus of what brought this couple to therapy was situated inside Karen and Bernd's inner lives but caught fire with their youngest son's increasing individuation. The parents were really confused by their son, who would distance himself with such ease, but then seek them out again. Bernd and Karen were familiar with the interplay of distance and closeness from their couple, and it could be said that this dynamic was this couple's Achilles heel. Pulling away from each other was how they defended against difficulty and pain within the couple but which also created pain between them. When their children were little, they felt more protected since as parents, they were so central in their children's lives. With the onset of their children's adolescence, their son in particular, this changed and their son's distancing touched on an existing emotional wound that had now started to become inflamed.

Bernd and Karen agreed that Ollie was a good student and had been "well behaved" until shortly before they sought therapy. Once he had started to become more interested in his friends and had started going to parties, this changed. Their child, previously respectful to his parents and their wishes, had now started to disregard them, and attempts to control him were often openly defied. There were pockets of open hostilities, and neither parent felt equipped to get through to their son. But he could equally revert to his charming former self and make his parents feel important and loved. He would suggest to play board games with the entire family, and they agreed to watch his favourite movies at home. But his friends proved to be more of a pull, and he would often slip out of family arrangements, regardless how much his parents protested or pleaded with him. Both parents could feel helpless, and both felt dispensable. This proved too difficult for Karen and Bernd, and they started to drift away from each other.

Karen was the stricter of the two parents, but she had a good relationship with both of her children. She felt particularly close to Ollie, and his growing independence left a hole in her life. She had seen him as friend and confidante, and she tended to confide in him. She now felt rejected as a mother, which hurt her. Karen felt she had lost a part of her son, as if she had been shut out and left behind. She started to engage differently with Ollie, more cautiously and with greater distance, trying to protect herself from further rejection.

Bernd appeared on the surface to be less disturbed but had started to "clamp down" on his son in an effort to control a situation that he experienced as increasingly problematic. As parents and as a couple, they struggled to explore together how they experienced their children and support one another.

The couple responded well to the container therapy offered, which allowed them to think about their feelings and their adolescent children's needs. They hit on a new crisis when their daughter started dating. There were angry outbursts from Bernd, and he started to bury himself in his work, withdrawing from his children and his wife. The couple again struggled to contain their anxieties, and Karen also started to withdraw again from the couple. It felt the work that we had done together was at risk of collapse; the pain was too overwhelming.

Bernd himself had experienced a tumultuous adolescence, with phases of reckless and risky behaviour and notably absent parents. Karen on the other hand had a very removed and aloof father and an overly close relationship with her mother, whom she never fully individuated from. They shared early experiences of feeling de-prioritised and unwanted.

We had started to explore how their own sense of importance felt diminished in light of their children's adolescence and their need to individuate. When their daughter started university and moved away, this again proved very difficult for the couple, with unexpectedly strong feelings of loss coming to the surface. Any closeness that had been regained had to be let go of, and the couple started to drift away from each other again.

They now felt they had lost both their children at once, and this unexpected and sudden shock proved too unsettling for the couple. They suddenly quit therapy and contact was lost.

## Case study three: Robert

Robert, a father of a 16-year-old son called Luke, attended therapy on his own when his son was in the throes of adolescence. He experienced quite debilitating anxiety, which he had never known before, and he was uncertain of its origins. His relationship with his only child had started to become challenging at times once he started puberty, but he still considered it to be a close and loving relationship.

He had separated from his son's mother early in the child's life, and whilst he was in a new relationship, it was casual, with little overlap between his son and his girlfriend, who lived abroad. Luke's mother had moved to Scotland, where she was from, two years after they separated. Robert was content with his life, with his son at the centre but with an active social life and a fulfilling career.

Robert's relationship with his son's mother was predominantly functional; the focus was on co-parenting their son. Their shared-care arrangement worked for their son and suited Robert since it gave him every second weekend to himself, and they shared the holidays.

Luke, formerly a little timid and compliant, started to develop into his adolescence as if by stealth. His peer group suddenly became very important, friendships were now also formed with peers Robert had never heard of and he quietly started to defy curfews set by him. He at times struggled to reconcile his view of his son with who Luke was turning into, and he occasionally found himself with jarring feelings, such as embarrassment, about this. His son's behaviour towards him had started to be challenging and occasionally denigratory, with upsetting language being used. He felt unable to control this and his previous ability to keep level-headed and thoughtful had started to fade. There were times when he felt violently pushed away, as if this was the only option available to his son to distance himself from him. This was painful, and the pain could be overwhelming.

Complications arose due to differences in how Robert and his ex-wife viewed what was acceptable behaviour, with the mother being very relaxed around setting any boundaries. Robert wasn't a strict parent, but he had a realistic sense of what was acceptable and age appropriate. He felt unease with his son choosing to spend so much time with his friends, which was a mixture of concern over not knowing what the friendship group were getting into and some stirrings that his son chose not to spend time with him anymore.

The pandemic inadvertently put Robert in touch with a feeling he had only fleeting awareness until then. His son, now aged 17, had started to make his own decisions which parent he would be staying with and how long for, initiated at first over concerns of spreading the virus between his parental houses but facilitated by school since teaching had moved online. This caused Robert inconceivable pain, with feelings of abandonment coming to the fore. In particular, sudden und unplanned departures could feel very hurtful to him, a rejection he could no longer ignore. He also started to get in touch with shame, centred around his perceived inability to hold on to his son. He feared he was driving him away. There was shame also in feeling deskilled, akin to the very early days of having his son, not knowing and not understanding, and having to learn about him from scratch again. A perfect storm was in the making, with Robert unable, or at least compromised, to contain his son's adolescent anxieties whilst in the midst of uncontrollable anxieties himself. He found himself feeling he was going through another divorce and again not initiated by him.

In therapy, Robert thought about the painful dynamic between him and his son, how he moved away from him in self-protection to feel less exposed to the pain of abandonment. He came to realise Luke also felt out of control with feelings of abandonment. His son's pulling away from him made him at times not like him, further adding to feelings of rejection in him.

The situation grew more testing as it became evident that his son felt overwhelmed by his adolescent anxieties and fled into numbing himself with alcohol and drugs. He experienced his son's struggles by getting in touch with very strong and unbearable feelings of helplessness, disappointment, guilt and fear. Robert's former wife, who was kept in the loop at all times, resorted to avoidance and withdrawal, to avoid any confrontation with her own painful feelings. This in turn left Robert feeling unsupported and very alone with managing the confusion and pain in himself and their son.

He often described feeling as if being inside a washing machine, on a high-speed spin, barely able to hold on. He also conveyed a sense of playing catch-up, having mastered bewilderment and confusion, and feeling back in the saddle, just to come face-to-face with another kink. The paradigm was constantly shifting, and his world felt unsteady.

Very slowly, the situation started to feel more manageable for him, with perhaps both Robert and Luke developing an increased capacity to contain their anxieties. Having a space to think what was going on for Robert led to a greater capacity in him to consider what his son was grappling with and helped contain him. He also started to make links to his own experiences, which he found helpful in understanding his relationship with his son, as well as any past relationships. There were some joyful moments between father and son again, and they started to see and understand each other through a different lens. This was not a linear process, however, which meant that time passing did not necessarily correspond in a linear way with their states of mind. But it was a process that involved them both and opened the door to a different way of understanding each other. Robert's capacity to think and contain had been supported and largely restored. Perhaps most importantly, Robert felt his foundations had been re-established and made stronger altogether. As time moved on and his son grew into an older adolescent, who was working on and realising his own hopes and dreams, he felt his importance diminishing not only in relation to his son but perhaps more widely in his place in the world, like a subtle awareness of having peaked. He felt able, however, to understand and tolerate this feeling within himself and support his son through this phase of his adolescence.

## Conclusion

The transformative aspects of adolescence can be thrilling as well as demanding, a puzzling paradox. It is a time of intensity, and it is the intense turbulence of adolescence which may generate a crisis in parents or the couple, or it may manifest more subtly, with the couple or parental dynamic not feeling as containing and supportive as it could do. These intense, at times overwhelming and confusing, emotions can result in couples and parents struggling to manage the challenges of parenting adolescents.

In this chapter, particular attention was given to the possibility of parental internal pressures re-emerging through the process of their children's individuation, which may impact their capacity to be available and contain their son or daughter's inner conflicts during adolescence. This immediately suggests the adolescent task is intertwined between the parents and the growing child. Not only is the adolescent in the throes of turmoil but their parents may also be in touch with inner anxieties. I found this thought to be extremely helpful in parenting my own teenager but also in a therapeutic capacity since it created more clarity where it was murky before, allowed for a different perspective to emerge and turned helplessness into the ability to cope and support.

It is my suggestion that having adolescent children may be the catalyst for parents and parental couples experiencing difficulties and seeking help, whether self-identified or not. As I have outlined in this chapter, parental couples can suffer as they get in touch with the more hidden anxieties in themselves, evoked by their adolescents' maturation process. Added to this, long-lived fractures in their couple relationship can be bought to the surface in the height of the stress of raising adolescents.

Knowing adolescent children are in the mix for any couple entering the consulting room ought to focus any therapist's antennae not only on the anxieties that can be re-aroused in parents but also on the opportunity for couples and parents to work through their own experiences afresh, perhaps offering a chance to grow and develop new ways of relating.

Creating space to help think and support the parents and couples to negotiate this fundamental new developmental phase takes on similar importance as the supporting of new parents with their first child; in fact, it is an exact reversal. New parents must forego the couple as two and reconfigure to become three. Parents of teenagers are facing not only a keen dependence on each other as they confront a new life stage but also a reverting back to being a pair, shedding their outer layer of children. This can pave the way for things to go better, or worse, and couples need a space to think about these changes. Handled thoughtfully, it can bring a period of fertile growth for all.

## References

Anderson, R. and Dartington, A. (Eds.) (1998), *Facing It Out: Clinical Perspectives on Adolescent Disturbance*, p. 166. London: Duckworth.

Diem-Wille, G. (2020), *Psychoanalytic Perspectives on Puberty and Adolescence*. London: Routledge. https://library.oapen.org/bitstream/id/053d47c2-d0a3-4c03-8551-51d621c0d40e/9781000336856.pdf

"DNA", Better Things, Fourth Season, Episode 4, FX (2020), *BBC iPlayer*. https://www.bbc.co.uk/iplayer/episode/p08my2w9/better-things-series-4-4-dna

Freud, S. (1909), 'Analysis of a phobia in a five-year-old boy', In *Standard Edition*, vol. 10, p. 122. London: Hogarth.

Jacobs, T. (1990), 'The no age time: Early adolescence and its consequences', In S. Dowling (Ed.), *Child and Adolescent Analysis: Its Significance for Clinical Work*. Madison, CT: International Universities Press.

Novik, K. K. and Novik, J. (2013), *Concurrent Work with Parents of Adolescent Patient*. https://pubmed.ncbi.nlm.nih.gov/26072560/

Smetana, J. (2011), *Adolescents, Families and Social Development*. Wiley Blackwell.

Soloman, A. (2012), *Far from The Tree. A Dozen Kinds of Love*, p. 1. New York, NY: Simon and Schuster.

Stokoe, P. (2023), Curiosity versus beliefs: The battle for reality and what this means for relationships and development (27th Enid Balint Lecture). *Couple and Family Psychoanalysis, 13*(2), 196–211.

Trowell, J. (2008), *Standing on their Own Feet. You and Your Younger Adolescent*. London: Karnac Books.

Waddell, M. (2002), *Inside Lives. Psychoanalysis and the Growth of the Personality*. London: Karnac Books.

# Chapter 7

# No sex please; we're parents

*Linsey Blair*

## Introduction

The adjustment of the couple relationship when a baby comes along can be a difficult time for many parents. The period following the birth of the first baby is a time that many couples enter therapy (Bischoff, 2004). Traditionally, in psychoanalytic couple therapy, the clients' physical and sexual transitions were often ignored in favour of their emotional consequences. However, the couple relationship must change and adapt both emotionally and sexually to accommodate a third into its dynamic, and as this chapter indicates, the emotional and sexual tend to be intertwined.

Belsky et al. (1994) cite sex as one of the main areas of parental conflict. This was echoed by Clulow (2009), who coined the acronym SHAME, incorporating sex (S) as well as housework, activities, money and employment as the chief areas of conflict for parents. When couples argue about any of these topics, they tend to be arguing about difference: Who does more? Who has more? Who gives more? Often, the conflict around sex also presents as a conflict around difference (e.g., 'I want sex, but my partner doesn't'). When couples argue around difference, they are communicating how frustrating it is that their partner is not the same as them. Sameness, it is believed, would make the relationship fairer, more predictable and easier to feel safe in.

When couples experience a transition, such as the decision to become parents, feelings of dependency and attachment to each other tend to increase and so, too, does the desire for sameness. This is because fears of abandonment, separation and merger can emerge alongside feelings of dependency. The closer we get to someone, the more we fear losing them, and conversely, yet simultaneously, the more we fear being taken over by them (Balfour, 2005). When couples feel an increase in dependency towards partners, their partner's difference can be experienced as threatening. This threat is a result of the reality that a separate, different partner has their own mind and thoughts which can never be wholly known by another individual. This affects how secure the relationship feels to both partners, raising fears of abandonment or merger.

The composite case studies I utilise in this chapter all present with concerns around difference. This conflict with difference links to shared fears concerning

DOI: 10.4324/9781003387947-10

vulnerability, separation, dependency or merger that have been stirred up by particular stages of parenthood. I am suggesting that underneath the presenting sexual difference is an emotional sameness and that this emotional sameness leads, in these cases, to a breakdown of physical intimacy.

Often in parenthood, the shared emotion is one of grief (Waddell, 2002). The changes that parenthood bring are real. Some are joyful and introduce a set of challenges that couples take pride in successfully navigating. If the woman carried the baby, her body will be different after birth, both internally and externally. The baby will undoubtedly impact a couple's routine, and in response, their roles in the relationship change. Libidos also change due to hormone fluctuation, as well as fatigue, physical pain and the emotional heft of parenting (McBridge et al., 2017). In fact, low libido is the most common presenting sexual issue for parents (O'Rosen et al., 2018), and hence, it features in three of the four case studies outlined later. Although these changes for new parents are not exhaustive and are not permanent, nevertheless, they can have far-reaching consequences. For instance, sex will not be as it was before the couple transitioned into parenthood since life will not be as it was. Therefore, the couple can only move forward once they have accepted that they cannot go back, and psychosexual behavioural work will reach an impasse unless emotional processing is part of the therapeutic intervention.

It is important to clarify the behavioural component of sex therapy. Sex therapists utilise the Masters and Johnson model of Sensate Focus (Masters et al., 1994) to set behavioural exercises for the couple to do at home at their own pace. Sensate Focus takes the couple back to exploratory sensual touch first to the self then to each other. In the early exercises, touching the classic erogenous areas such as breasts, bottoms and genitals is forbidden. This allows the couple to relax and play without any pressure to perform. Sensate Focus, when used correctly, encourages curiosity and creativity towards one another. It allows couples to slowly reveal themselves both emotionally and physically with the help of weekly therapy to aid communication around what is happening in their bodies and minds (see O'Connor, 2019; Hawton, 1985).

The four case studies in this chapter all brought sex as their presenting problem. I will view the parenting 'journey' through a psychosexual lens, so as to explore the couple's sexual relationship from the decision to conceive, through to pregnancy, the process of weaning and early separations and, finally, teenage years. The case studies will highlight how sex can become a place where emotional issues around a fear of separation and merger, stemming from unprocessed grief, are played out. They also emphasise how these emotional issues are shared by the partners, even if only one partner is presenting with the sexual symptom.

## Stage one: The decision to conceive

When the decision to have a child is made, the transition to parenthood begins (Clulow, 1982), and changes to a couple's sexual relationship are inevitable (Scharff, 1982). For a heterosexual couple, birth control ceases, fertility tests might be carried out, the timing of the sex might change to match ovulation and penetration to ejaculation becomes the ultimate goal. Any one of these changes could signify a massive shift for the couple, causing anxiety in one or both partners. It is common for couples to present to sex therapists when they are trying to conceive with issues such as erectile disorder, delayed ejaculation, low libido and sexual pain. Understandably, this is disturbing for couples relying on their own and their partner's sexual performance to get pregnant. These sexual problems could be related to natural anxiety or ambivalence concerned with starting a family, but they can become catastrophised when the pressure to perform is turned up. The fact that many couples in the Western world are trying for pregnancy later in life (Furstenberg Jr, 2010) only serves to increase the pressure. This tension is sometimes replicated in psychosexual work, where the couple and therapist are all aware of a disruptive, invisible, ticking clock. This pressure is partly reality based, but if combined with increased emotional vulnerability, then the transition to parenthood can result in sexual dysfunction, as illustrated in the following case.

## Case example

Colin and Lily, both aged 38, presented for couple psychosexual therapy because of Colin's erectile disorder, which had been occurring for six months. They both agreed that this was Colin's problem, as Lily was sexually available and willing.

In the initial session, the couple explained that they had been trying for a baby for about a year, and given Lily's reduced fertility due to her age, they were feeling pressure to conceive quickly. It transpired that Lily and Colin's sexual encounters were stressful and focused solely on conception. To give an example, Lily had a watch that tracked her ovulation, and the watch indicated the optimum time for sex by beeping reminders during her fertile period. When the watch beeped, they both dropped what they were doing in order to have sex. Lily would take off her clothes and lie on the bed. Colin would go into the bathroom and masturbate whilst watching porn. Once he was erect, he then entered the bedroom and attempted to penetrate Lily. If Colin didn't get an erection, they would argue. In these arguments, Lily would accuse Colin of being a closet homosexual or of having an affair. Penetration didn't work 70% of the time.

As the couple told me this story in the session, they noticeably started to cringe. I acknowledged their emotional reaction, and Lily said that this was the first time they had described their sexual intercourse in such detail to another. Now their process was laid bare, it seemed blatantly obvious why Colin was not getting an erection. 'Why?' I asked. 'Because the sex is not sexy', Lily replied.

Before this couple's attempts to get pregnant, Colin and Lily reported a largely satisfactory but infrequent sexual relationship, with mutual initiation and foreplay. It was the idea of having a baby that had turned their sex life upside down. As the sessions with Colin and Lily progressed, it transpired that both had a history of childhood sexual abuse. Lily recalled lying still and frozen on her bed while her uncle touched her, and Colin remembered masturbating to porn magazines in his neighbour's attic with a group of older boys who then touched his genitals. The couple's sexual relationship now, in different ways, appeared to be replaying the abuse they had suffered as children. Contemplating becoming parents had triggered shared memories of their own sexual abuse and shared fears that they, as parents, would fail their children and each other. Lily's accusations towards Colin could be understood in terms of her fear of her dependency on him, and Colin's loss of erection served to increase Lily's assumption that Colin would abandon her. Their resulting conflict upped the anxiety and pressure and created an atmosphere at odds with sexual arousal.

As a next step, Lily and Colin's relationships with their own parents were explored in an attempt to identify any repetition or reaction in their current relationship (see Di Ceglie, 1995; Ruszczynski, 1993; Morgan, 2004). Colin's parents were both teachers who had a functional and, he imagined, fairly sexless marriage. He said he couldn't see them as anything other than parents and couldn't imagine why they had married in the first place. He believed he and his siblings were the glue that held his parents together. Conversely, Lily's father left when she was only 2 years old. As the fourth child, Lily believed her birth had tipped her parents over the edge.

So directly linked to their childhood experiences, Colin believed that children trapped parents in a dead marriage, while Lily believed children broke a happy marriage in two. Their sexual interaction, while also replaying aspects of their abuse, unconsciously confirmed both their beliefs around the impact of babies on the parental couple relationship. Colin could identify that just the thought of having a baby led to him feeling trapped in a repetitive, lifeless sexual interaction. While Lily felt that Colin's loss of erection was a sure sign they were breaking up.

This couple were attempting to create a baby without having processed any of their own shared fears around parenthood and their grief at how they were parented themselves. It was not hard to adjust Colin and Lily's sexual script and offer some behavioural interventions to help with the erectile loss to enable the couple to achieve their goal of penetration to orgasm. However, this was only possible when both partners could trust that they weren't going to be rejected, abandoned or trapped by each other. Colin and Lily left therapy after they had reached their desired outcome, so I did not get to see them through conception and pregnancy, which is the second stage of parenthood for many couples.

## Stage two: Pregnancy

If the couple are able to negotiate the physical and emotional changes that occur when the idea of conception takes hold, then, if all goes according to plan, the next step to becoming parents is the conception. Again, this requires physical and emotional change through which the couple relationship must adapt. Some couples report sex as celebratory during pregnancy; one or both partners are aroused by the female bodily changes as they occur. However, other individuals are put off by it. Some clients report fears of damaging the foetus, and subsequent growing baby, via penetration and mutual orgasm, though the evidence around this suggests the contrary (Jones et al., 2019).

There is also evidence that women's libido drops during pregnancy (Aslan et al., 2005), possibly due to nausea and fatigue. Panea Pizarro et al. (2018) note that the more difficult and desired the pregnancy was, the more that sexual intimacy is reduced, especially during the last trimester.

Another factor to consider is the impact on the sexual relationship for couples who are not able to achieve pregnancy via intercourse. Many studies emphasise the difficult impact in vitro fertilisation (IVF) has on the couple's sexual relationship (Smith et al., 2015). The intrusiveness of the IVF process can greatly impact a woman's relationship to her own body; she may feel like she has little control over who has access to her vagina and womb, and consequently, her body starts to feel desexualised. Her partner can also feel powerless, like a voyeur to the process rather than a needed equal. This might be especially true for heterosexual men, but as seen in the case example later, it can also be true for lesbian couples. Many couples who go through IVF or intrauterine insemination (IUI) describe physical factors around tiredness and hormone disturbance that can result in sexual initiation beginning to wane. In gay male couples, the adoption route or surrogacy can cause emotional stress that can also impact the sexual relationship. Whatever the route to parenthood, it is not uncommon for fears around vulnerability, attachment and dependency to get stirred up. In all of the aforementioned situations, both partners are reliant on the other to help the journey to parenthood go smoothly. In the case example later, this reliance can stir up historic attachment issues that impact the current relationship.

## Case example

Claire and Jen presented for therapy because of Claire's low libido following a birth. Claire had desperately wanted children, while her partner had been ambivalent, but when Jen finally did come on board, there was a sense of taking their couple relationship to a deeper level, and because of this, both felt that their sexual relationship had become more imaginative.

The couple used donor sperm, but Claire suffered three miscarriages, which led to concern that her womb was not viable. Given that the couple's relationship felt so strong at this stage, Jen stepped in and offered to carry the baby, and this time, the pregnancy was successful. At this point, Claire, who had so wanted to be the birth mother, started to feel depressed. She described watching Jen's body change and wishing that it was she who was pregnant. She began to withdraw. Jen, having never desired a pregnancy, was alarmed at the changes in her body. Feeling abandoned by her partner, she started to attack Claire, describing her as useless and unsupportive. Unsurprisingly, sex stopped for the couple during the pregnancy, and this also included any intimate touching. Almost a year later, the couple were functioning well as parents but were unable to recover their physical relationship, mainly because Claire did not feel any sexual desire and rejected Jen's tentative advances.

Thinking about their past histories, I discovered that Claire was the fifth of nine children and, as a middle child, often felt lost and overlooked. Her route to parental praise was looking after her smaller siblings, which fed her desire to have her own children. She assumed sex between her parents must have been functional, predominantly focused on having babies. She also believed they were disappointed when she came out as a lesbian and linked this to their staunch Catholicism.

Jen was adopted as a baby. Her birth mother had died in one of the mother and baby homes in Ireland. She was one of two adopted children, but her adopted sister was sickly, and Jen quickly fell into the role of being the strong child. Her adoptive mother was the caregiver, while her father took Jen under his wing. Neither parent was surprised when Jen came out as gay, and both were accepting. She noted that while her parents were tactile with each other, she wasn't sure if they were having penetrative sex.

From looking at these individual histories, we can surmise why this couple struggled so much through Jen's pregnancy. Claire remembered feeling threatened by every pregnancy her mother had. How would the family survive another baby? Would there be enough food? Enough love? During the pregnancy, she felt entirely at the mercy of Jen, who was carrying the coveted baby. This stirred up her childhood fears of dependency on her mother, and she started to feel that the baby she wanted so much could separate them. Claire feared losing Jen but was also scared of losing the baby. She also felt she had let Jen down by not being able to be the birth mother, evoking memories of how she felt a disappointment towards her parents. Jen's anger with her only served to reinforce this. Despite Jen's sexual advances, by the time I saw them, Claire felt unattractive and unlovable.

Jen felt weak and needy in the pregnancy, while she had prided herself in childhood on her independence and self-sufficiency. She was alarmed by her need for Claire's physical and emotional support. For Jen, Claire's withdrawal triggered her fears of loss. She had lost both her mothers, firstly through death and, secondly, by being overlooked because of an unwell sibling. On the cusp of becoming a mother herself, she now believed she was losing her partner. In therapy, Jen spoke about how she was always reactive to others' needs rather than being in touch with her own. She acknowledged that, probably, she had felt that her parents were not able to handle her needs as well as her sisters'. She now felt Claire wasn't able to handle her needs either.

Claire eventually began to articulate how she felt that she'd disappointed Jen by not being able to carry the baby and how she feared Jen didn't need her anymore. Jen was able to let Claire know that she did need her, more than ever, especially since she felt at sea in her role as a mother. She could also own a need for being mothered herself. The couple were able to express their mutual sadness for some of their historic pain, freeing them to acknowledge the sadness they both felt at their distance from each other. We proceeded with the behavioural work alongside the emotional, and through this integrated model, the couple tentatively became more physically intimate and resumed their connection again (cross ref Sandor chapter).

## Stage three: Early separation

Clulow (1982) suggests that, for some marriages, the crisis is not immediately postpartum but occurs when the baby begins the process of separation from the mother or main carer. The total dependency of the baby, especially on the primary caregiver, naturally means physical intimacy between a couple is limited. The nursing mother might feel tired and craving physical space rather than physical closeness. Also, like Max and Christina (in the next section), for practical as well as emotional reasons, couples tend to keep their infants in their bedroom. When breastfeeding stops and/or the baby is moved out, then the absence of physical touch between the couple can become more apparent, with its lack harder to avoid.

## Case example

Max and Cristina presented when their daughter, Sophie, was 2 years old and they had just moved her into a room of her own. Max was eager to get back to a sexual relationship, but Cristina complained of pain on penetration. She'd experienced it once, following the birth, and was now too afraid to try again. Both Max and Cristina assured me that they'd had regular and enjoyable sex before and during their pregnancy, although they lived separately up to Sophie's birth.

Max grew up in a matriarchal household. His father was quiet and withdrawn which his mother was openly critical of. Max, on the other hand, was close to his mother and considered himself the 'man of the house'. His mother approved of Cristina, after having been disapproving of Max's previous partners. Cristina was the youngest of three and the only girl. Her father expected her brothers to work in his business but had no expectations for Cristina other than marriage and children. Her mother was passive, often absent, and the children were left to the care of nannies. Cristina had been told by one nanny that her mother had suffered from postnatal depression after all three births. Cristina's previous long-term sexual relationship had been with a much older, married professor.

When a baby arrives, oedipal issues can re-emerge, dominating the lives of the parental couple and their sexual relationship. In modern psychoanalytic thought, oedipal issues are concerned with negotiating the threesome (Balfour, 2005), a triangular configuration where one of the three protagonists can feel excluded from the relationship between the other two (Britton, 1989). The birth of a first baby immediately brings this to the fore for couples since one partner tends to be the main caregiver to the infant, leaving the other to feel excluded. How both partners manage their feelings around this merger and separation speaks to how childhood oedipal issues were negotiated and how they as children fitted into their parents' couple relationship. In other words, did they feel totally left out of their parents' bond, were they both included and gently excluded or were they attached to one parent at the expense of the other?

If we look at the parental couple relationships Max and Cristina describe, we can see that their blueprint didn't involve mutual, loving and balanced relationships between the children and their parents. Max felt partnered with his mother and responsible for her wellbeing, while his father appeared absent. Cristina felt unable to connect to either parent and was also excluded from the father-son relationships.

When Sophie was born, Max and Cristina had to negotiate a triangular relationship with their daughter. They did so in the only way they knew how, namely, encompassing both merger and exclusion. Cristina merged with Sophie, giving her the relationship that she had been deprived of with her mother, whilst Max was left on the outside, relieving him of an intrusive mother figure and unconsciously repeating the distant role associated with his dad. The fact that the sexual relationship had ceased was linked to this merger-exclusion dynamic; Max had no access to Cristina emotionally or physically while she was merged with Sophie. However, on exploration, there were further reasons as to why sex was central to this couple's presenting issue.

It transpired that Sophie's birth had been traumatic, as the baby had become detached from the placenta leading to an emergency Caesarean section. Post-birth Cristina was separated from Sophie, who was in intensive care for six days. She was beset with anxiety of not attaching properly to her baby because of the separation, and she started to blame herself for the placenta detaching. When her and Sophie returned home after hospital instead of talking about her fears, Cristina sought physical comfort from Max in the form of sex, but no one had told her about the impact of breastfeeding on a woman's body.

Hormonal changes during breastfeeding can lead to a lack of vaginal lubrication (Polomeno, 1999). Without lubricant, penetration led to Cristina suffering soreness and vaginal bleeding. This incident became quickly catastrophised, as Cristina was already vulnerable. She started to feel her body was letting her down, and she was failing as both a wife and mother, but she didn't know how to explain this vulnerability to Max. Instead, she pulled away from him, focusing entirely on Sophie to fight against the depression and withdrawal she identified in her own mother.

On the surface, Max seemed desperate to connect physically with Cristina, but in reality, he also wasn't available. In the therapeutic relationship, I experienced a connection with Cristina but couldn't connect with Max. He would often glance at his phone during sessions and sometimes absent himself last minute from the therapy, blaming crucial work meetings. In supervision, I spoke about the repeat within therapy of a triangular relationship in which Max was being positioned on the outside.

As therapy unravelled Cristina's emotions, she started to explore her vulnerabilities and, utilising Sensate Focus, began to uncover her buried desire. Interestingly, Max then began to suffer erectile disorder. It was as if the symptom had switched from one partner to the other, with Max now keeping his distance, increasingly unavailable at home as well as in therapy. This exchange of rejection and need is common in couples who are mutually wary of intimacy (Mattinson et al., 1979). The couple stopped their behavioural touching exercises because Max was too 'busy' to engage. In a session, where we acknowledged the 'stuckness' in the therapy, Max became angry with me and Cristina, complaining he was being put under pressure. He'd experienced the sensate exercises as restrictive and demanding, and I'd morphed into his critical mother, suffocating his freedom with my own agenda. After exploring this, Max was able to speak about how he wanted Cristina to desire him but not to take him over with her needs. Her emerging sexuality scared him because he experienced it as pressure to perform. It transpired that his fears about his sexual inadequacy, that he'd not be 'good enough', were linked to his early feelings of not being good enough for his mother.

Slowly, the couple became more united, openly discussing their anxiety around dependency, exclusion and merger brought about by Sophie's arrival. They were more able to grieve past hurts whilst working on the present. They worked hard to create a new way of relating sexually, alongside a new understanding of their emotional connection. This paved the way for Sophie to establish a relationship with the parental couple and to both mother and father separately, who were, in turn, better equipped to protect the boundary of their own relationship.

### Stage four: Later separation

As noted in the previous cases, the idea to become parents, pregnancy and the initial physical separation from the baby, whether via weaning or moving rooms, is often a time when couples present with sexual issues. Less is published about parents' sexuality as their children develop into teenagers. Scharff (1982) and Morgan (2019) both note that teenage years can trigger a renegotiation of the oedipal conflict for parents. Though it could be argued that parents have more space and time to have sex during this period (Scharff, 1982), the evidence suggests parental satisfaction in their relationship reaches an all-time low when children reach adolescence (Gilbert, 2005). As Sonja Vetter describes in her chapter (6) on raising teenagers, this particular stage sees parents facing their own fears of separation and dependency as their children become more independent. This can stir up grief around how they as teenagers negotiated their own individuation from their parents.

The final case presentation is one in which the couple were able to maintain a sexual relationship on and off throughout a strong marriage. However, when their children became teenagers, the couple presented with female low sexual desire.

### Case example

In their initial assessment, Aayat and Raj blamed Aayat's low sexual desire on the menopause. Aayat was in her early 50s and had hot sweats, dry vaginal canal, thinning vaginal walls, mood swings, inability to sleep and sensitivity to bodily touch and smell. Everything physiological she was going through communicated 'keep out' to Raj.

The couple had three children, 19- and 17-year-old boys and a daughter, aged 15. Raj spoke about his sons' growing sexuality and how free they seemed compared to him at their age. Both Raj and Aayat were raised in Indian communities in England. While Raj's parents were more liberal, he said his freedom was nothing compared to that of his sons, who brought young women to the house and spoke openly about sex. Raj was simultaneously impressed that he and Aayat had created such an open, liberal environment and yet envious that his sons were benefiting from it. Raj noted that he had always idealised his father but felt his sons did not respect him in the same way. In addition, his boys were becoming sexually active at a time when he felt his own sexual activity waning.

It transpired that Raj's fear of his own sexual decline was partly why Aayat had withdrawn from him. She said that he had become penetration focused, getting Viagra from the GP to make his erection harder and last longer, which he did without consulting her. She complained he was paying less attention to her needs and behaving like a rampant teenager, demanding sex in strange places at odd times. It is important to remember that when one partner presents with low desire, it often needs renaming as 'different' desire. Female and male desire cycles often are different (Basson, 2020); withdrawing from sex can be a partner's way of passively communicating that they want something different sexually than what's on offer.

On exploring Aayat's reaction to her teenage children, she spoke about her own strict family background, headed by a controlling father. Her mother had fled the marriage when Aayat was 15 years old. Throughout her childhood and adolescence, there were restrictions on Aayat's sexuality. Her father had wanted an arranged marriage for her, rejecting Raja as a result. Aayat had been forced to cut all ties with her father and older brothers when she was 18 as the cost of being with Raj.

As children negotiate their own sexual development, so parents must renegotiate theirs. Raj and Aayat described their own difficulties in separating from their families. While Aayat had initiated a permanent, harsh spilt, Raj had not yet negotiated real separation from his family of origin. It transpired that he still harboured this strong, idealised image of his father and maintained a boyish persona in his mother's eyes. As the youngest of three boys, he had been teased for being the smallest and his mum's favourite and recognised he felt 'less' of a man than his father and brothers. When he met Aayat, he was attracted to her fiery personality, and their sex life was always initiated by her. Her blatant sexual attraction to Raj and the fact she left her family to be with him helped him feel potent and strong. Now that his sons didn't look up to him and his wife no longer seemed to desire him, his identity was shaken. He resorted to Viagra to try to regain his potency.

Aayat had been attracted to Raj because he seemed quiet and kind, different form the other men in her life. She felt safe with him sexually because he allowed her to take control. Aayat was feeling 'at sea' now because of the unpredictability, both physically and emotionally, of the menopause. She was in touch with the fact that her daughter was the same age she was when her mother disappeared and, as a result, spent any spare time she had with her. She was aware that her sons were leaving home and was frightened they wouldn't return, like her mother.

Although Aayat had looked forward to her and Raj being alone again once the children had flown the nest, she was surprised to discover a growing fear of sex within her. She experienced her husband's urgent sexual need as controlling and aggressive as if he was transforming into her father. Surprisingly, Aayat also spoke about how alone the couple would be once Raj's mother died. At 87 years old, she was the only surviving parent. It seemed that both Raj and Aayat were feeling vulnerable, as they reflected on the changes happening to them and what had already passed.

Thankfully, through the slow sensual build-up of Sensate Focus, along with a deepening mutual understanding, Raj and Aayat were able to reconnect and to 'play' physically again. Raj was no longer the hounding teenage boy, and Aayat was no longer the scared, angry teenage girl. Penetration stopped being the sole focus of their sexual relationship. Aayat was able to access her desire once more and allow Raj to initiate sex freely, within some new agreed boundaries.

## Conclusion

In the case studies outlined earlier, couples presented with frustration and hurt related to their feelings of difference. Lily felt that she was sexually open and available whilst Colin was not. Claire and Jen were threatened by their difference when one was pregnant and the other was not. In the latter two case studies, both couples experienced different levels of desire. The differences in all cases were normal and natural, resulting from a mix of physical and emotional change in one or both partners. However, the couples felt unable to negotiate their differences, mainly because of the feelings that were evoked. These feelings were not only in the symptomatic partner but in both partners, and they referenced echoes of historic childhood feelings.

I suggest that, at specific times in parenthood, feelings of dependency on one's partner may be aroused which can lead to vulnerability within the parental couple relationship. These feelings come especially alive in sexual relationships, mainly because sex is so physically and emotionally exposing for couples. In sexual intercourse, the need for the other is apparent but so, too, are differences between couples. Couples struggling with fears of dependency and difference unconsciously find ways to physically distance from each other. This is particularly painful since, in an effort to assuage vulnerability, many couples require physical comfort.

Although I have not detailed the psychosexual treatment for these couples, nevertheless, I wish to emphasise the importance of an integrated model. Sometimes, when childhood fears resurface, couples may struggle to put words to their fears, instead just wanting to be held physically. This echoes infancy when the infant's greatest comfort was given by physical care. Winnicott described the physical comfort parents give children as 'handling' and 'holding' (Winnicott, 1962). Sensate Focus encourages such holding. Throughout the case examples, the couples were literally holding each other every week, more than once a week, in a sensual and nonsexual way. I think this physical touch can be soothing for couples experiencing transitions in parenthood because their infant and adolescent selves come into consciousness while supporting their children's development. It was noticeable from these couple's stories how few had received physical comfort as children when they most needed it. I believe that this is why couples withdraw from physical intimacy when, as adults, they feel vulnerable. They are simply not familiar with receiving physical comfort when it's needed and have not developed the confidence to ask for it. That is why it is important that the therapist helps to give voice, direction and permission to these unspoken needs via setting behavioural work. When these needs are met, I think the couples are more able to be vulnerable and experience shared grief.

In this chapter, I have mostly emphasised psychodynamic repeated patterns, linked to childhood experience, that can lead to sexual dysfunction in later life. That said, it is also important to acknowledge the macro impact of religion, education and socioeconomic and sociocultural issues on the couple's ability to negotiate their sexual relationship through these transitions (Pacey, 2004). Certainly, Claire and Jen were affected as adults from growing up within a Catholic community which did not affirm their sexuality. Couples may be emotionally attuned, but if they haven't learnt the language, then they cannot talk about sex. The way parents raise their children and how they name and talk about their bodies, sex, desire and pregnancy will have a huge impact on how their children sexually relate to themselves and others and how, in turn, they parent their own children and help them develop.

## References

Aslan, G, Aslan, D, Kızılyar, A, et al, 2005: A prospective analysis of sexual functions during pregnancy. International Journal of Impotence Research 17, 154–157. https://doi.org/10.1038/sj.ijir.3901288

Balfour, A, 2005: The Couple, their marriage and Oedipus or problems come in twos and threes. In Grier, F (ed): Oedipus & The Couple, Routledge, London.

Basson, R, 2020: The circles of sex: Basson's sex response cycle. In: Lykins, A (eds): Encyclopedia of Sexuality and Gender, Springer, Cham. https://doi.org/10.1007/978-3-319-59531-3_37-1

Belsky, J & Kelly, J, 1994: The Transition to Parenthood, Dell, New York.

Bischoff, R.J, 2004: The transition to parenthood. Implications of recent findings for couple therapy. Journal of Couple & Relationship Therapy 3(1).

Britton, R, 1989: The missing link: Parental sexuality and the oedipus complex. In Steiner, J (ed): The Oedipus Complex Today: Clinical Implications (pp. 83–101), Karnac Books, London.

Clulow, C.F, 1982: To Have and To Hold. Marriage, The First Baby and Preparing Couple for Parenthood, Aberdeen University Press, UK.

Clulow, C.F, 2009: Becoming Parents Together, Tavistock Centre for Couple Relationships Publication, London.

Di Ceglie, G.R, 1995: From the Internal Parental Couple to the Marital Relationship in Ruszczynski, S & Fisher, J (eds): Intrusiveness and Intimacy in the Couple, Karnac, London.

Furstenberg Jr, F, 2010: On a new schedule. Transitions to adulthood and family change. Transitions to Adulthood 20(1), 7–81.

Gilbert, D.T, 2005: Stumbling on Happiness, Vintage Books, New York.

Hawton, K, 1985: Sex therapy. A Practical Guide, Oxford Press, London.

Jones, C, Chan, C & Farine, D, 2019: Sex in pregnancy. Canadian Medical Association Journal 183(7), 815–818. https://doi.org/10.1503/cmaj.091580

Masters, W.H, Johnson, V.E & Kolodny, R.C, 1994: Heterosexuality, Harper Collins, New York.

Mattinson, J & Sinclair, I, 1979: Four Theoretical Themes. In Mate and Stalemate: Working with Marital Problems in a Social Services Department, TIMS, London.

McBride, H.L & Kwee, J.L, 2017: Sex after baby: Women's sexual function in the postpartum period. Current Sexual Health Reports 9, 142–149. https://doi.org/10.1007/s11930-017-0116-3

Morgan, M. (2004) On being able to be a couple: The importance of a "creative couple" in psychic life. In Grier, F. (Ed.) Oedipus and the Couple (pp. 9–30). London: Karnac.

Morgan, M, 2019: A Couple State of Mind. Psychoanalysis of Couples and the Tavistock Relationships Model, Routledge, London.

O'Connor, M, 2019: Lets talk about sex. In Balfour, A, Clulow, C & Thompson, K (eds): Engaging Couples. New Directions in Therapeutic Work with Families, Routledge, London.

O'Rosen, N, Bailey, K & Muise, A, 2018: Degree and direction of sexual desire discrepancy are linked to sexual and relationship satisfaction in couples transitioning to parenthood. The Journal of Sex Research 55(2), 214–225. https://doi.org/10.1080/00224499.2017.1321732

Pacey, S, 2004: Couples and the first baby: Responding to new parents' sexual and relationship problems. Sexual and Relationship Therapy 19(3), 223–246. https://doi.org/10.1080/14681990410001715391

Panea Pizarro, I., Dominquez Martin, I. I., Barragan Prieto, V., Martos Sanchez, A., Lopez Espuela, F. (2018) Behaviour and attitudes towards the sexuality of pregnant women during the last trimester: Phenomenological Studies. Atencion Primaria (2019), March 51(3), 127–134.

Polomeno, V, 1999: Sex and breastfeeding: An educational perspective. The Journal of Perinatal Education 8(1):30–40. https://doi.org/10.1624/105812499X86962. PMCID: PMC3431754.

Ruszczynski, S, 1993: Thinking about and working with Couples. In Ruszczynski, S (ed): Psychotherapy with Couples (pp. 3–27), Karnac Books, London.

Scharff, D.E, 1982: The Sexual Relationship. An Object Relations View of Sex and the Family, Routledge, London & New York.

Smith, N.K, Madeira, J & Millard, H.R, 2015: Sexual function and fertility quality of life in women using in vitro fertilization. The Journal of Sexual Medicine 12, 985–993.

Waddell, M, 2002: Inside Lives. Psychoanalysis and the Growth of the Personality, Routledge, London.

Winnicott, D.W, 1962: Ego integration in child development ch 4 pp 56–63 in the maturational processes and the facilitating environment. The International Psycho-Analytical Library 64, 1–276.

# Chapter 8

# Falling or flying

## Managing the 'emptying of the nest'

*Krisztina Glausius*

American psychoanalyst Paul Marcus (Marcus, 2007, p. 641) in his essay *I'm Just Wild about Harry!* says:

> *"Like both my children, Harry was a bad sleeper who would frequently come into our bed in the middle of the night, forcing me to get up and put him back in his own bed. As with my children, however, there were many nights when I was too tired or lazy to get up, or simply enjoyed his warm company, and Harry slept next to us."*

At first glance, he appears to describe a common parenting situation, instantly recognised by so many sleep-deprived new parents. When baby comes in, sleep and, rather too often, the parental couple's intimate life goes out of the window. Indeed, beyond the very real external explanations for this state of affairs, various chapters in this volume address some of those possible hidden unconscious reasons that could account for the waning intimacy parental couples can experience in this most private domain, their marital bed.

However, Marcus' essay is not quite about that. It is subtitled *A Psychoanalyst Reflects on His Relationship with His Dog*. Harry is, in fact, the couple's pet dog whom they have adopted after their youngest child left home. The essay, however, is not so much about the dog but about the middle-aged couple's capacity to reflect on the meaning and challenges of this new stage of life, the emptying of their nest.

## Being able to think

This chapter draws attention to the central importance of reflective functioning, that is, the mature parental couple's capacity to think about and work through this new stage of their shared life. Children leaving the parental home ushers in considerable intrapsychic and interpersonal changes, and the extent to which each couple can manage the psychic work involved in working through varies a great deal, highlighting anew some major structural strengths or fault lines in their intimate

DOI: 10.4324/9781003387947-11

relationship. New fissures can open up, and incomplete or botched psychic repairs might not hold when exposed to the sharp light of this new childless reality.

*"With an empty nest, individuals in middle age experience the need to reconfigure their relationships not only with their departed children (and their newly acquired sons and daughters-in-law), but more importantly, with their spouses."*

(Akhtar & Choi, 2004, p. 184)

Couples' reflective capacity fluctuates throughout the life cycle of their journey through parenting and ebbs and flows under the varying pressures from conception onwards through managing infants, toddlers, teenagers and then, later, young adults. When children grow towards adulthood and begin the frequently stop-and-start process of fleeing the nest to strike out on their own, a monumental change has to be worked through by all parties involved. Whilst there are some universal themes, this life stage carries different meanings and stirs up different anxieties for each parental couple navigating and, if all goes to plan, psychologically surviving this stage and thriving in later life.

Indeed, research into this area of couple functioning comes to no definite conclusion. Firstly, a recent comprehensive study (Tracy et al., 2022) notes the relative scarcity of high-quality research into the effects on the reported level of couples' satisfaction during and after their transition to the empty nest stage, that is, when couples live with no children after having raised one or more children together. And secondly, and rather unsurprisingly, they find that ultimately, the picture is mixed.

In some studies, the empty-nest status has been linked to better marital quality (Gorchoff et al., 2008; White and Edwards, 1990) and lower rates of conflict (Mackey & O'Brien, 1999) whereas other research documents an increase in divorce likelihood when grown children leave the home (Heidemann et al., 1998).

So what makes the difference between falling or flying? Why is it that some couples stumble afresh over reawakened ghosts from their individual and couple past, whilst others feel that now that their life is theirs again, they will take this opportunity to fully inhabit it? The temptation to turn a blind eye to the psychic task ahead, to subtly mould internal or external reality to avoid fuller psychological awareness of the demanding process of working through some of these changes, is considerable.

*'Are we crazy?' Having just sent off our second of two children to college and having spent many of the preceding months fantasizing about how nice life would be without any children to look after – call it a neurotic decision to deal with our 'empty nest' 'we nevertheless decided to adopt Harry'. 'Maybe we will get it right the third time', I joked to my wife!*

(Marcus, 2007, p. 640)

It is not easy to let go of this central pillar of the day-to-day caring function of the parental couple, and despite the lightness of his tone earlier, Marcus recognises that this is no joking matter and that the stakes are indeed high:

> "Harry satisfies a very basic need that I have, which for that matter seems to be a constituent part of the human condition: He blunts the horror of separation and abandonment that most of us somewhere feel deep down in our infantile selves and spend considerable conscious and unconscious psychic energy managing."
>
> (Marcus, 2007, p. 642)

It would seem the impulse purchase of the puppy is a defensive manoeuvre to keep something terrifying at bay, to paper over an abyss that might otherwise open up when the children leave home.

> "In infancy, such terror of annihilation or disintegration was based on the infant's primitive state of physical and psychological vulnerability, and for some people late life can bring a new coinage of such anxieties. . . . the threat of vulnerability and dependency in later life can be felt as a trauma to be avoided at all costs."
>
> (Balfour, 2015, p. 57)

The gradual moving on from the sometimes benign and often much complained about clamour and chaos of parenting can terrify some couples. Busyness can be confused with liveliness. The newly descending quiet can feel deadly and is often likened to a bereavement. There are indeed considerable losses to mourn, and it is a hard truth to face that the parental couple is moving just that much closer to the grave.

Limitations of space in this chapter will not allow for full consideration of the many different shapes and sizes of families arriving at this stage of life. Couples who have their children young might just about be entering their middle years, whilst late parental starters are nearing pension age by the time their youngest leaves for university. These couples might worry about how little life there is left for them to live. Some children, on the other hand, might have arrived too soon, conceived by accident before their parents felt fully ready or got to know one another well. Other babies now grown into young adulthood might have come about following years of fertility struggles and multiple complex losses.

Some couples, at this point, can look back at decades of shared history, whilst others have come through separations and remarriages and now negotiate the complexities of blended families, with children at different developmental stages, their parents juggling conflicting pressures and divided loyalties. There are same-sex parents, single parents, widowed or adoptive parents and couples who parent disabled, neurodiverse or otherwise complicated children. There are couples who need to come to terms with the painful fact that for various reasons, their child or children will never reach full independence and will always require care.

In this chapter, I focus predominantly on the psychological pressures impacting the couple dynamics of those empty nesters whose children, on entering young adulthood, are no longer or differently present in the home and are differently dependent on their parental couples. The illustrative vignettes that follow are composite examples drawn from the author's clinical and supervisory practice.

## The squeezed middle

Often, in tandem with their children's newly established independence, the no-longer-youthful parents will have to face up to their own increasing dependence brought about by the physical effects of aging. Just when dependence on reading glasses, hearing aids, health services and other forms of care become part of the late-middle-aged couple's daily reality, they need to draw on seemingly inexhaustible reserves of stamina. They continue to have to meet the needs of their young adult children whilst rising to the emotionally, financially and physically crippling cost of caring for the increasingly frail generation above. The dual responsibilities of care for both the generation above and below can make middle-aged couples feel caught in a pincer movement on the battlefield of life. Meanwhile, there are some significant emotional challenges to rise to. The empty-nester couple is faced with the work of mourning for the psychological loss of no longer occupying the centrally potent position as the actively parenting couple. Little wonder that couples entering therapy at this point can feel terribly worn out.

## Case example: Mark and Joanna

Mark and Joanna, both in their mid-50s, applied for therapy in a polite, almost tentative manner. Mark, making his initial enquiry, stressed that their need was not pressing and that they were happy to wait for a vacancy to come up in due course. When an appointment did become available, they made every effort to fit in with their therapist's schedule and accepted a time that was slightly too early for them both, necessitating an exhausting and rather frantic drive through the post-work rush hour. They always made it to their sessions just in time, at once slightly jittery and sluggishly exhausted. Each arrival was a triumph and a disaster, as they staggered into the consulting room, weighed down by what seemed like a fair bit of psychic luggage.

The atmosphere, particularly during the opening minutes of each session, was a heavy combination of defeat and resentment. Their description of the current state of their 33-year marriage had a similarly contradictory feel. They explained that although they were ploughing through life in tandem, twin-like and seemingly joined at the hip, despite such proximity, they seemed to have entirely lost sight of one another. When either of them did become visible to the other, as if emerging from the fog of exhaustion, neither liked what they saw. They clearly described the jolt of displeasure nearing disgust they suffered when glimpsing in their partner a reflection of some of their own aging – a sagging of both mind and body. It's not that they couldn't recognise what they saw. It was more that they did not feel that they could bear it. Their past was idealised but forever lost, the present unbearable, the future unthinkable.

Mark and Joanna had every success in their professional and personal lives, and central to their achievements, the foundation of their self-regard, was the success of their four now-grown-up children. All graduates of good universities, two of them recently married, all well-established in their young adult lives and were well supported by the generosity of their parents. This appeared all the more remarkable when the couple went on to consider the emotional and material deprivation from where they themselves had come.

Joanna's parents were immigrants fleeing conflict, arriving traumatised with their baby daughter who remained their only child. They lived an isolated, somewhat bewildered, hard-working life. Joanna's mother never mastered the language of her new country and had always relied heavily on her daughter for getting by. This both burdened and gratified Joanna when she was a girl. Her father, a skilled labourer, worked multiple jobs to provide for the family and made it clear that Joanna's success was all that mattered. Joanna felt she had no choice but to feel grateful, even though her father was largely absent from the home. He died young, at a similar age to that of Joanna now. Joanna continues to navigate life for her mother, whose capacity to manage is further eroded by her encroaching dementia and sharp decline.

Mark's background was, on the surface, entirely different. His mother is a successful artist, and his father an eminent scientist, both still active and respected in their field. Mark's childhood was characterised by relative material comfort and benign neglect. His celebrated mother in her studio and formidable father in his study, Mark and his younger sister were left to fend for themselves.

When Mark and Joanna met at university, their attraction for each other was immediate. Mark was hungry to be at last properly held and cared for, and Joanna, through years of practice, was very good at providing just that. She cared for herself vicariously through him, and his gratitude gratified her. They knew they wanted to give a different and better upbringing to their children than the one they had experienced themselves. The couple went on to share all aspects of parenting whilst also supporting each other professionally. Despite their packed schedule, they never missed a school event, and their family of six was very much admired and envied within their local community.

In the course of their therapy, a different story began to emerge, hinting at the 'gritted-teeth', aggressive-competitive nature of the way they parented their children. As neither partner could ever really allow themselves to be in touch with their unconsciously held grievance towards their own parents about their differently deprived childhoods, they carefully wrapped these feelings up into self-sacrificial, masochistic perfection. Living in this exemplary way meant to semaphore to their own, now internalised parents: *'You see, this is how it's done'*. Mark and Joanna parented their children the way they as children had longed to be parented, a childish approximation of idealised perfection which ended up feeling like a rather competitive sport. The couple's unconscious pact about meeting their own needs in this way held so long as they were employed in a particular hands-on way by their children. When this was no longer necessary, they felt utterly lost. Whilst, for decades, and much like Joanna's father, they masochistically overextended themselves, secretly hoping for gratitude but fearing an early grave, their couple relationship had fallen victim to the same pattern of benign neglect that was the hallmark of Mark's childhood.

Entering couple therapy, however ambivalently, was a tentative departure from this continuing neglect. Initially, Mark and Joanna used their sessions to complain, somewhat competitively, about their enormous workload, seemingly necessitated by exhaustively meeting the financial and emotional needs of those around them. Mark's parents still needed their son's regular homage to their talents; Joanna's mother needed her as a guide to navigate and provide her care. Their children needed deposits, advice and occasional rescue via cash injection. Whilst there was undoubted external reality to these demands, it has become increasingly clear that the couple, exhausted though they were, also felt a certain satisfaction from being exploited in this way.

Their therapist with the inconveniently timed sessions and monthly bills could easily have become another one of those hungry mouths to feed, a person into whom the couple could project their own hunger. Careful work in the transference helped Mark and Joanna to become more aware of, and less embarrassed by, their own needs and wants. Regular interpretation of their hidden fury over feeling unfairly treated by their therapist each time they were billed for sessions that they were unable to use due to conflicting commitments helped Mark and Joanna to recognise that such feelings can be known about and discussed without fracturing the therapeutic relationship. Their therapist's steady holding on to the importance of the couple's regular time as well as her valuing her own time supported the couple's incremental discovery of the value of what they have now and what they imagined for themselves for the future. They gradually became more ambitious for themselves, both individually and as a couple. As they no longer relied almost entirely on others to carry their own needs, they were able to be more ordinarily resentful about their adult children's continuing demands. This brought them closer to each other and allowed for a more lively solidarity between them. Letting go of long-established defensive solutions is never an easy or straightforward process, and the couple's therapy proceeded in fits and starts, characterised by periods of regression. Their complaints and long-held grievances were hard to give up, and at times, maintaining things unchanged had a near-addictive quality to it (Joseph, 1982; Feldman, 2008).

It also has become increasingly clear that the couple were, above all, terrified. Terrified that if they should set a limit to what they can willingly give, they will no longer appear boundless in their capacity and will be regarded as a couple in decline – an aging couple, who, if they cannot be central, will end up being nothing.

A long-hidden fear was stirred up by the emptying of their nest. Fundamentally, this was an anxiety about managing intimacy, a fear of not being enough for each other when left with each other to face the challenges and reap the potential rewards of being in a couple. Neither Joanna nor Mark had ever felt secure about being loveable just for who they are, and their busy lives and caring responsibilities contained an element of psychic procrastination. It helped them postpone seeking an answer to this fundamental enquiry about their worth.

And most of all, somewhere deep down, they were terrified that they don't have what it takes – a feared lack of capacity to mourn some of their real and unavoidable losses.

## Discussion

When Mark and Joanna's children flew the nest, the couple were left alone together. They were left with their 'marital triangle' (Ruszczynski, 2005) which is composed of the couple and their relationship. The structural soundness of this formation, like with any structure, matters enormously when it comes under pressure. Change is pressure and always carries within itself elements of loss, particularly so for a couple like Mark and Joanna, who relied so heavily and for so long on a form of conscious and unconscious arrangement, a sort of golden age, to keep certain anxieties at bay.

As much as the children needed their parents psychologically, the parental couple also relied on their children in a similar way. Some parental couples need their children for their psychic survival, and they might feel unsure about being able to manage without their actual presence. When children are unconsciously used to plug certain psychic gaps between their parents, the couple might exert considerable pressure to keep things as they are, which can make it harder for their children to mature and individuate. Letting go is an experiment with loss.

Parents can feel anxious that if their children grow up and leave, they, the parents, might become cut off from and lose touch with those split-off, unbearable aspects of themselves they had originally and for so long projected into their children. At the same time, this could equally be an important opportunity to reclaim such aspects of the parental couple's personality which, if not exactly lost, have been dormant, as if on loan, residing solely projected into the psychic structure of their children. Couples who, in the course of satisfying their children's lustful demands, might have become cut off from their own lively appetites can discover or rediscover these aspects as parts of their own internal make-up. This, in turn, can help balance and enrich a previously somewhat impoverished, uneven personality structure, and the mature empty-nester couple, if things go well, can look forward to a rewarding period where they can be in touch with what they need but also bear it when these needs cannot be perfectly or immediately satisfied.

Mark and Joanna together had a great unconscious need for their children to carry their own unmanageable infantile feelings of neediness, greediness, messiness and dependency for them. When their children became adults and their hard-earned independence and fledgling adult capacity have become undeniable, the couple panicked and, in order to ward off internal collapse, worked ever harder to maintain the status quo. They had an unconscious need for their children to remain resource hungry and weak so that they could cling on to the illusion of remaining forever strong. But it was clear that, on one level, both Mark and Joanna had an inkling of the futility of this desperate rear-guard action. Even if they could not bear to acknowledge signs of advancing age in themselves, they could not remain blind to this when glimpsing them in their spouse. They had to begin the work of mourning.

## Mourning and its failures: melancholia and mania

As Freud first noted in *Mourning and Melancholia* (Freud, 1917), mourning is a complex but necessary process. In this seminal paper, he describes the psychic work of mourning as one of gradual, painful letting go, untying, bit by bit every emotional anchor that once tied the mourner to that what was lost. Mark and Joanna earlier could not bear to recognise that a period of their couple and parenting lives was now in the past and, therefore, lost to them through the ordinary passage of time. Their glory days of a particular type of parenting were over. However, if the painful mourning process could be managed, new links with life can be established, and the mourner would not become impoverished but enriched by the experience.

> *"Facing the suffering that comes in the wake of change and loss, we have two options. In our minds, we can cling desperately to what is slipping out of our lives . . . or, taking courage, we can let go."*
>
> (Polden, 2002, p. 303)

Letting go requires considerable internal resources accumulated, if all goes well, from our earliest infancy. Joanna and Mark, who both have come from emotionally deprived beginnings, doubted their capacity to manage the new reality of this later stage of life, that of the 'empty nester', and protected themselves by establishing a depressed and depressing reality, maintaining a caricature version of their permanently busy younger couple self. Their way of trying to manage incorporated both melancholic/depressed and manic elements.

Nathans (2012), surveying those various losses that might fall beyond a couple's shared capacity to mourn, specifically highlights the crisis brought about by the couple's youngest child leaving home, the emptying of the nest, as well as the physical and psychological challenges of aging. The following vignette describes a couple's *'manic attempt to replace depression or psychic pain with excitement'* (Nathans, 2012, p. 166).

## Case example: Mike and Mia

Mike and Mia came to therapy following Mike's discovery of Mia's affair. Mike felt shocked, angry and humiliated and was threatening to file for divorce. Mia immediately ended her eight-month affair with her personal trainer and asked Mike for a chance to understand together what had happened and, if possible, try and repair their marriage. She herself was also bewildered by her own actions, and she could neither make sense of this period of lustful infatuation nor the ongoing cover-up of evasions and half-truths, which shattered Mike's trust. She said, however, that, in many ways, she was relieved that she was discovered and hoped that therapy will help to see if they can find a way through.

During their sessions, their story emerged gradually. Mike, at 64, was 15 years Mia's senior. He had been married before and had two grown-up sons and a grandson from his first marriage. Mia had met Mike five years after the collapse of his first marriage, a little over 20 years ago. His first wife had also been unfaithful to him, and it took Mike a long time to recover from the hurt.

In therapy, Mike and Mia described a happy, well-balanced partnership, where they have always been able to accommodate and even enjoy their differences. Mike was a hard-working man, he managed the large business he had inherited from his father, and from modest beginnings, under his stewardship, the business thrived. In fact, the couple met through work when Mia took a job as Mike's office manager. He described falling for her not only because of her considerable beauty but also because, despite her being so much younger, she was uncommonly caring and capable, even maternal. Mia instantly fell for Mike's rugged good looks, his energetic masculinity and his gentle and sensitive parenting of his two young sons from his first marriage. There was an immediate, powerful physical attraction, and until relatively recently, the couple had always enjoyed a good sex life.

They married after a brief courtship, and their daughter, Lilly, was born the following year.

19-year-old Lilly, their only child, was currently away on a gap year before taking up her place at university. Because their daughter came about so soon after they had met, on one level, the couple were rather looking forward to her becoming independent and flying the nest. They wanted to spend more quality time together and had planned the next phase of their lives with excitement.

Mia had always been a homemaker, keeping family life running smoothly, like a well-oiled machine. With their daughter gone, she was finally planning to rejoin Mike's company. Things did not go to plan. Mike suffered an unexpected health scare. What was initially feared to have been a serious heart attack turned out to be a more benign bout of angina. Nevertheless, the couple decided that it was time to pass on the business to Mike's sons, and Mike took retirement earlier than he had planned.

During the first couple of months of their therapy, a lot of time was given to Mike's fury over Mia's betrayal. He felt that there was a flavour of cruelty to the affair, as Mia must have known only too well that this was a particularly sensitive, even traumatic area for him. His own father was a notorious womaniser, and Mike vowed never to be like him, only to suffer a double betrayal by his first wife and now in his second marriage. Perhaps to compound the pain and share some of his sense of humiliation, he interrogated Mia obsessively about the details of the affair. He particularly wanted to know everything about what happened in the bedroom between his wife and her lover. Mia was mortified and felt tortured by his insistence but tried her best to oblige without becoming vulgar or overly hurtful.

In time, it became clear that Mike was secretly convinced that it was his own recent infirmity and his general aging that was behind Mia seeking comfort in the arms of a younger presumably more virile man. Mia could not see this but felt relieved to be able to finally speak about her own predicament. At 49, she was now perimenopausal and was suffering the encroaching hormonal and emotional storms of an imminent menopause. She has always measured her worth by her success as a sexually alluring woman and feared that the loss of her fertility will naturally lead to the loss of her sexual desirability. Consciously, she tried to hold up the encroaching tide by her daily intensive workouts in the gym, whilst unconsciously, she found the young man's attention irresistibly affirming, soothing away her anxieties about herself. The affair was a manic denial of the reality of the loss of what Mia considered her primary identity. It was an avoidance of the mourning for a much-enjoyed earlier period in her life. In this way, the affair also arrested her progress into that unknown land she so feared to enter, that place where she imagined all women languished after their menopause. The psychic work of realistic mourning might have given her a passport to enter and more fully map out this unknown terrain, but with the manic affair, she held back from finding out that there is much life to live on the other side.

Mia was also anxious about no longer being needed in the same way by her daughter, and there were clearly some maternal projections mixed in with her affair with her much younger lover.

But she was not the only one of this empty-nester couple who manouvered to avoid the work of mourning. Mike has always been a man whose sense of wellbeing and self-esteem was based upon his sexual virility, as well as on his authority and his capacity to perform well in all areas. He was hit hard by the health scare, his unexpected retirement and by the other uncontrollable losses of midlife. He has become withdrawn, even morose at times, and had trouble sleeping. The couple realised that he had become rather depressed and needed some help. Mia, whose own father had always been a withdrawn, depressed man and whose alcoholic mother's vitality had prematurely withered away, was terrified of living out her own life in this rather mournful atmosphere.

Nathans clearly identifies infidelity as a manic defence against losses, such as those couples might suffer midlife:

> *"When each partner has a capacity for mourning, they will be more likely to face loss in a shared way and experience their relationship as a source of containment. However, when there are deficits in the capacity for mourning in one or both of the partners, difficulties in facing their losses individually, and together, will more likely lead to defensive enactments that serve to deny loss, leading either to severe depression (melancholia) or to manic defences. In these circumstances, infidelity may serve as a possible vehicle for the manic attempt to deny both dependency and loss, and to replace pain with excitement."*
> (Nathans, 2012, p. 178)

Freud (1923) identifies manic avoidance as an unconscious attempt at warding off depressive feelings. Klein added to our understanding by detailing the particular defensive functions of manic activity, primarily aimed at denying unbearable aspects of reality, such as experiences of loss, vulnerability, dependency and – ultimately – of mortality (Klein, 1935, 1940). This couple represented two sides of these principal methods of avoidance of true mourning. Mia acted out in a manic way, whilst Mike has become quietly depressed.

## Managing envy

Just when Mike's 'crown and kingdom' has passed on to his sons, Mia was following obsessively through social media the confident progress of their daughter through exotic lands, making new friends and boyfriends along her way. On one level, they congratulated themselves on a job well done. The sons, so capable, the daughter, so confident and bright. But on another level, hidden beneath the surface, envious feelings were stirred up in the couple. Envy is present between the generations, and it goes both ways.

The newly child-free couple need somehow to bear their young peoples' envy. Their children, just starting out in life, might find it hard to know just how much their parents might have accumulated both in material and emotional terms. At the time of writing, there exists in the UK a particularly stark generational divide in terms of wealth and property, and it might feel particularly difficult for young people to climb those mountains which their parents had successfully scaled. Young people might also feel trapped by old people's politics, hemmed in by decisions made about their futures by the generations above. Perhaps some of these decisions by their elders are partly influenced by their unconscious envy for being no longer young. After all, most young people stride out into the world with their whole life ahead of them. They have their young and vital bodies, fresh and lively minds, livelier libidos and flowing sexuality and a full life left to live.

## Oedipus returns

Mike and Mia, like so many other empty-nester couples, were watching their young adult children's lives unfold from their new position, that is, supporting from the side-lines. They had to contend with a fresh version of a familiar and demanding psychic situation. This time, it is the older adult couple who can feel left out, looking in, as it were, from the outside. At this time of life, Oedipus can return with a vengeance, except in reverse. As Britton points out, oedipal struggles have to be 'reworked in each new life situation, at each stage of development, and with each major addition to experience or knowledge' (Britton, 1992, p. 38). After so many years of trying to close their bedroom door, oedipally frustrating their children by leaving them out of the real and imagined exciting goings-on in the parental bedroom, now *they* are the couple left out of their children's couplings.

This new situation can expose cracks in the structure and functioning of the parental couple that might have previously been papered over by various defensive uses of the couple's involvement with their children. Grier points out that '*partners often share a history of inadequate working through of certain aspects of the Oedipus complex*' (Grier, 2005b, p. 201), resulting in various defensive solutions unconsciously maintained to prevent coming in touch with aspects of reality that are felt to be too painful and thus unmanageable. Negotiating the challenges of the oedipal situation is a lifelong task. Of course, none of us ever fully 'resolves' it. Whether in fantasy or reality, the experience of being left out can always stir up disturbing feelings. There are certain junctions in all parental couples' lives which are particularly challenging in this respect, and two of these are going in and coming out of parenthood. Both these stages involve a comprehensive and wide-ranging reorganisation of existing internal, as well as external structures. When partners become parents, even when things go well enough, certain psychological defences are established to operate throughout the active parenting life of the couple to support them in managing both the conscious and unconscious psychological challenges of this period. When this stage of life is drawing to a close, it is 'all change' again, and this later time of life may threaten to weaken or dismantle a couple's entrenched defensive solutions. Many of these defences were originally established to protect both partners from coming into contact with what Lanman (2005) calls '*the painful truth*', inherent in the oedipal situation: the truth of a parental intercourse that excludes us. This perceived threat can, in turn, bring about a desperate rear-guard action to fortify defences. Some couples, who never have come to terms with being left out of their own parents' coupling, might continue their envious and destructive internal attacks but, this time, targeting their own potentially successful and exclusive coupling. Such attacks likely undermine the couple's own potential, their capacity to fully own what they can create together. This then weakens the couple and depletes much-needed internal resources at this important transition point to later life, and the internally impoverished couple might struggle to support one another or feel held and contained by their relationship.

## Falling or flying: the couple reinvented

Although challenging, this later life stage can bring about new opportunities for working through an entrenched or stagnant system of defences, perhaps even loosening a long-standing 'projective gridlock' (Morgan, 1995), breathing new life into the unconscious relating of the parental couple. There can be a real opportunity for the empty-nester couple to disentangle the 'who is who' of their previous way of functioning, and this gradual working through and withdrawing of projections allows the couple to plant their feet on psychologically more solid grounds, with deeper roots in reality. Couples need to be able to draw on both internal and external resources to manage the psychic work of this transformation. Colman (1993a) outlines an important function of the couple's relationship, whereby the relationship itself can function. '*as a psychological container or secure base for each partner, a container within which each partner might be helped by their relationship*' (Cudmore & Judd, 2001, p. 153). Morgan (2005) similarly emphasises the importance of those internal resources that can be provided by the couple relationship itself. In her conceptualisation, the *'creative couple'* is as follows:

*"an unconscious internal representation of the link between both partners, that functions in the couple's mind as a 'third' which they can turn to for containment at times when conflict and high levels of projection of unwanted parts threaten the relationship. This internal couple object represents the interaction and quality of emotional interaction between a couple: each contributes to it, but neither is sole creator or solely responsible. It functions as part of the couple's shared psychic life that each has in mind as a resource to draw on during difficult times."*

(Wrottesley, 2017, p. 198)

It is clear that the secure internal establishment of a 'creative-couple object' contributes to the development of reflective capacity. It is equally important for supporting the necessary process of mourning all that has been lost through the aging process. If this capacity exists, it will be called upon as the couple will have to recreate their relationship once again in this new life stage.

## In summary

This chapter aimed to take up some of the challenges with which parental couples are faced when their children grow up enough to leave the parental home. Much like some of the earlier challenges of parenting, many of which are explored in other chapters in this book, this change can also impact heavily on the couple's relationship quality. Psychic pain is expected, and complex changes and often regrets need to be worked through.

It is clear that there are losses to be mourned. Mourning, as illustrated earlier, can be a resource hungry and inevitably painful process, and when resources are scarce, perhaps because one or both partners are poorly equipped and the relationship itself lacks resilience, various evasive manoeuvres might be unconsciously put into place. Some of these are more depressive, others are manic in nature. Sometimes a couple together resort to one way of managing, at other times, the partners might polarise and a division of psychic labour results. This can then leave the partners feeling cut off from one another and the relationship suffers.

The beginning of this chapter pointed at a more light-hearted evasion, that of the purchasing of the dog, Harry. But this was more procrastination than a true solution, and the couple's reflective capacity was called upon to work through of what was actually happening to them and to make sense of their new situation.

When the reality of this most important fact of life (Money-Kyrle, 1971), that is aging and ultimately mortality, can be truly borne, something fresh and new and vital might be created. Couples, at this stage, often benefit from external therapeutic support to help them gather up those resources that might never have been sufficiently established or have become temporarily lost under the pressures of change.

Many parental couples find that working through brings considerable gains to this stage of life, which can usher in fresh psychic development, bringing increased wisdom, intimacy and fulfilment to the relationship. Waddell, writing about later life, sums it up movingly:

> *"Development, at whatever age, is founded in the capacity to go on engaging with the meaning of experience with imagination, courage and integrity . . . now, as ever, for those who have the capacity to learn, the passing of years certainly grants more time further to integrate their life experiences."*
>
> (Waddell, 1998, p. 217)

## References

Akhtar, S., & Choi, L. W. (2004). When evening falls: The immigrant's encounter with middle and old age. *American Journal of Psychoanalysis* 64:183–191.

Balfour, A. (2015). Growing old together in mind and body. *Fort Da* 21:53–76.

Britton, R. (1992). The Oedipus situation and the depressive position. In: R. Anderson (Ed.), *Clinical Lectures on Klein and Bion* (pp. 34–45). Tavistock/Routledge.

Colman, W. (1993a). Marriage as a psychological container. In: S. Ruszczynski (Ed.), *Psychotherapy with Couples: Theory and Practice at the Tavistock Institute of Marital Studies* (pp. 126–141). London: Karnac.

Cudmore, L., & Judd, D. (2001). Thoughts about the couple relationship following the death of a child. In: F. Grier (Ed.), *Brief Encounters with Couples: Some Analytical Perspectives* (pp. 33–53). London: Karnac.

Feldman, M. (2008). Grievence: The underlying oedipal configuration. *International Journal of Psychoanalysis* 89: 743–758.

Freud, S. (1917). Mourning and melancholia. In: James Strachey and Anna Freud (Eds.), *The Standard Edition of the Complete Psychological Works of Sigmund Freud, Volume XIV 91914–1916): On the History of the Psycho-analytic Movement, Paper on Metapsychology and Other Works* (pp. 237–258). London: Hogath Press.

Freud, S. (1923). The Ego and the Id. In: James Strachey and Anna Freud (Eds.), *The Standard Edition of the Complete Psychological Works of Sigmund Freud. Volume XIX. (1923–1925): The Ego and the Id and Other Works* (pp. 1–66). London: Hogarth Press.

Gorchoff, S., John, O., & Helson, R. (2008). Contextualizing change in marital satisfaction during middle age: An 18-year longitudinal study. *Psychological Science* 19:1194–1200.

Grier, F. (2005b). No sex couples, catastrophic change, and the primal scene. In: F. Grier (Ed.), *Oedipus and the Couple* (pp. 201–219). London: Karnac.

Heidemann, B., Suhomlinova, O., & O'Rand, A. M. (1998). Economic independence, economic status, and empty nest in midlife marital disruption. *Journal of Marriage and the Family* 60(1):219–231.

Joseph, B. (1982). Addiction to near-death. *The International Journal of Psychoanalysis* 63(Pt 4):449–456.

Klein, M. (1935). A contribution to the psychogenesis of manic-depressive states. *International Journal of Psycho-Analysis* 16:145–174.

Klein, M. (1940). Mourning and its relation to manic-depressive states. *International Journal of Psycho-Analysis* 21:125–53.

Lanman, M. (2005). The painful truth. In: F. Grier (Ed.), *Oedipus and the Couple* (pp. 141–162). London: Karnac.

Mackey, R. A., & O'Brien, B. A. (1999). Adaptation in lasting marriages. *Families in Society* 80: 587–596.

Marcus, P. (2007). "I'm just wild about harry!": A psychoanalyst reflects on his relationship with his dog. In: *Psychoanalytic Review* 94: 639–656.

Money-Kyrle, R. (1971). The Aims of Psychoanalysis. *International Journal of Psycho-Analysis* 49:691–698.

Morgan, M. (1995). The projective gridlock: A form of projective identification in couple relationships. In: S. Ruszczynski & J. V. Fisher (Eds.), *Intrusiveness and Intimacy in the Couple* (pp. 33–48). London: Karnac.

Morgan, M. (2005). On being able to be a couple: The importance of the "creative couple" in psychic life. In: F. Grier (Ed.), *Oedipus and the Couple* (pp. 9–30). London: Karnac.

Nathans, S. (2012). Infidelity as manic defence. *Couple and Family Psychoanalysis* 2:165–180.

Polden, J. (2002). *Regeneration: Journey through the Midlife Crisis.* London: Continuum.

Ruszczynski, S. (2005). Reflective space in the intimate couple relationship: The "marital triangle". In: F. Grier (Ed.), *Oedipus and the Couple.* London: Karnac.

Tracy, E. L., Putney, J. M., & Papp, L. M. (2022). Empty nest status, marital closeness, and perceived health: Testing couples' direct and moderated associations with an actor-partner interdependence model. *Family Therapy in Alexandria, VA* 30(1):30–35.

Waddell, M. (1998). *Inside Lives: Psychoanalysis and the Growth of the Personality.* London: Karnac (Revised edition published in 2022 by H. Karnac Books Ltd.).

White, L., & Edwards, J. N. (1990). Emptying the nest and parental well-being: An analysis of national panel data. *American Sociological Review* 55:235–242.

Wrottesley, C. (2017). Does oedipus never die? The grandparental couple grapple with "oedipus". *Couple and Family Psychoanalysis* 7:188–207.

# Part 3

## Challenges to parenting

Chapter 9

# Perinatal loss
## The impact on the couple and the next generation

*Marguerite Reid*

## Introduction

While thinking about writing this chapter, I visited the Museo del Paesaggio, Verbania, on Lake Maggiore. The museum showed paintings and sculptures from the late nineteenth century to the early twentieth century. Whilst there, I discovered the work of Prince Paolo Troubetzkoy (1866–1938), a sculptor and painter described by the playwright George Bernard Shaw as 'the most astonishing sculptor of modern times'. As I looked at his bronze sculptures, which were originally formed with layers of gesso or plaster of paris, I not only became aware of the complexity of his work but I also began to think about the subject of perinatal loss and its impact on the couple and the next generation in a different way. The words that kept coming into my mind were 'complex emotional layers'.

I have worked in the field of perinatal loss for many years, initially as a child and adolescent psychoanalytic psychotherapist and then as a perinatal and couple psychoanalytic psychotherapist. In my work with children, I had observed the feelings of distress, terror and fear that children brought to sessions when their birth followed a perinatal loss (Reid, 1992). Within my clinical work, I encountered the same atmosphere of distress in subsequent clinical sessions with women referred following a perinatal loss, some of whom had given birth to the next baby (Reid, 2007a). The sense of rawness was equally present when I saw the parental couple together, but I also observed the different experiences that the parental couple struggled with and how differently they might mourn. There was a quality to Troubeztkoy's work that left me thinking about the layers of emotional experience for a couple and their children when there has been a perinatal loss. How emotional states might change from day to day and year to year and the difficulties associated with finding the language to communicate these experiences.

There was a sculpture by Troubetzkoy of his wife and muse, Elfin, with their son, Pierre, which showed the depth of her loving feelings and his understanding of those feelings. I wondered how the depth and loss of this experience could be thought about or imagined by the couple who have lost a baby. In my work, I have been aware that mothers often compare the developmental milestones of the baby born following a perinatal loss with thoughts about the dead baby. Mothers will say

DOI: 10.4324/9781003387947-13

that their new baby has begun to crawl but then follow this comment with a thought about the dead infant: 'She would be starting school now'. I had always thought that it was difficult for the live child to have their developmental steps shrouded in sadness for the lost child, but on reflection, I realised that this comparison was perhaps the only way that the mother could access these thoughts, these layers of emotional experience.

## Historical perspective

Historically, it was only in the 1970s that people working with couples who had suffered a perinatal loss began to acknowledge that the unknown child was not simply forgotten and that couples mourned. As with many changes in society during the last century, an acknowledgement of psychological need had stemmed from the developing awareness of psychological processes and a major shift in medical knowledge and practice. Davidson (1984) linked an awareness of psychological need associated with the death of a child to a rapid drop in both maternal and infant mortality during the first 50 years of the twentieth century.

Kirkley Best and Van Devere (1986) commented on a surge in the literature at this time. Forest et al. (1982) noted that it was only during the past ten years that obstetricians, paediatricians and psychiatrists had realised that families needed help in adjusting to perinatal loss. Caplan (1964) in Giles (1970) discussed how the proper management of bereavement prevented the development of psychiatric difficulties. However, Bourne (1968) produced statistical evidence that showed reluctance on the part of family doctors to know or remember anything about a patient who had suffered a stillbirth. He attributed the difficulties associated with stillbirth to it often being perceived as a 'nonevent' that could not be categorised within a conception of illness.

## Terminology and hospital management

The terminology associated with perinatal loss is important, as couples usually refer to their loss using the same language as that used by medical staff. It is also important from another perspective; I have found that women and couples talk differently about their experience depending on the time when the loss occurred, a point I will expand upon later in this chapter. The definition of miscarriage is that it occurs from natural causes before the 24th week of pregnancy in the United Kingdom and before the 20th week in the United States of America, accounting for between 14% and 20% of pregnancies. A stillbirth is a baby born with no sign of life after 24 weeks, and recent figures estimate that this occurs in approximately 1 in 250 pregnancies. Intrauterine death specifically refers to the death of a baby whilst in utero. Neonatal death is the death of a newly delivered infant in the first 28 days.

Gradually, recommendations were made that resulted in hospital practice following perinatal loss being changed. The following composite clinical vignette describes the experience of one couple in their 60s, whose experience of perinatal loss preceded these changes being implemented.

## Clinical vignette

Iris and Edward were referred to me by their General Practitioner, as they were experiencing difficulties in their long marriage. Both thought they had lost the ability to communicate with one another and felt lonely within their relationship. When I went to the waiting room, they were sitting close together as though communicating to me in the transference that they wished to keep the world at bay. Because of this impression, I felt surprised when they both acknowledged that they talked to friends outside of their relationship, rather than each other.

Together, we thought about their long marriage, and later in the session, I asked about children. They told me about their daughter and how much she had achieved. I felt an acute sense of sadness as they spoke, which I commented on, and Iris said that it was always difficult when people ask about their family because they have a lovely daughter, but there was another baby who died.

The couple went on to describe the death through stillbirth of their first baby. Iris told me that everything seemed all right when she went into labour at the right time but then the baby died. Edward said that he had only just realised that they both thought the death was the result of hospital negligence. They had never talked together about this. Iris said she was in labour for many hours in excruciating pain and that she was on her own much of this time. This was before partners were encouraged to be part of their baby's delivery. The baby, a little girl, was eventually delivered stillborn.

Edward spoke of Iris being badly torn and that she was anaesthetised for the tear to be repaired. Edward had been at the hospital, and he had held their baby girl, but when Iris came round from the anaesthetic, the baby was no longer there. Neither had any idea what happened to their baby. Iris was discharged from hospital two weeks later, and their understanding was that they were told to forget about the baby and to wait two years before they conceived again. When their second daughter was born, they gave her the name they had planned to call their first child. They said they now felt awful about this because their daughter had understandably found this knowledge unbearable and yet had never felt she could change her name, as it was special to her parents. Iris said, 'It was simply the name we had always wanted to call a little girl'.

The trauma of this couple's experience had remained with them throughout their long marriage, but they had never talked about it in depth. My sense was that the trauma had remained on the periphery of their relationship as a couple, but they had never been able to bring it to the centre. This perhaps mirrored my thoughts about Troubetzskoy's layers of emotional experience. It was only after they had acknowledged to one another that they both thought the hospital had been negligent that they requested help from their General Practitioner. The loss of their first-born daughter, however, was not mentioned initially in our session, and I questioned whether they thought their distress would not be understood so many years later.

To summarise, the importance of careful management following stillbirth or neonatal death, Bourne and Lewis (1984) listed the following points that they thought might be helpful: parents seeing and holding the dead baby, registering a proper name and keeping photographs, a funeral and a decent marked grave. They concluded by saying:

> *"Careful management helps to preserve the dignity and poignancy of the experience and to initiate the difficult mourning process."*
>
> (p. 33)

These changes and recommendations gradually became part of hospital practice, although there was also recognition that many staff were unaware of hospital procedure concerning recommendations around formal ritual following miscarriage and stillbirth.

In the 1980s and 1990s several clinicians and researchers further mentioned the risk of mindlessness if procedures following a perinatal loss were too rigid. Bourne and Lewis (1983) drew attention to a state of mindlessness that could evolve if staff automatically expected women to see and hold their dead baby. Leon (1992) raised the issue that there is a risk of bereavement becoming 'institutionalised' with the use of checklists and protocols.

More recently, there has been acknowledgement that it is essential that the couple has an opportunity to discuss the death with their obstetrician and midwife. Wool and Caitlin (2019) stressed the need for bereavement support, guidance with the completion of mandatory forms and, if the gestational age permitted, sensitive discussion concerning post-mortem and whether the placenta should be sent to pathology. O'Leary and Henke (2017) acknowledged the need for standardised clinical tools to assess those women more likely to be at risk of an intense grief response. Elklit and Gudmundsdottir, in their 2006 Danish study, assessed guidelines for good psychosocial practice for parents who had lost an infant through perinatal or postnatal death. They found that photographs of the dead infant did not appear to raise distress levels, whereas other articles of remembrance did (Eklit & Gudmundsdottir, 2006). Hughes (2002) had also found that mothers who kept articles of remembrance had a worse outcome than those who did not. This may be associated with the concreteness of articles of remembrance and the importance attached to them, which may impact on the parent's ability to symbolise their experience as part of the mourning process.

## The emotional experience of the couple during pregnancy

Just as the emotional impact on the couple of the loss of their baby was not recognised until the mid-twentieth century, there was a similar perception that mothers or couples did not bond with their baby during pregnancy. The importance of bonding and emotional attachment to the infant during pregnancy developed with a growing awareness of psychoanalytic thinking and child development research.

When working with couples during pregnancy, I keep in mind the three psychological trimesters of pregnancy and the states of mind associated with each trimester. This frame of reference is also important when there is a perinatal loss. Caplan (1959) described the three psychological trimesters of pregnancy, with the first trimester beginning with conception and continuing until the woman becomes aware of her baby's movements at around 16 weeks.

The period of preconception might also be thought of as the first trimester. Couples often say that they conceived too quickly and that they have not adjusted to their pregnancy because of this. It is as though couples have a conscious or unconscious time frame in which they expect pregnancy to occur. When there are fertility issues, the period of preconception becomes even more significant for the couple.

The pregnant state is often experienced as an unknown landscape, and even the most planned pregnancy can stir feelings of ambivalence. The considerable hormonal changes in the woman's body during the first trimester can result in malaise, nausea and mood swings, and this may put a strain on the couple's relationship. By the end of the first trimester, there is usually an acceptance of the pregnancy, but if there are complex unresolved feelings, it would be helpful if the couple was given an opportunity to discuss these, rather than wait until later in pregnancy.

The second trimester lasts from the time the mother feels her baby's movements until she has a sense that the infant would be viable in the outside world. Couples should feel more settled in their pregnancy, with the paternal figure offering containment and support of the protective feelings the woman has towards their baby. The parental couple may play with ideas about the future identity of their new baby and be strongly aware of the impact of the emotional environment.

During the third trimester, there should be preparation for the birth and a sense of readiness for the baby to be born, as the couple prepares for the delivery by making space in their minds as well as in their home. Throughout pregnancy, the importance of the pregnant couple's relationship with their own parents should not be underestimated.

## The emotional experience of the couple following perinatal loss

More than 80% of miscarriages occur during the first twelve weeks of pregnancy, with the highest incidence occurring between six to eight weeks gestation. This is described as an early miscarriage. There is often a tendency for people to dismiss the emotional impact of this loss. However, the meaning of the pregnancy to the couple is significant and a factor in their emotional response. There is a high incidence of early miscarriage following IVF treatment, when couples are already worried that they might not conceive.

When there is a miscarriage before twelve weeks or early in the second trimester of pregnancy, women speak of feeling that their bodies have let them down. There is a tendency at this stage in pregnancy to think of the baby as being a part of the mother's body, although I have noticed in recent years that couples speak more of 'our pregnancy' as though indicating a shared positive experience. If there is a late miscarriage once the mother has felt the baby's movements, couples often speak of having thought all was going well and that they were beginning to make plans that included their child.

When there are complications in pregnancy, couples become aware of a risk of perinatal loss. The experience of a normal pregnancy is suddenly lost. If a baby survives a premature delivery with admission to a neonatal intensive care unit, parents struggle with continuing anxiety that their infant may not live, as well as having to negotiate emotions stirred by observing often intrusive medical procedures and the distress of other couples who are going through a similar experience.

After the loss of a baby, it is the woman who is supported medically and emotionally. It is usually the partner who informs family and friends, registers the death and initially discusses funeral arrangements. The emotional impact on the couple and on their relationship is rarely the focus. If the baby dies during delivery, perhaps during an emergency Caesarean section, both the couple and the obstetric team suffer shock and experience trauma. This may impact on the way that feelings of distress and grief are acknowledged or communicated. The loss is experienced as having taken place as part of a medical emergency. The complexity of processing feelings stirred by meeting death in birth means that this is a unique bereavement experience. At this stage, there is a preparedness to become parents and couples speak of the terrible feeling of loss that they do not have their baby to love and care for. Women speak of longing to hold a baby in their arms and the sadness they feel that there is no baby to feed when lactation commences.

## Mental health following late miscarriage and perinatal loss

It is not within the remit of this chapter to consider in detail the mental health difficulties of women and their partners following a perinatal loss. It is, however, generally accepted that pregnancy and the postpartum period is a time when women's mental health can be adversely affected, even when there has been no previous mental health history. Brockington's (2004) review of postpartum psychiatric disorders highlighted the fact that historically, there had been an oversimplification of the mental health problems that can arise during the postpartum period, such as maternity blues, puerperal psychosis and postnatal depression. He stressed the importance of psychiatric assessment during pregnancy and the postpartum period. More recently, Howard and Khalifeh (2020) noted that the early postpartum period is a time of high risk for new and recurrent episodes of mental illness. They questioned whether there was an under-detection or undertreatment of possible depressive and anxiety symptoms during pregnancy. They ascertained that women were more likely to receive treatment in the postpartum period than during pregnancy. This may be associated with a couple's unwillingness to acknowledge depression and/or anxiety during pregnancy, perhaps pressured by the Western world's tendency to idealise pregnancy and childbirth.

There has been less research into the area of antenatal or postpartum depression in men, but studies have shown that maternal and paternal postpartum depression are moderately correlated. In fact, the strongest predictor of male postpartum depression is postpartum and/or antenatal depression in his partner.

These are important factors when considering the emotional health of the couple when they have suffered a perinatal loss. They are in a postpartum state – something often not acknowledged and have suffered trauma. Research shows that women who experience a perinatal loss are at risk of a severe grief reaction and post-traumatic stress disorder, as well as depression and anxiety. They may become pregnant again sooner than women who have a live baby, which again may put them at emotional risk. Blackmore et al. (2011) found that depression and raised levels of anxiety experienced following a perinatal loss are likely to continue following the birth of a healthy baby. My work with couples has also shown that fathers are at risk of depression and post-traumatic stress disorder and may require a psychiatric assessment. Partners may try to avoid emotional pain by retreating into work or self-medicating with alcohol or recreational drugs. Unwanted feelings of emotional distress may be denied but then projected into their grieving partner, who is a vulnerable receptacle.

## The impact on the couple following perinatal loss

As we are aware, the couple's ability to communicate with one another is at the centre of a strong couple relationship. It is often difficult for couples to talk to one another as they struggle to come to terms with the traumatic experience of perinatal loss. On another level, couples speak of the experience bringing them closer together, only to find that this may be followed by their becoming distant as they mourn in different ways. The loss may impact on their sexual relationship, as their baby-making has resulted only in loss as opposed to new life. Self-blame or blame of the other may be present. If the pregnancy was less welcomed by one member of the couple, there may be feelings of guilt or perhaps even a sense of relief. Couples describe feelings of isolation from friends and family who have become parents. This sense of being alone can be exacerbated when one member of the couple feels ready to think about a further conception when the other does not. It is important for clinicians to hold in mind that anniversaries can stir heightened feelings of distress for the couple with significance attached to the time of conception, the date of the loss and the expected date of delivery. If a further conception takes place before the expected date of delivery some couples experience confusion between the two babies.

## Clinical vignette

Georgina and Daniel were referred for couple psychotherapy by their obstetrician four months after they had suffered an intrauterine death at six months gestation. When I went to the waiting room, both members of the couple were sitting on opposite sides of the waiting room. Georgina immediately began to weep when I introduced myself and kept apologising for doing so.

Once in the consulting room, Daniel told me what had happened. This had been their first pregnancy, and they were delighted. On the day the loss occurred, Georgina had telephoned Daniel to say she was worried that the baby did not seem to be moving as much. She was not sure what to do. Daniel was in the middle of a complicated transaction and on reflection thought he had not realised how worried his wife was. He just reassured her and said he was sure everything was fine. Georgina called an hour later, and this time, Daniel recognised how anxious she was. He said she should call her midwife. Georgina was told to come into the hospital immediately, and Daniel said he would meet her there.

A scan revealed that the baby had died. Georgina spoke of the way that everyone was so nice, but she was told that she would now have to wait until she went into labour. She became even more distressed as she spoke of their much longed-for baby being dead inside her and how she just could not get this thought out of her mind. They both thought the delivery had been managed sensitively, and they spoke of their daughter, whom they named Louisa, as looking perfect.

Daniel explained that the obstetrician thought there might have been a problem with the placenta, but she did not really know. I said that this was so often one of the most painful factors, not knowing why the baby had died. Then both members of the couple spoke of their feelings of guilt. Daniel said he should have dropped everything. It was ridiculous that he could possibly have thought a business transaction was more important than their baby. Georgina said that she should have gone to the hospital immediately. She could not blame Daniel. His job is so stressful. She should simply have gone. Why did she wait? I said that sometimes fear paralyses us, but did their obstetrician think it would have made any difference? They agreed that she had said it would not, but could she be sure? It was clear that they both felt that they had not done enough for their daughter. They had let her down. I gently voiced their feelings about this. I went on to stress that this is the way that couples so often feel when they lose a baby because they feel so helpless.

A referral for psychological help is often made close to a significant anniversary, and I had noted that they had recently passed the expected date of delivery. I asked about this, and they both agreed it had been a terrible day. Georgina said that they had visited the church where Louisa's ashes were interred, and she added that they were married in the same church.

This couple were struggling with their feelings of grief and distress following the loss of their baby. As is so often the case when there is a perinatal loss, there was uncertainty about why the death had occurred, which always leaves the couple searching for clarity. As our work continued, I became increasingly aware of the strength of their relationship. I had noted this during their first session when neither blamed the other for what had happened.

## The next pregnancy

There is a recommendation that following a stillbirth, it is helpful if a further pregnancy can be delayed for twelve months to enable mourning and to lessen the possibility of confused states of mind. Many couples find it difficult to wait this long, particularly when the biological clock is ticking. Others have spoken of feeling that they cannot grieve their lost infant until they have a baby that they can love and care for. In terms of unconscious states of mind, the need to rush into a further pregnancy may not only be an avoidance of mourning but also a wish to make reparation in the internal world. This may lead to an unconscious sense of a concrete repair in their inner world and subsequent feelings of disappointment with the self and perhaps the next baby.

From a psychiatric perspective, there may still be evidence of post-traumatic stress disorder as well as a diagnosis of depression and anxiety. There is often hypervigilance during the pregnancy, which may continue after a live birth. Couples often speak of the painful feelings they experience when friends and family assume they will now 'feel all right', as for them, pregnancy is a time of mixed emotions: joy that there is another conception but sadness as memories of the previous pregnancy and loss come to the fore. Couples often go to the grave and tell the dead baby about their new pregnancy. Although couples speak of the reassurance of regular scans, they also describe their sense of dread before each scan. I think it is helpful if it is noted in the woman's hand-held notes that there has been a previous pregnancy loss and if the couple are agreeable that mention is made that they are receiving therapy and that the therapist can be contacted.

## The next baby

Cain and Cain (1964) used the term a 'replacement child' to describe an infant who is consciously conceived by either one of the parents to replace another child who has died a short time before. Some parents may wish to replace their lost baby, and replacement dynamics are complex, but I have found that many do not. I prefer the term 'penumbra baby', Reid (2007a) as my work has shown that many babies conceived following a perinatal loss are born in the shadow of the dead baby. Couples often need help in thinking about their complex feelings and an acknowledgement that these feelings exist. I usually find that during initial sessions, the couple will focus on the dead baby before talking about their live infant. If a subsequent pregnancy has quickly followed the loss, couples may not have begun the mourning process. I see this work as a way of facilitating the mourning process, as well as enabling them to connect more strongly with their new baby.

The birth that follows a perinatal loss often takes place close to an anniversary, and this can lead to complex feelings of wishing to celebrate the birth but at the same time to mourn and acknowledge the loss. Mothers have told me that they have felt guilt that they have sometimes called the new baby by the dead baby's name and have difficult feelings about caring for the genitalia of their new baby if the gender is different.

Bion (1962) wrote of maternal containment whereby the mother receives and detoxifies painful projections from her baby before returning these detoxified feelings. Within this concept, Bion stressed the infant's need to project a fear of dying. When there has been a perinatal loss, I think it is often difficult for the mother to receive painful projections associated with death. They stir considerable anxiety for her, and as a result, the dialogue that forms the basis of maternal reverie and mother-infant interaction is inhibited.

## Clinical vignette

Michael called the clinic to make a couple appointment with his partner, Jane. He asked if I would telephone them so that he could explain what had happened. When I called, he said that they had recently had a baby and Jane was finding it difficult to manage. He felt very worried, and it was their General Practitioner who had suggested they make an appointment. I asked if there was anything in particular that was contributing to his partner's distress, and he told me that this time last year, Jane suffered a late miscarriage of a baby girl. Their new baby was a little boy, and he was now 7 weeks old.

I think it is important to work flexibly as a perinatal couple psychotherapist, as there is a risk of bereaved parents disappearing, as if mirroring the loss of their infant. I like to see the couple with their new baby.

The couple arrived early for their appointment, and I thought Michael looked relieved when I went to the waiting room. Jane looked as though she had been crying but made an effort to smile when I introduced myself. Michael was carrying the baby snugly wrapped in a sling. Once in the consulting room, he gently unwrapped the baby and looked towards Jane as if asking if she wanted to hold their son. She took him, I thought reluctantly, and said she hoped he would not start crying. I commented that it was fine if he cried. We would just have to think about what he might be saying.

I went on to say that Michael had spoken to me on the telephone and told me what had happened. Jane acknowledged that she knew this and started to cry. Michael told me that Jane had gone into premature labour when she was 20 weeks gestation. The hospital was wonderful. They could not have done more. Jane, however, said, 'It was all so sudden. I still feel shocked. The pregnancy had been going so well and then everything changed, and it was all over'. As she spoke, the baby started to cry. I said it sounded awful and this baby seemed to be letting us know that he was aware that something very sad had happened. Jane looked at the baby and said, 'It is not that I do not think he is lovely. It is just that I keep remembering our little girl and what we have missed'. I agreed that it was so hard and asked if they could tell me what they remembered.

We thought about the memories they had of their daughter, the way she looked and how they had held her and named her Sophia, Jane's grandmother's name. They had a small service for her at the hospital. Their parents and Jane's sister had come. Michael said that they had scattered Sophia's ashes in one of their favourite places not long before their son was born. It was so hard to do, but they thought they must.

Soon after telling me this, Jane used the baby's name for the first time, when she said that Oliver seemed so unsettled. I asked about this, and she said he did not settle for long. I queried if they both kept checking that he was all right, and Jane immediately agreed that she did. She said she was so worried that she would be able to keep this baby alive. She had been so confident about being a mother before. Now she felt unsure what she should do. I commented that many parents feel unsure when they have a tiny baby to look after, but this was even more difficult for them as a couple. Michael immediately said that he just gritted his teeth and got on with it, but really, he didn't feel at all confident about what he was doing either. Jane looked surprised and said she thought he did not have any worries, that caring for Oliver seemed so easy for him. I pointed out that each member of the couple parents in different ways. Perhaps Jane just felt that Michael was the expert and she couldn't begin to feel that way. They smiled, and I noticed that Jane looked at Oliver and held him more comfortably.

I regretted that this couple had not been referred either following the loss of their baby or during their next pregnancy, as this might have given them space to begin to process some of their distressing feelings. My description at the beginning of this chapter of complex emotional layers associated with the experience of perinatal loss is, I think, clearly demonstrated.

## The next generation

As can be seen from the last clinical vignette, parents may struggle with caring for their new infant when the birth follows a perinatal loss. I have always thought that it must be confusing for the baby to see feelings of grief in the mother's eyes, as well as those of love and joy (Reid, 2007b). Children who come for therapy have spoken of thinking there is another baby in the mind of the mother. Others worry that they do not know if their parents would have had another child if their sibling had not died. These children can struggle with their sense of identity and feel they do not have a rightful place. This may lead to the child being scapegoated, always perceived to be to blame and in the wrong place. Older children in the family may not accept the new baby following a perinatal loss, and there may be fear that this baby will not survive.

Children may feel haunted by the loss. One little boy whom I shall call Gregory spoke of the dead baby being angry with him for taking his mummy and daddy away and spoke of a robber breaking into their house. Louisa, another child, whose adoption followed a perinatal loss, complained that her house felt like a mausoleum. Why should this be? Sibling rivalry can be a problem in any family, but for the child who follows a loss, there is always the sense that they do not know who their rival is. They can only imagine. The lost infant may be idealised, there may be survival guilt or the next child can feel triumphant that they have survived. Perhaps alluding to this, parents can complain of hyperactivity as though their children are racing around so that they do not have to think.

These difficulties may continue through the life stages with adolescents feeling they are living in someone else's shoes whilst trying to find a sense of self. Survival guilt may present as risk-taking behaviour to prove they can survive, and there may be concentration or behavioural difficulties at school.

As a result, these young people may find it difficult to reach their potential as they continue to struggle with their sense of identity. Committing to a relationship may prove difficult, and there may be fear of pregnancy and a terror of childbirth – tokophobia. When a couple presents with difficulties associated with a fear of pregnancy and childbirth, the area of perinatal loss in the family of origin should be explored.

## Conclusion

At the beginning of this chapter, I considered the complexity of emotional layers associated with the experience of perinatal loss. In writing about this subject, I have tried to give a historic perspective so that there may be awareness of the intergenerational difficulties associated with this experience of trauma. I have described the couple's experience following a perinatal loss and the risk of psychiatric difficulties which may present at this time and continue following the birth of the next baby. Psychiatric problems may affect parenting behaviours and impact upon the new infant's emotional development. Finally, I have described the problems encountered by parents as they care for their new infant and the difficulties that the next generation may experience.

## References

Bion, W.R. (1962) Learning from Experience. London: Heinemann (Reprinted London: Karnac Books, 1984).

Blackmore, E.R., Cote-Arsenault, D., Tang, W., Glover, V., Evans, J., Golding, J., & O'Conner, T.G. (2011) Previous prenatal loss as a predictor of perinatal depression and anxiety. The British Journal of Psychiatry, 198(5): 373–378.

Bourne, S. (1968) Support after perinatal death: A study of support and counselling after perinatal bereavement. Journal of Royal College of General Practitioners, 16: 103–112.

Bourne, S., & Lewis, E. (1983) Support after perinatal death: A study of support and counselling after perinatal bereavement. British Medical Journal, 286: 144–145.

Bourne, S., & Lewis, E. (1984) Pregnancy after stillbirth or neonatal death. The Lancet, 3: 31–33.

Brockington, I. (2004) Postpartum psychiatric disorders. Lancet, 363: 303–310.

Cain, A., & Cain, B. (1964) On replacing a child. Journal of the American Academy of Child Psychiatry, 3: 443–456.

Caplan, G. (1959) Concepts of Mental Health and Consultation. Washington, DC: US Children's Bureau.

Caplan, G. (1964) Principles of Preventive Psychiatry. London: Tavistock Publications.

Davidson, G.W. (1984) Stillbirth, neonatal death and sudden death syndrome. In H. Wass & A. Charles (Eds.), Childhood and Death. USA: Taylor & Frances: 243–257.

Eklit, A., & Gudmundsdottir, D.B. (2006) Assessment of guidelines for good psychosocial practice for parents who have lost an infant through perinatal or postnatal death. Nordic Psychology, 58(4): 315–330.

Forest, G.C., Standish, E., & Baum, J.D. (1982) Support after perinatal death: A study of support and counselling after perinatal bereavement. British Medical Journal, 285: 1475–1479.

Giles, P.F.H. (1970) Reaction of women to perinatal death. Australian and New Zealand Journal of Obstetrics & Gynaecology, 10: 207–210.

Howard, L.M., & Khalifeh, H. (2020) Perinatal mental health: A review of progress and challenges. World Psychiatry, 19(3): 313–327.

Hughes, P., Turton, P., Hopper, E., et al. (2002) Assessment of guidelines for good practice in psychosocial care of mothers after stillbirth: A cohort study. Lancet, 360: 114–118.

Kirkley Best, E., & Van Devere, C. (1986) The hidden family grief: An overview of grief in the family following perinatal death. International Journal of Family Psychiatry, 7(4): 419–437.

Leon, I.G. (1992) Perinatal loss. A critique of current hospital practices. Clinical Pediatrics, 31: 366–374.

O'Leary, J.M., & Henke, L. (2017) Therapeutic educational support for families pregnant after loss (PAL) A continued bond/attachment perspective. Psychotherapy, 54(4): 386–393.

Reid, M. (1992) Joshua life after death. The replacement child. Journal of Child Psychotherapy, 18(2): 109–138.

Reid, M. (2007a) The loss of a baby and the birth of the next infant. The mother's experience. Journal of Child Psychotherapy, 33(2): 181–201.

Reid, M. (2007b) Grief in the mother's eyes: A search for identity. In C. Bainbridge, S. Radstone, M. Rustin & C. Yates (Eds.), Culture and the unconscious. Basingstoke: Palgrave MacMillan.

Wool, C., & Caitlin, A. (2019) Perinatal bereavement and palliative care offered throughout the health care system. Annals of Palliative Medicine, 8(Suppl): S22–S29. https://doi.org/10.21037/apm.2018.11.03

# Chapter 10

# Great expectations

## Blame, shame, and mourning in work with adoptive couples

*Simon Cregeen*

## Introduction

A common feature in work with adoptive parents is the presence of shame and guilt, leading to blame being projected and located in the other. The other may be the parental partner or one or more of the couple's adopted children. Persecutory guilt is often experienced by adoptive couples, who feel internally and externally criticised for not making a better job of parenting in the way which they feel is required to repair the damage their children suffered in their birth family or in subsequent care settings. Notably, adoptive parents can feel that it is not permissible to feel regret and hatred towards their adopted children, whilst in their private thoughts feeling just like this.

Shame is experienced in relation to the adoptive parents' feeling that they are failing to match their internal, idealised standards for being parents, including being 'much better ones' than the birth parents. The presence of an idealised ego ideal which the adoptive parents can so readily feel is impossible to attain. Any evident family difficulties can result in excoriating feelings of shame – an experience of a fundamental deficit, exposed and judged, fit only for hiding from.

The pressure to discharge these feelings can lead to couple conflict and fragmented parental functioning. At other times, the adopted children may be held responsible for the trouble. They can be seen as the carriers of a legacy of failed parental couplings, which through enactment in the new family contribute to the adoptive parents suffering the distressing collapse of their shared ego ideal. Child psychotherapy literature shows that many adopted children are significantly troubled by early deprivation, trauma, loss, and associated developmental difficulties, and these experiences inevitably inform their relationships to the adoptive parents (e.g., Boston & Szur, 1983; Briggs, 2012; Fagan, 2011; Hindle & Shulman, 2008; Roy, 2020; Rustin, 2018).

In considering what emotional work may be needed to help adoptive couples struggling with such issues, difficulty with mourning is a central concern. In the assessment process that prospective adoptive parents undergo, assessing social workers are sensitively alert to the painful losses which the majority of couples have experienced in their efforts to conceive a child. Consideration is given to whether

DOI: 10.4324/9781003387947-14

the couple have grieved their losses: the determined efforts to conceive, the miscarried babies, and the possibility of becoming birth parents with all its privileges and joys. In many cases, the powerful drive to become parents, the intensely painful nature of such losses, and the adoption agency's urgent imperative to assess couples and place children can combine to privilege a shared narrative of sufficient grieving having taken place. The cumulative traumatic loss for couples in this position cannot be underestimated nor the courage required and difficulties encountered in mourning the loss of an imagined 'ordinary' family experience.

My work with adoptive families has encompassed many cases where there has been a struggle to mourn, which restricts the parents' capacity to fully take in their adoptive child. This can lead to a stuck dynamic of mutual blaming, melancholic in character. The distressing reality of what has been lost and not been possible is aroused once the adoptive family is finally created and a different sort of family reality is being grappled with. The parental desire to 'overcome' loss can impede the creation of mental space for the adoptive child, of a satisfying coupling between the partners, and of a fulfilling, albeit previously unimagined way, of being parents.

In contrast to the family celebration of a couple's sexual procreativity when a baby is born, for couples adopting due to infertility, the fact of their sexual coupling not leading to them becoming birth parents becomes known by others. This can bring support and expressions of sorrow, but less helpfully, it can attract pity or manic denial. For the couple, this painful reality can come to represent a fundamental failure of their coupling, specifically their most private intercourse.

## Psychotherapy with adoptive couples

Much of the therapeutic attention by health and social care post-adoption agencies is focused on either the troubled child or on providing advice, support, and psychological guidance on the parenting of the child. There is, however, a strong evidence base for the global effectiveness of couple psychotherapy as an intervention (Hewison et al., 2016) and a developing evidence base for the efficacy of couple-focused therapy for adoptive parents (Polek & McCann, 2020). The absence, therefore, of funded provision (at least in the UK) specifically concerned with the adoptive couple relationship is a significant gap.

In their paper exploring melancholic reaction to loss in adoptive families, Glausius and Humphries (2018) reference the Selwyn report (2015):

> "indicated that the challenging behaviour and needs of the adopted child places such a strain on the parental couple that it can leave many feeling powerless, and as if they need to make a stark choice between saving their relationship or keeping their adopted child in the home."

> (Glausius & Humphries, 2018, p. 4)

These authors go on to argue that 'working therapeutically with adoptive couples can help prevent adoption breakdown that is often linked with unmetabolized losses and earlier traumas suffered by both the parental couples and their children' (Glausius & Humphries, 2018, p. 3), and they suggest that couple psychotherapy is 'uniquely placed to address this particular challenge' (p. 4).

Ludlam (2008) discusses the couple's un-mourned loss and sense of failure, and how there can be 'a gulf between the idealised family which has developed in the minds of the parents and of their adoptive child, and the actual family which they discover in real life' (p. 177).

## The ego ideal

The ego ideal, a psychoanalytic concept first described by Freud (1923), can be understood as an unconscious aspiration for oneself and may include personal qualities which are admired in others and which one hopes could also be one's own. Sedlak (2019) describes the links between the ego ideal and a critical internal figure, the superego.

'The ego ideal is how one would wish to be; when one fails to achieve such ambitions one is judged by a different but related mental structure: the superego' (Sedlak, 2019, p. 73). Money-Kyrle (1960, p. 357) proposes that 'while to please the superego arouses guilt, failure to live up to an ego-ideal arouses only shame'.

We could say that shame arises when the gap between who we narcissistically imagine ourselves to be (an idealised ego ideal) and the actual reality of who we are becomes known to ourselves and to others. Under the critical eye of a persecuting superego, this gap can be felt as a failure at root, a fundamental lack, and a source of shame, a reality to be hidden from (Cregeen, 2009). As Horne succinctly puts it, 'when we fall short of our ego-ideal, shame stalks in' (2019, p. 49).

Sedlak proposes that in contrast to an idealised, impossible-to-reach ideal, we can also have what he calls a 'reparative ego ideal' (2019, p. 70). This is one which is arrived at through some mourning of the relinquished narcissistic state, with omnipotence tempered by recognition of internal and external realties and a capacity to bear the pain, conflicts, and anxieties associated with this. Importantly, such a mental state enables gratitude and appreciation of what is, a movement forward, rather than grievance and regret and a backward-looking preoccupation with what isn't possible.

In the context of couple psychoanalytic psychotherapy, Grier (2006) has described how we can unconsciously hold 'an absolute ideal of the kind of relationship for which we wish, and to which we consider ourselves entitled' (p. 37). He suggests that when a real relationship fails to meet this ideal, 'we tend to feel betrayed' (p. 37), and blame may be directed towards the partner.

I suggest that for periods of time, and in relation to important life matters, couples create a joint ego ideal, which could be considered a form of shared unconscious phantasy (Hewison, 2014). For some adoptive couples, when ambitions for a procreative coupling and imagined family life are thwarted by painful realities and losses, their shared ideal may become deeply persecutory. A couple's difficulty in managing the associated pain, anxieties, and conflicts, and their inability to let go of this ideal and mourn the loss of it, can inhibit the couple's development of new shared aspirations, most notably those with a reparative quality. Further to this, the partners in the couple may blame one another for the loss and the pain or together blame the adopted child for not being or becoming the imagined child in the original ideal family. Sometimes a cycle of mutual blaming ensues between all family members.

One couple, Sara and Richard, described feeling 'overwhelmed and persecuted' by their children and the task of parenting. They described adoption parenting courses they'd been on – 'where we don't match up as adoptive parents . . . we don't match up with what we see other families managing'. They felt tyrannised by the demands of their children, by what they saw as the expectations of the adoption agency, and by not living up to their shared ideal. Their sense of being overseen, or seen to fail, was clear. They ceaselessly tried 'to analyse what is happening with the kids, understand what all their behaviour means'. Inevitably, they felt they had failed in this, too, and agreed they were not the parents they'd imagined, as if there was something fundamentally lacking in them. This led them to avoid doing things with others as a family.

## Loss in adoptive couples

In considering the experience of couples who seek to conceive children but fail to do so, I wonder what happens to their shared ideal of themselves as birth parents? What sort of encounters with emotional reality are necessary to mourn the loss of what has been so desired, to enable the development of new, more realistic aspirations for themselves as adoptive parents? What can help potential adopters with this deeply painful emotional work? The ordinary narcissism and omnipotence which underlies most couples' background assumption of the possibility of parenthood will, for these particular couples, come under much pressure. In the adoptive context, the couple's capacity to grapple with the losses, mourn what is not possible, and develop a new and more reparative shared family ideal are essential to equip them for the previously unimagined reality of themselves as adoptive parents. When possible, such a couple development represents a mentally fertile intercourse.

It is unlikely that the mourning associated with infertility is ever complete. As with the mourning of other forms of loss, it is likely to be lifelong, coming and going in intensity and importance as life events and life stages happen. In my experience, insufficient mourning prior to adopting children can lead to extremely difficult adoptive family dynamics. The acute, and usually more temporary, emotional states of grief may be conflated and confused with the interior working through associated with mourning, an extended and sober experience (Freud, 1917).

One way in which failure to mourn reveals itself is when overcoming of loss is privileged by the couple over the mourning of loss. This can be taken as a sign of resilience by the couple and often, too, by adoption agencies. A narrative of 'overcoming' may be idealised as a denial of the depth of mourning needed. In a similar way, Glausius and Humphries note:

> "*exploring the couples' preceding losses is widely understood by professionals to be an indispensable part of the assessment process for adoption. Nevertheless, it is our experience that many parents feel that they have not been able to fully understand or process what has happened to them.*"
>
> (Glausius & Humphries, 2018, p. 6)

### Shame and blame

In considering what impedes mourning in this context, shame is likely to be a factor. Weiss (2020) describes shame as 'a dismal and mortifying affective state', where 'the shamed one is faced by an observer who *watches* them critically and *looks down* on them' (p. 30, italics in original). For some adoptive couples, shame may be particularly acute, as they may critically judge themselves as being as compromised a couple as the birth parents and as equally unable to provide what the children need. The associated unconscious defensive manoeuvres may include blaming one another, insisting that the fault is in the other partner. In the clinical situation, the therapist can also be experienced as a disappointing parent and partner to the couple and may be experienced as casting judgement – perhaps even contempt – for what the couple feels to be their failures.

In some adoptive couples who are under considerable strain, a state of excessive and fixed mutual blaming may develop. Such a state has been described by Morgan (1995) as 'projective gridlock', where the couple 'create between them a relationship in which they feel locked together in a defensive collusion within which there is only very limited growth' (p. 33). Morgan links this to the experience of there being an insufficient capacity within the couple for emotional containment (Morgan, 1995, p. 47).

Although Morgan is describing couples who struggle to be separate from one another, with this being part of their 'couple fit', I think a state of projective gridlock may also be created within an adoptive couple for whom this wasn't necessarily originally present. It may be formed as a consequence of the adoptive family's experience, most particularly the parents' feeling of failure, a compromised capacity for containment, and difficulties in maintaining their couple relationship. An important factor would be the children's projections into the parents which may be intrusive and attacking. As infantile experiences of neglect and deprivation are so common within adopted children, a sense of something essential which is lacking is an inevitable characteristic of that which is projected. Central to this dynamic is the rigidity of relating, insufficient containment, and the denial of separateness. In such situations, a family projective gridlock may develop.

Following traumatic birth family experiences, many adopted children are susceptible to beliefs that they suffer from deficits at the core of their being, and it is these intrinsic fault lines which are the cause of their birth parents' inability to care for them. We can imagine that while living with their birth family, such beliefs are strengthened by unconscious enactments by birth parents, with projections into the child of their own feelings of failure and helplessness. In some birth families, a more knowing cruelty and humiliation of the infant is evident, with the adults gaining perverse pleasure at the child's distress and sense of inadequacy and wrongness. Such experiences are carried forward into the adoptive family, and negative projective cycles become entrenched. This can result in a breakdown of the parental couple and the child's capacities to see the other as having any good intentions or impulses to relate lovingly. The following clinical material serves to illustrate this sort of family dynamic.

## Julia and Sean

Julia and Sean adopted Milly following several miscarriages and unsuccessful IVF interventions. Milly had suffered greatly in her birth family, and she came to Julia and Sean as a traumatised young girl, who often rejected their efforts to care for her and yet intrusively sought proximity. She would hurt herself and others, with words and actions.

Julia and Sean were senior professionals in their fields of work, and neither had close family relationships due to unresolved familial traumas and conflict. Services were intensively involved, and the post-adoption support network was concerned at how split the parents were in their attitudes and approaches to Milly, now aged 9, and the many occasions when an angry and depressed mood would take over the family.

When I met with Julia and Sean, it was quickly clear that neither of them was able to be emotionally available to the other, there was resentment at what each felt the other demanded or required of them, and they had retreated from any impulse towards intimacy. There was significant hostility and fixed, well-established battle lines regarding their views as to what Milly needed from them. Julia was the primary carer, and Sean's career was increasingly demanding. Emotionally, Sean lived much of his life outside of the family, except for occasional harsh judgements on Julia and Milly. Julia lived most of her emotional life within the family, or more accurately, within the relationship with Milly, and felt bitter at Sean's lack of care towards her.

Milly persistently followed Julia around and spoke and touched her mother in ways which were intrusive, provocative, or humiliating. Julia was in touch with, and often unhelpfully identified with, Milly's experiences of loss and trauma. This included Julia's own experience of protecting her depressed mother from a frightening father. This led Julia to try and understand Milly's aggression as an inevitable consequence of her early experiences; she believed that tolerating Milly's intrusion and aggression was a necessary burden to enable Milly to feel accepted.

In contrast, Sean's teenage experiences of being bullied by his siblings over a long period, a situation which apparently his parents had failed to manage, led to his conviction that Milly's aggression and intrusions were unacceptable, and she needed to learn this through him becoming an impermeable father, who withheld care until the aggression ceased.

My understanding was that Sean experienced Julia and Milly as if they were siblings locked together and fighting. He seemed to feel terrified of Milly's aggression and consequently of identifying with Julia as a powerless victim. Sean managed this by becoming a parental figure who abdicated responsibility, turned away, and let them get on with it. Julia carried a burden of guilt about what she saw as her childhood failure to save her mother from her father's violence. She was also afraid of Milly's aggression but submitted to the pull of a frightened and rather masochistic position, as if this was inevitably a mother's fate.

Sean seemed to have abandoned Julia to being the repository for Milly's anxieties, hatred, and terror, and Julia had unconsciously agreed to this, protecting Sean in the process. Julia was required to experience all the vulnerability and claustrophobic neediness, and Sean was to carry all the need for separateness and boundaries. However, each position was held in extremis, and the lack of linking between Julia and Sean led to Milly invading one parent and being repelled by the other.

What Julia and Sean shared was a view that Milly's aggression was within her control, that she felt triumphant at tyrannising her parents, that her personality as the aggressive child of violent birth parents was a fixed entity, and that she had little capacity for anxiety, guilt, or vulnerability. The exception to this was when she tried to hurt herself and made evident something of her desperate state, assailed by terrifying states of mind and persecutory figures, internally and externally. In these moments, they were in contact with her vulnerability and need of them, but this raised many fears for them about the perils of dependency.

I think the family were living in a chronic state of distress, with pervasive feelings of inadequacy and each family member blaming the others for this catastrophe. Their common survival strategy was to almost never spend time together, often remaining in separate rooms, losing themselves in online games, music, and television.

Julia and Sean idealised their life as a couple prior to Milly's arrival, who in their most difficult moments was blamed for ruining the couple's life together. As their therapist, I found it difficult at times not to leap (at least in my mind) to Milly's defence, blaming them for their parental inadequacies and their retreat from their vulnerable daughter. Such splitting in my mind could be framed as 'the fault's not in her, it's in you two'.

There is no doubt that Milly was enacting damaging birth family experiences in an effort to evacuate and communicate these to her adoptive parents. What alerted me to Julia and Sean's feeling of shame was finding myself feeling moralistic towards them, finding fault in how they were thinking, and becoming judgemental about their difficulty in holding together as a couple. There was an impulse in me to want to blame and shame them into behaving better, as if I was a critical and rather contemptuous parental figure, who was sure I'd be doing better in their circumstances. In thinking like this, I felt ashamed of myself and of my failure to draw upon my own internal parental couple to help me achieve a balanced way of reviewing the situation. Instead, my internal figures became judgemental in my mind, ashamed of me and would want to disown me.

I talked to Julia and Sean about how they, and Milly, were all overwhelmed by needs and emotions and how perhaps they believed there was no choice except to pursue individual survival, as there were no helpful figures with containing capacities anywhere – internally, between them, or others, including myself.

This line of interpretation, along with the slow growth of trust in my interest and concern for them all, gradually made a difference, and we began to talk about how Milly had started to tell them that she was 'invisible', not existing. They were alarmed at this but able to become interested in what she might mean by it. Their curiosity allowed us to consider how Milly might have doubted the availability and security of her parent's minds, feeling impelled to force her way in and colonise them. The difficulty is that in making such an aggressive entry, the parents she was so desperately in need of were then perceived by her as damaged or threatening.

With the less persecuted atmosphere of the sessions, I was able to describe what I thought might be happening for Milly and how her damaging early experiences were resonating so painfully with their own. Through this untangling of the projective family dynamic, some separation of their individual experiences and distress could be made. This process seemed to enable Milly to become more visible to Sean and Julia and for them to see one another more clearly.

In thinking about their own childhood and teenage experiences, Sean and Julia were able to recognise how they each had felt unseen and unprotected by their parents in the context of familial violence. They had hoped that by becoming parents to a birth child, they would have a chance to repair the conflicted and insecure child-parent relationships which they carried insides themselves. Not being able to have a birth child had been a terrible blow, which they had felt unable to talk about together. Becoming adoptive parents to Milly didn't allow for repair; instead, it confronted them with repetitions of the un-mourned traumas of their own childhoods and Milly's. This was simply unbearable.

With the opening up of some mental space, Julia and Sean were able to speak more freely about their experience of one another without feeling attacked or attacking. Julia described how Sean's way of talking 'makes me feel stupid, like a child', to which Sean responded that he felt this too. It wasn't 'I think you've got the wrong idea or approach' but more 'you are the wrong thing, the wrong person'. When this is in the ascendancy, there is not a coupling in which curiosity about Milly, parenting together, or couple intimacy can develop.

## Mourning

In this final section, I want to pay attention to mourning and provide some clinical material to describe something of the losses being borne by one adoptive couple and how they began the long process of mourning. This included, what I understood as, them beginning to relinquish their grip on a shared ego ideal, associated with their original hopes to be birth parents.

As Freud evocatively described it, in experiencing loss, there is the following:

*"an identification of the ego with the abandoned object. Thus, the shadow of the object fell upon the ego."*

(Freud, 1917, p. 249)

What Freud is referring to is how the lost figure or ideal can't be let go of so that the individual can get on with life as it is now for them. Rather, the individual becomes bound up with that which has been lost, and this casts a depressive shadow within the individual's psyche. This may lead to feelings of hopelessness, unexpressed anger, and an absence of liveliness in their continuing relationships.

I'm suggesting that for those couples who must make the difficult transition from imagining themselves as birth parents to imagining themselves as (and becoming) adoptive parents, there is the need to mourn the specific aspiration that their sexual coupling will produce children.[1] When this is not possible, a state of depressive identification with that which is lost may take hold. If this happens for adoptive couples, their children meet parents who are preoccupied with what isn't there, rather than parents emotionally available to the child who lives and who needs them. For children carrying their own losses and often traumatic experiences, too, this is clearly problematic. For adoptive parents in a melancholic state, it is not only that they are suffused with sadness and anger, but their incapacity to make connection with the liveliness and developmental imperatives of their child leads to a restriction of the capacity for pleasure and growth associated with parenthood which, in turn, limits family life for all.

Barrows (2008), writing about a different clinical context, eloquently describes how, in some cases, a parent's difficulty in mourning lost figures can lead to their child experiencing the parent 'as *pre*-occupied by a dead internal object' (p. 262, italics in original). In an adoptive family, there are the parent's individual losses, the adoptive couple's un-mourned losses, the un-mourned losses of their child, and finally, the un-mourned aspects of the child's internal objects associated with their birth parents – a dense constellation of multiple losses to bear and to work through. The main responsibility for this daunting task falls upon the adoptive couple. The clinical vignette which follows illustrates something of these ideas and shows just how difficult the task of mourning can be.

### Marcia and Tyrone

Marcia and Tyrone had a well-established relationship which overall they found satisfying. Both worked in professional jobs that offered them much fulfilment. Efforts to conceive led to multiple miscarriages and failed IVF attempts. Their grief was recognised but unattended to, as neither were good communicators of their feelings. They were determined to assuage their losses by becoming adoptive parents.

Unknown to everyone involved at the point of adoption, Ruby, a little girl in early toddlerhood, had developmental difficulties which manifested in her learning, social relationships, and in extremely challenging behaviour. This was particularly marked at home with Marcia and Tyrone. When I met the couple, Ruby was 10 years old, and a network of services were involved with the family.

From our first meeting, it was clear that Marcia and Tyrone were exhausted from what they experienced as Ruby's insatiable demands, needs, and intrusive projective states. The continuing impact of their losses felt relentless. These included their early years together when they might have conceived but didn't try, miscarried babies, IVF possibilities, a family life as hoped for and expected, their imagined happy adopted child, family events and outings with friends and their children, their adult couple relationship, feeling themselves to be good and competent and in control of their lives, and their emotional and mental steadiness.

Marcia felt 'defective as a woman'. They were both acutely aware of how public their struggles were, both prior to becoming adopters as well as since. They knew that mourning was needed but were overwhelmed by the size and complexity of what this would entail. Marcia spoke:

> *"grief can suddenly come over me . . . even though this has been going on for years. . . . I was driving the other day and suddenly I was crying and there was nothing particular going on around me and I wasn't even thinking about babies or Ruby and how shit my life is."*

Tyrone was less frequently taken by sadness but would occasionally lose his temper in outbursts of frustration and hurt. He seemed lost in a vacuum between what he thought a father was and the father he seemed to be, as if, years after adopting Ruby, he was still struggling to find a satisfying paternal identity.

Ruby's way of managing the complexity of a parental couple was to split them, and she stuck herself remorselessly and tyrannically to Marcia and ignored, denigrated, or physically attacked Tyrone. There was room only for two, and her dad was to carry all the experience of an unwanted outcast. Unsurprisingly, emotional and physical intimacy between Marcia and Tyrone had ceased, supplanted by a grim sense of an unwanted and unfulfilling task, where they depended upon one another but without much sense of a joint endeavour. Ruby's splitting connected with pre-existing vulnerabilities for the couple, in that as a child, Tyrone experienced a rather uninterested, distant parental couple, and Marcia had a rather intrusive, over-involved mother.

As an adult couple, I think Marcia found Tyrone's emotional distance a relief and a frustration, while Tyrone found Marcia's emotionality as bringing life to the relationship, which was sometimes over-intense. Ruby's splitting pushed her parent's positions vis-à-vis the other into extreme territory, and they lost emotional contact with one another.

In the therapy relationship, I sometimes found myself preoccupied by Marcia, who was able to forcefully command my whole attention, and Tyrone would drift into the background. Their family histories and couple transference dynamic led to them often feeling that they couldn't turn to one another for support and containment, or it didn't occur to them to try.

Although there were at times conflicting views about how to manage Ruby and family life, it was the emotional gap between Marcia and Tyrone which was most notable. In the consulting room, I sometimes felt this as if it were a physical reality, a palpable absence. This led to a loneliness in each of them, feeling that the experience was solely theirs and that the other wasn't able to share the pain or be in contact with what they were going through. As Marcia put it, *'I know Tyrone is really struggling, I know it, but I can't get any feel of it. . . . anyway I have no space, no space inside me for it. . . . sorry'*.

As we worked together, one of the factors inhibiting mourning was that privately, each of them felt bad about their hatred towards the difficulties Ruby brought with her, resentment at what parenting had taken from them as a couple, and disappointment in how unsatisfying family life had turned out to be. Associated with this was their shame at having such feelings towards their vulnerable daughter. There was also guilt at feeling, at times, some regret at having adopted Ruby and imagining other children they could have adopted in Ruby's place. When these phantasies were able to be shared, Tyrone and Marcia were relieved and able to reintegrate some of their projections into Ruby. They could see how most of the time, she was being driven by forces within her which she was as powerless over as her parents felt. This also allowed them to realise that they shared these feelings of grievance and guilt and that they were more bearable when held between them, finding me to be a figure who didn't condemn or criticise them for how they felt was containing.

Marcia and Tyrone had an enduring and acutely painful sense of having failed themselves, their parents, and their child. Consequently, they felt observed, judged, and at times, abandoned by friends, family members, and services. Added to this list, they also felt abandoned by internal parental figures, whose approval and admiration they sought, individually and as a couple, and which they sorely needed to sustain their internal buoyancy. Each felt that, in childhood, they'd been let down by their own parents, and they now felt inadequately equipped to become good parents in their own right. They expressed resentment about this. Unconsciously, perhaps Marcia and Tyrone experienced their internal parental objects as interfering with their procreative intercourse, preventing them from having a satisfying experience as a parental couple.

What was particularly painful for Tyrone and Marcia to bear was the helplessness they felt when experiencing their grief. At times, this brought sorrow beyond words. As an adult couple, they had developed an impressive capacity to manage life and find solutions to problems. However, their conception and adoption related grief couldn't be fixed nor would it go away. They felt the compulsion to repair this but didn't know how to go about it.

In a recent article, Steiner (2021, p. 8) notes that people 'commonly make great efforts to repair their objects but fail because the attempts at repair are concrete'. Marcia and Tyrone's insistent advocacy might have represented, amongst other things, a desperate plea for reality to be different and for containment of the family's overwhelming emotional states. This might also have been linked with a refusal or inability to recognise the reality of what could and could not be repaired in their own history as a couple and in Ruby's early life and developmental difficulties.

As their therapist, I was also required to bear some measure of their despair and helplessness. I could feel the pressure within me to either try to make concrete repair by giving advice or to give up and sink into despondency. What they needed from me was to be as emotionally receptive as possible and not flinch from painful reality.

## Concluding thoughts

The main premise of my discussion is that for adoptive parents who have been unable to conceive and carry their own babies, the imperative to mourn this loss and their somewhat idealised image of themselves as ordinary parents can be impeded not only by the pain of such losses and the difficulty of mourning but also the shame of a self-perceived intrinsic deficit, seen and known by others. The couple may experience themselves as not only burdened by an incapacity to conceive but as having a fault in their capacity for emotional intercourse, for creative relating. When an adoptive couple find themselves in such a position, I suggest this makes it more difficult for them to be fully emotionally available to all that their adoptive children may need to communicate, project, and seek respite from, most particularly the emotional states arising from deprivation, trauma, and loss, which the children have suffered and which now seek a psychic home (Cregeen, 2017).

I suggest that for adoptive parents, an important aspect of mourning involves the relinquishment of an ideal which embodies their aspirations to be birth parents and their ordinally imagined version of family life. If adoptive parents can mourn the idealised image of themselves as a biologically fertile couple, something more creative may be possible. I think that the development of a shared ego ideal that is aspirational *and* realistic is necessary. When this is possible, the closer contact with emotional reality enables growth in the adoptive couple relationship, increased mental space as parents for their children, and a more satisfying family life.

## Note

1 In the case of same-sex couples, although their sexual coupling *per se* doesn't carry the possibility of conceiving a baby, I would argue that their sexual intimacy and relationship can be the ground upon which their shared aspiration grows.

## References

Barrows, K. (2008). Keeping the ghosts at bay: An autistic retreat and its relationship to parental losses. In K. Barrows (Ed.), *Autism in childhood and autistic features in adults.* London: Karnac.

Boston, M., & Szur, R. (1983). *Psychotherapy with severely deprived children.* London: Routledge and Kegan Paul.

Briggs, A. (Ed) (2012). *Waiting to be found: Papers on children in care.* London: Karnac.

Cregeen, S. (2009). Exposed: Phallic protections, shame and damaged objects. *Journal of Child Psychotherapy*, 35(1), 32–48.

Cregeen, S. (2017). A place within the heart: Finding a home with parental objects. *Journal of Child Psychotherapy*, 43(2), 159–174.

Fagan, M. (2011). Relational trauma and its impact on late-adopted children. *Journal of Child Psychotherapy*, 37(2), 129–146.

Freud, S. (1917). Mourning and melancholia. *Standard Edition*, 14, 237–258.

Freud, S. (1923). The ego and the id. *Standard Edition*, 19, 3–66.

Glausius, K., & Humphries, J. (2018). The road between Corinth and Thebes: Adoption and loss. *International Review of Couple and Family Psychoanalysis*, 18(1), 1–18.

Grier, F. (2006). Ideals, betrayal, guilt and forgiveness in couple psychotherapy. *British Journal of Psychotherapy*, 23(1), 37–48.

Hewison, D. (2014). Shared unconscious phantasy in couples. In D. Scharff & J. Scharff (Eds.), *Psychoanalytic couple therapy*. London: Karnac.

Hewison, D., Casey, P., & Mwamba, N. (2016). The effectiveness of couple therapy: Clinical outcomes in a naturalistic United Kingdom setting. *Psychotherapy Theory Research Practice Training*, American Psychological Association, 53(4), 377–387.

Hindle, D., & Shulman, G. (2008). *The emotional experience of adoption; A psychoanalytic approach*. London: Routledge.

Horne, A. (2019). Reflections on the ego ideal in childhood. In C. Harding (Ed.), *Dissecting the Superego: Moralities under the microscope*. London: Routledge.

Ludlam, M. (2008). The longing to become a family: Support for the parental couple. In D. Hindle & G. Shulman (Eds.), *The emotional experience of adoption: A psychoanalytic perspective*, 177–184. London: Routledge.

Money-Kyrle, R. (1960). On prejudice: A psychoanalytic approach. In *The collected works of roger Money-Kyrle*. Perthshire: Clunie Press.

Morgan, M. (1995). The projective gridlock: A form of projective identification in couple relationships. In S. Ruszczynski & J. Fisher (Eds.), *Intrusiveness and intimacy in the couple*. London: Karnac.

Polek, E., & McCann, D. (2020). The feasibility and effectiveness of a time-limited couple-focussed therapy for adoptive parents: Preliminary evidence from the *Adopting Together* project. *Adoption & Fostering*, 44(1), 75–91.

Roy, A. (2020). *A for adoption: An exploration of the adoption experience for families and professionals*. London: Routledge.

Rustin, M. (2018). Psychoanalytic work with an adopted child with a history of early abuse and neglect. In P. Garvey & K. Long (Eds.), *The Klein tradition: Lines of development – evolution of theory and practice over the decades*. London: Routledge.

Sedlak, V. (2019). *The Psychoanalyst's superegos, ego ideals, and blind spots: The emotional development of the clinician*. London: Routledge.

Selwyn, J., Meakings, S., & Wijedasa, D. (2015). *Beyond the adoption order: Challenges, interventions, and adoption disruption*. London: BAAF.

Steiner, J. (2021). *The psychoanalytic attitude: Implications for technique*. New York: The Melanie Klein Trust conference 2021. Melanie Klein Newsletter.

Weiss, H. (2020). *Trauma, guilt and reparation*. London: Routledge.

# Chapter 11

# Holding the line

## An exploration of the difficulties in maintaining a boundary around the couple for parents raising a child with a disability

*Kate Thompson*

## Introduction

In this chapter, I aim to explore the experience of parents of disabled children, gleaned from my work as a couple psychotherapist over many years. Often, parents of disabled children describe an increase in patience, empathy and compassion, of reaching a calmer place of acceptance, where what makes life tick alters from the more mundane or acquisitive to simpler priorities of care and love. Frequently cited is an important sense of purpose to these parents' lives which others more caught up in ambivalence might envy.

Alongside these more positive outcomes, these parents also face particular difficulties. These challenges are particularly acute at specific times of development, both within the couple relationship itself and around the physical and emotional development of their child. At its worst, a couple can feel besieged by an overwhelming combination of external and internal pressures. These pressures can gather at specific junctions in a couple's timeline, threatening to bulldoze the secure boundary around their relationship, splitting them in two.

I liken the boundary around the couple to an elastic band. What's inside it belongs to the couple relationship. The band can be wound double, keeping the partners secure and close, or loosened to allow space between them and the freedom to individuate whilst still being within the bounds of the band. This slackened, flexible boundary leaves room for a child to be invited in, elderly relative to be cared for or a work challenge to be absorbed without causing the band to become overly tight or rigid. An affair by one partner can challenge its bond, stretch it to its limits, and sometimes it is broken beyond repair. I think raising a disabled child can mean the elastic band, for some couples, is taut to breaking over a prolonged period of time, placing a particular burden on this would-be safe couple boundary that surrounds them. Many couples face hurdles that pull and distort the shape of their protective intimate boundary, but I argue that the lifelong nature of the pressure and the loss these particular parents of disabled children need to process, whilst still living alongside its source, makes the threat to their couple boundary unique.

Using composite clinical vignettes and case examples, I will describe the tensions that can beset couples in such circumstances. External forces provoking

DOI: 10.4324/9781003387947-15

anxiety in the relationship may include the reaction of friends, extended family and medical, social care and teaching professionals as they respond to the disabled child. Reading the paper or turning on the radio is likely to bring stories of disabled children being misdiagnosed and mistreated by police or care providers. Added to this is an inevitable additional financial pressure in raising a child with a disability, likely extending throughout the parents' lifetime and beyond.

Internal pressure within the two individuals and their couple relationship when raising a child with a disability varies and is often linked to their own emotional make-up and valence. For some, it comprises their emotional reaction to what might be perceived as 'failure' to produce a 'healthy' child. For others, it is the difficulty in letting go of a fantasy of a 'cure' which can result in repeated waves of disappointment and frustration. Another unconscious reaction can result in a defensive expert-non-expert split between parents, over the care of their child, which leaves them isolated from one another. There is also disparate mourning, fear, regret and blame. Coping with a surfeit of anxiety and depression, resulting from these internal pressures, is common among the parents of children with special needs.

For a couple used to their share of personal success, be it school prefect when they were young or manager of a successful business in later life, the psychic shock of finding themselves joining the ranks of a minority of parents of disabled children and the alarm, sympathy, or defensive negation this evokes in their peers can cause a narcissistic injury from which it is hard to recover. For those adults more used to misfortune, having a disabled child returns them to a familiar place of hopelessness and victimisation which inevitably makes the tasks they face, in nurturing their child and their own relationship, all the harder. These internal pressures give rise to defensive reactions within the couple relationship and between them and the world, casting them adrift from the mainstream, a dangerous place to dwell.

In his book *Far from the Tree*, Solomon (2013) describes a goal for parents of disabled children; wherein they no longer suffer. Solomon writes of a parental state of mind that can accept their child's difficulties and disabilities, a mindset that lies beyond loss and railing against injustice and hardship, a mark of healthy development for all. I argue that the psychological growth required to reach this hard-fought-for transcendent place needs support, understanding and challenge that couple psychotherapists are well qualified to give. In order to do so, therapists need to know how important it is for the couple relationship to survive this onslaught and learn to flourish alongside what I describe as a 'living loss reality' as they raise their disabled child. It's a complex mental manoeuvre; balancing feelings of mourning while encouraging living and development in their child. Partners may defend against this confusion and pain at different times and in different ways.

Leader of the Free French Forces against the Nazis during World War II, Charles de Gaulle, on burying his 20-year-old daughter, who suffered from severe Down's syndrome, is reputed to have said, "Now she is like the others" (James, 2007). This simple statement hints perhaps at what de Gaulle had often longed for. Parents of children with life-limiting illnesses or rare genetic disorders must work, often day and night, alongside their child's pain, and it is common to hear the phrase, "If

I could take it away, if I could suffer instead of my child, I gladly would". Parents of a blind or deaf child or a child with Down's syndrome will all encounter hurdles in their parenting and emotional relationship with their child. Parents of a child with cerebral palsy will likely face huge physical demand on their own bodies, particularly as they age and their child matures.

For the purposes of this chapter, however, I will focus on the parents of children diagnosed with autistic spectrum disorder (ASD), although the disparity in diagnosis of this condition is infinite. Around one in 57 (1.76%) children currently living in the UK are on the autistic spectrum, significantly higher than previously reported, according to a 2021 study of more than 7 million children carried out by researchers from Newcastle University in collaboration with the University of Cambridge's Department of Psychiatry and Maastricht University. The team drew on data from the school census from the National Pupil Database, collected by the Department for Education from individuals aged 2–21 years old in state-funded schools in England.

Autism is a lifelong neurodevelopmental condition characterised by significant deficits in the social and communication domains and by restrictive, repetitive and ritualistic patterns of behaviour, interests or activities (American Psychiatric Association [APA], 2013). It affects how individuals interact with others, communicate, learn and behave. Difficulties can occur when interpreting nuance, abstract ideas, making generalisations, understanding facial expression, coping with change and forming friendships. The condition can result in self-injurious behaviour, anxiety, depression, problems understanding people and difficulties in expression of affect. Autistic children, and adults, often self-soothe with repeated behaviours or words, sounds or phrases (echolalia), with little apparent comprehension of how they affect those who hear them.

Autism can be more invisible in very young children and is likely to emerge as a toddler develops. Parents report a gradual creeping awareness that their child is going to be different and face challenges that will set him or her apart. Having facilitated groups for parents of children with autism and supervised therapists who do the same, as well as offering both long- and short-term therapy to parents at many stages of their autistic child's development, I will hone in on this particular condition, although many of the hurdles this chapter explores are applicable to the parents of children with a variety of disabilities.

## Parents' experience of medical, social care and educative interventions for their child

Scenario 1: *"The first paediatrician who assessed Charlie said he was un-assessable. We were devastated, it took almost a week to recover from the shock of it. We couldn't understand what it meant. When we finally found a second paediatrician, the report she wrote floored us. It just arrived in the post. We could barely speak to each other for the first 48 hours. It said Charlie had the mental age of a 12-month-old".*

(Father of 5-year-old Charlie, who has ASD)

"The idea of a couple coming together to produce a child is central in our psychic life, whether we aspire to it, object to it, realise we are produced by it, deny it, relish it or hate it" (Britton, 1995). The private lives of parents, largely operating without public glare and interference as they raise their children, for good or ill, are denied to a couple raising a child who is different. In order to access vital medical and educative help, their private family lives must be exposed, predominantly to professionals working in the field. Scrutiny from professionals and fantasies of judgement are likely suffered and absorbed by such parents as either benign or malign. This 'fracture' to their contained parental autonomy needs to be tolerated – a big ask for those who are, most likely, lacking in confidence and unsure of their parental agency.

As Charlie's father, quoted earlier, can attest, a common complaint from parents is how universally unfeeling and unaware professionals charged with the vital job of making a diagnosis of ASD can be; this has significant bearing on the mental health of the parents. How and when a diagnosis is delivered is an important part of the family's care.

> *"A recent empirical study found that one of the best predictors of how a child responds to treatment, regardless of the type of treatment, is how the mother is faring psychologically. . . . Mothers and fathers of children suffering from autism are more likely to feel less confident in their parenting and to experience greater marital distress than parents of typical or mentally retarded children."*
> (Rodrigue et al., 1990; Wolf et al., 1989)

### The couple expert/incompetent split

Scenario 2: *"We had termly round table meetings at the school about Sasha's progress. They were attended by the Special Educational Needs Assistant, Sasha's form teacher and the educational psychologist. All 3 addressed their comments only to Rob. He's Sasha's main carer, while I work. It appears Rob's day to day knowledge of her social and learning challenges at school disqualify or dwarf my thoughts about how she's doing. Rob and I would always have massive rows after those round table meetings"*.
(Paula, mother of 7-year-old Sasha)

As Sophie Corke describes in her chapter entitled 'Good cop – bad cop', all couples can find themselves split unhelpfully into 'good and bad' as they attempt the complex task of raising their child. This often links to similar experiences of feeling 'good or bad' as children in their families of origin. For parents raising disabled children, this defensive reaction to challenges is perhaps doubly understandable.

Faced with acute stress and uncertainty in raising a child with ASD, this 'good cop – bad cop' split can manifest in a slightly different way, with one parent becoming the expert in ASD and the care of the child while the other feels redundant and incompetent. Of course, much like all 'good cop – bad cop' splits, in reality, neither parent 'knows' what the best treatment, or diet, for their child is but this split stance perhaps provides an illusion of certainty to both.

Both parents are likely lacking in confidence in raising a child that neither recognises as similar to themselves. The primary carer, however, maybe through greater research, can become the more 'skilled' parent in the eyes of both. In this more authoritative position, the more knowledgeable partner often fails to sufficiently share their discoveries.

If not recognised and checked, this competent-incompetent split can trigger unprocessed feelings linked to oedipal transitions for the parental couple, with the 'incompetent' feeling left out and rejected, while the 'expert' temporarily triumphs. The boundary around the couple in such cases can reconfigure to encompass the disabled child and one parent. Although this 'coupling up' between one parent and one child can be evident in relationships where there is no disability, having a disabled child increases its likelihood, as it's much harder for parents to impose an 'excluding' couple boundary, which is, at the right time, necessary for children to bear.

## Case example

One couple I worked with, Sally and Michael, were parents to Simon, aged 18, when they entered couple therapy. Simon 'ruled' at home. To help him with intense anxiety and storms of seemingly out-of-control emotion, the parents had adapted their home and shut down their emotional intimate life as a couple. There wasn't the space or time for their relationship, and sex had stopped a long time ago. Sally and Michael slept in separate rooms and never went out together or treated themselves to anything. Lists were stuck around the house because Simon needed to know exactly what was happening and when. Only limited foods could be included on the family menu because Simon was so picky. The couple spent all of their time together talking about Simon and thinking about strategies that could help him.

The couple themselves seemed timid and thoughtful, which exacerbated the monstrous image of their demanding and domineering son. Simon's throwing of plates and his rude insults dwarfed their couple relationship, rendering it insignificant in comparison. Working with them in therapy, my countertransference registered something curiously deadened about their relationship, and I found myself being pulled into moving quite quickly and taking risks as to the interventions I used. I was also more challenging than normal, perhaps a keenness on my part to bring the sessions – and their relationship – to life.

I was conscious of Michael, in particular, needing support in creating a boundary around himself and his wife and in reducing his 'inhabiting' of his son's experience. By 'inhabiting', I mean a complex set of projections between father and son which resulted in Simon's anxiety and depression residing within Michael. Sally would often turn to Michael to find out what Simon was thinking and feeling, partly to absolve herself of the frustration and sadness of not being able to understand her own child.

As we worked to create a safe space in the consulting room for this couple to try and build, almost for the first time, a boundary around their relationship, I became increasingly aware that their timidity towards their son and their inability to create a structure of benign parental authority to protect him was as much a result of their own childhoods as the circumstances in which they found themselves.

In a particularly moving session, Sally wondered if she had killed off a part of herself in order to live alongside Simon. I gently challenged this view and wondered to what extent her relationship with her own feelings of anger and agency, linked to growing up with a violent, alcoholic father, were activated around Simon. Having Simon had perhaps allowed her to deny a split-off part of herself, but in doing that, her relationship with Michael was denied any intimacy. In turn, Michael's childhood had been restrictive and joyless. He had needed to go 'undercover' within himself with his creativity, to keep it secret, creating his own psychic retreat. He didn't experience any closeness with either of his parents, and as it turned out, Simon's demands allowed him to maintain this undercover internal life, separate from those he loved.

Progress in the couple therapy was slow. Getting the balance between what material belonged to the three individuals in the family, or to the couple relationship or was in the domain of parenting a child on the spectrum, was difficult for all to identify with any clarity, partly because it seemed to move around the relationship dynamic and in the therapy itself. Sometimes I would think this is Simon's disturbance we are thinking about here, only to recognise it was also something that was the direct opposite of the repression Michael or Sally had experienced in their childhoods. At times, it seemed Simon exhibited a gross exaggeration of all that was denied in his parents by their parents, and therefore, parts of them both were alive in him.

I faced dangers in the couple dismissing me as simply having no idea how difficult things were for them and how the alarm of Simon throwing plates around the kitchen left them in bits. Over time, they were able to trust that I could recognise their distress and carry the hope that they would be able to withstand it and venture towards a couple intimacy that they had hitherto not managed. This might, in turn, relieve Simon of the guilt he may have felt in causing his parents to shut down their lives and orbit around him to the exclusion of anything else.

## The rest of the family and friends

Scenario 3: "*Adam and I were stretched trying to get Emily into the right secondary school, one that could cater for her special needs. It took up much time and was stressful. Plus the money we spent on expert witnesses in our fight with the council. I came across a local charity while doing some research for the education tribunal. It was about siblings of children with ASD. I was horrified to read about the depression and anxiety they suffered. It had never occurred to me that Emily's sister would be affected that much*".

(Tracey, mother of 11-year-old Emily, diagnosed with ASD, and her 7-year-old Jessica)

Parents can be awash with the emotional fallout of raising a child on the spectrum. In the consulting room, these parents may dismiss their neuro-typical children as being unaffected by having an ASD sibling. Alternatively, neuro-typical children are evident in their absence in the material explored in the consulting room, as all the couple want to focus on is their child with special needs. If these neuro-typical siblings are mentioned, it is perhaps inevitable that these offspring are considered 'luckier', that their efforts at school will be taken more for granted and that the burdens and added responsibilities they experience at having an autistic sibling will be overlooked. They, in turn, will witness the strain their parents are under and believe that their own concerns and worries may overload them or appear insignificant to them. The challenge for these parents is to accept that, like themselves, these siblings may suffer embarrassment and protective fury in equal and confusing measure in relation to their ASD brother or sister, especially in public as a family. They may consider themselves unimportant to or neglected by their parents or be tempted into creating their own problems, to siphon off some parental anxiety for themselves.

Despite siblings of ASD children often gaining in resilience and compassion as they grow up, if their parents do manage to realise how difficult life might be for them, it can simply add another layer of shame or source of despair for all. As for the parents, they are confronted with a sense of guilt about the burden they have placed on their neuro-typical children, both in the here and now and in the future, when they will no longer be there to help. At best, this realisation simply adds to the long list of anxieties over which parents believe they have no agency or control.

When children are young, many parents resort to 'tag-team' strategies to spread themselves between their disabled and able children, meaning these parents spend much time apart, sometimes resulting in an impoverished sense of unfairness and mutual resentment.

Whilst parents of children with ASD may well be supported by extended family and friends as they bring up their child, their fantasies about 'what other people think', perhaps a projection of some of their own darker or ambivalent feelings about their child, can result in anger, envy and all manner of defensive reactions. This can create a vicious cycle, with these couples tending to avoid the company of other families so as not to be confronted by their different, mainstream parenting experience or find themselves in positions where they feel rejected or second best.

Scenario 4: "*I love my nieces and nephews and celebrate all their successes. I want to hear about them, I really do, although I suspect sometimes my brothers keep their children's triumphs to themselves. What would help though, would be a sign from my friends or siblings of the on going challenge Colin and I face, in raising Adam. Rather than the silences. Not to feel sorry for us but just to say, we know it is hard for you. We get it and that it doesn't go away*".

(Julie, mum to Adam, aged 22)

## The school gates

Scenario 5: "*At the Year 5 end-of-term picnic, the other mothers would literally lean across me and discuss the sleepovers their sons were having that night. It was as if I was invisible and didn't have a son in Year 5 myself. I could have broken down each time they didn't invite my boy*".

(Joanna, mother of 9-year-old Joseph)

Social isolation is the enemy of parents of children with ASD. It is often experienced in parallel with the exclusion difficulties their child may face. This perception of being 'spat out' of the safe circle created by their peers and communities, whether imagined or real, can be deeply painful. Many young people with autism and learning difficulties are bullied or ostracised in school by children and young people who experience their difference as threatening or frightening.

The distrust of difference, the desire not to dwell near it for fear of contagion, is hard to shift in the collective psyche. Parents of autistic children are emotionally bruised each time they sense it. One mother of an ASD boy told me of arriving to pick up her son at school only to find herself walking across a playground and seeing a gathering of parents looking up at the gym roof where her 7-year-old son was perched. She described her acute anxiety for his safety, although this wasn't the first time he had done this. She also felt an overriding shame that *this* was the reason she and her son were at the centre of everyone's attention. "*No-one came up to me and asked how I was, they just parted to create a clear path for me to half-drag a screaming Seth home*".

Parents of a child who died commonly describe finding it agonising to be among young people who mirror the age their child would have been, had they lived. Others find it helpful to be surrounded by the youth and energy of the young, to make contact with the essence of the child they have lost. For parents of a child with ASD, therapists may uncover much material as they explore the couple's feelings towards and relationship with their child's peers and parents. Is there envy at the successes of their child's classmates, who seemingly sail through exams or take the lead in the end of year school play, mobbed by friends as the final curtain falls? Perhaps most identifiable in its absence, these parents may need their therapist's tacit permission to express their envy and hatred, to purge themselves of it and pave the way for authentic recognition of their child's different development and achievements.

While some ASD children and young people excel at school, the majority are likely to suffer comorbid conditions such as learning difficulties and auditory processing impairment, which will impact their ability to forge an independent pathway through life. Their parents must undergo a profound shift in what constitutes success for their children in school since it will be different to that of their child's contemporaries. At various points, parents will face the outcome of, for example, selective streaming of children into the top and bottom sets, or exam results, all of which constitute the benchmarks against which parents judge themselves and are sometimes judged by others. These benchmarks can feel like a defeat for parents of children on the autism spectrum, if they aren't given enough support or helped to recognise their own child's successes, different though they may be.

## Stress, depression and anxiety

Scenario 6: *"In the early years, the anxiety about Ollie's future was intense. When I changed his nappy aged 9 months, I wondered if I would be changing his nappy at 9 years. Later, when we were on holiday in Cornwall and I saw all these families on the beach, it hit me like a bullet . . . the thought that I would never have grandchildren. Other times, when I saw homeless people on the streets, I wondered if that would be my boy when I was dead".*

(Susie, divorced, single mother of Ollie, aged 15)

Caring for a child with a developmental disability (DD) such as ASD has been widely used as one model for examining the effect of chronic stress on psychophysiological functioning (Lovell & Wetherell, 2016). Indeed, the challenges of caring for a child with a DD, which include financial hardship (Kogan et al., 2008), social isolation, negotiating a fragmented service system (Griffith & Hastings, 2013), stigma and social judgement far outstrip those of parenting a neuro-typical child.

Diagnosis of ASD is a particularly difficult time for parents. Arguing with local authorities for the proper provision of care for their child is common to most families with a disabled child, and the toll of this can be devastating on a couple relationship.

As with all children and their parents, key developmental stages of the adult relationship and maturation of their child are likely to dovetail and cut across one another. The birth of subsequent children, serious illness in the family, the onset of menopause for mothers, retirement plans for both parents – all these significant life changes take on an added dimension for parents of children with ASD.

The first decade of a disabled child's life is necessarily novel and confusing. Parents are getting to know their child, but in many cases, this child is unrecognisable to them. The second decade, when their child is grappling with disabled adolescence, bodily changes and the formation of a sexual self, whilst coming to terms with their difference, is perhaps the hardest to accept. It often coincides with parents beginning to lose their energy and agency as they face worries for their future, a potentially cruel junction for both adolescent and parent.

If the task of the adolescent is to "take ownership of his own body and mind, because he can be the one who chooses to exclude himself from the couple and develop his own identity" (Morgan, 1975), this challenge is often denied to the autistic child. Adolescence and autism are a potent cocktail for parents to contain. For teenagers with ASD, depending on where they fall on the spectrum, navigating the pull to individuation whilst accepting a dependency on parents that may never change is confusing. Resulting stress, anxiety and depression in the young person with ASD is likely, alongside similar affect states in their parents, creating a perfect storm.

Parents can appear to feel persecuted, sometimes by each other, their child or the wider world. This sense of paranoia might identify as a defence against guilt – the guilt of bringing their child into the world. One mother of an autistic 19-year-old ruefully told me, *"all autistic boys hate their mums. Who can blame my son, after all, I brought him into this world that doesn't give him a break"*.

Coming to terms with loss is an integral part of parenting, alongside many other enriching aspects. First, on becoming parents, there is the loss of being only two. Next, as the child develops, there is the loss of being utterly depended upon. As the young person moves towards adolescence and individuation, parents submit to this separation and all that it can throw up for them. These stages are simultaneously longed for and dreaded, as parents mourn what has passed. For the parents of a disabled child, who may never have an independent life, proper mourning is thwarted. There is no lost object. Rather, the loss lives alongside the living child and parents. Anxiety and depression are likely to fill the gap left by this un-mourned loss for parents and, compounded by the likely sense of social isolation, experienced vicariously through their disabled child.

## Acceptance of 'living loss reality'

Scenario 7: *"I've learnt over the years not to predict the future for Rosie. As she grows, I have tried to reassure myself she continues to develop, so I can't possibly 'know' how it will be. But terrible sadness sometimes takes the wind out of me. That my gorgeous girl is hidden away and I can't ever reach her"*.

(Susan, mother of 8-year-old Rosie)

Acceptance of a child with a disability can bring richness to families who can learn to prioritise what is important to them, be patient and have compassion in ways sometimes denied to those who have an easier path through their lives. To remain open, hopeful and optimistic about life whilst having a child who may never reciprocate your communication of love, who might always struggle with day-to-day living and need to be cared for, soon erases any King Lear–like fantasies of being taken care of by adult children.

These parents need space for their ambivalence; children are loved but loathed in a more visceral way than families with no disability amongst their progeny. Understanding that there is no contradiction between loving a child and feeling heavily burdened by that child, even wishing the child away, is needed. Unlike Marley's ghost in Dickens' *Great Expectations*, these parents are not in chains due to past misdemeanours but weighed down by thoughts of an unknown future for their child. They must learn to contain these fears, a considerable imaginative feat.

In *Paradise Lost* (X.743–45), Milton wrote:

*"Did I request thee, Maker, from my clay*
*To mould me Man, did I solicit thee*
*From darkness to promote me?"*

The relationship between an autistic child or young person and their parents is complex, and therapists are well advised to devote time and space attempting to understand how it is constructed. The normal projective identification between infants and their mothers, between parents and their children, and vice versa, is subject to a confusing overhaul. Emotions are still projected, of that there is little doubt, but the taking back and ownership of projections can be more problematic.

In couple psychotherapy, my client, Stella, described the kind of bewildering exchange she regularly had with her teenage son:

*"he would burst into the kitchen and berate me for being angry. I was usually*
*just peeling spuds, or something similar, whilst listening to Radio 4. I'd try to*
*reassure him I wasn't cross. After half an hour though, of being told how 'bad'*
*I was, I started to feel angry, which was utterly confusing."*

Stella, her husband, and I slowly attempted to untangle her son's projections into her and recognise his terror of individuation away from her. This kind of 'me/not me' muddying of boundaries and identity is undiluted in families where there is a young person with a disability, who has little 'outside life' to enliven, distract and absorb his 'inside' life as an the adolescent. We came to understand, however, that if the boundary around the couple relationship was steady enough, their son felt safer, less stuck and less inclined to project his disturbance and anxiety into them.

I have also worked with couples where I felt that some of their autistic child's out-of-control anger was linked to their shared inability to get in touch with their own. Alternatively a couple's mutual fear of intimacy that might start to surface in couple therapy and be an additional reason for the couple relationship to be neglected. All focus is channelled into the child, a burden on young shoulders that needs to be lightened if therapy is to be successful.

Parents need to be able to trust that their therapist can understand and empathise with the losses they have to face, as parents, as partners and as members of wider society. It is a careful balance for the therapist to sufficiently acknowledge the unique 'living loss' that can threaten to saturate their lives whilst containing their anxiety and sense of injustice that this is happening to them. Alongside an under-standing of the past, the present must be attended to, with all its disappointment and fatigue. At the right time, parents may be helped to acknowledge an unknown future that they will encounter together, as opposed to a known catastrophic one which, in a state of panic, parents can resort to 'knowing' in their minds.

## Resource and containment in the couple relationship

Scenario 8: *"There are days when Bob and I are too stressed and exhausted to talk to each other. Most of the time though, when it gets bad, he throws me a look as if to say, 'I'm here and I understand' and, although it doesn't take the bad day away, at least I don't feel alone in it. He's with me and together we can face down pretty much anything".*

(Susanna, wife to Bob, and parent of two autistic boys, aged 12 and 10)

There have been numerous quantitative studies on the life experiences of parents of children with autism. The results are not difficult to predict.

*"Parental quality of life (QoL) deficits could be understood in the context of the challenges that these parents face. Increased levels of stress, sleep deprivation and fatigue have been associated with parents of children with ASD and are likely to compromise their mental and physical functioning."*

(Giallo et al., 2013)

Few studies link information on the relationship between QoL and parental self-efficacy, by which I mean people's beliefs in their ability to influence their lives. Parental self-efficacy in managing their children's disability and belief in their shared ability to achieve this, needs encouragement and validation, possibly contained in couple psychotherapy.

Couple therapists know the potential resource in an intimate, boundaried couple relationship that is strong enough to form a receptacle for shared joy, distress and despair. 'Rehearsing' first in the safety of the consulting room, couples experience the containment of a shared safe space. This space can withstand, at times, hatred even of a beloved disabled child, if only as a precursor to parents picking themselves up and pushing forward again. It is a space in which to feel accepted and understood and, most importantly, not be alone. Their partner is perhaps the only other person who knows what has had to be given up and what can push either one into depression or an acting out that they will later regret. Their partner can engender a sense that they are in this 'together' and can weather the storm, despite not knowing what will happen next. They don't know if their child will develop further nor how their child will fare in society, both with and without them being around. They can't know their child's separate experience, pleasure or pain – admittedly, the preserve of all parents. What's unique with a child on the spectrum, however, is that parents and child do not speak the same 'language' and never will.

One father disclosed that although he loved his son, at times, their life together felt like a lifelong catastrophe, with no escape and no end, except in death. For parents who have undergone their own catastrophic losses in early life, living alongside their children who may be in a perpetual state of daily crisis, the anxiety of vicariously being in touch with early trauma tests them to the extreme.

If a couple relationship is a good enough container, it can withstand this level of pressure. To do so, however, the couple must reserve some capacity and agency for themselves, both as individuals and adults joined in an intimate relationship. To siphon off all their attention to their child will ensure neglect between them, providing the perfect breeding ground for resentment and rejection.

Warren Coleman (1993) identifies the marital container:

> *"a capacity to make an identification without losing the sense of one's own identity and, by implication, confusing the self with the other, couples are then able to create a sense of 'us' that acts as a third factor – the relationship that contains them."*

The capacity Coleman describes ensures creative space within the relationship allowing the couple to feel held during the times of regression that inevitably arise in life transitions and points of crisis, for both them and their child.

Hopefully, parents of children with ASD have the good sense to surround themselves with friends and family who can support them when they need it, a kind of wider, outer container, reinforcing the couple boundary. These supporters of the couple can sensitively acknowledge the burden they carry, occasionally relieving them of some of that burden and, in turn, celebrate their own able children's successes alongside the different achievements of the disabled child within their midst.

## Conclusion

Parenting a disabled child is a lifelong, defining feature of a couple's relationship. A medical cure to change things or a practical solution to fix things is not possible however much parents fight or hope for one. Parents of disabled children go on a crash course to understand the "emotional experience of difference" (Fisher, 2008). They need emotional empathy to imagine the feelings, lived experience and world view of their child one which they are unlikely to have experienced themselves.

All parents must accept their children's different identities as separate and unique. To borrow from Shakespeare's Hamlet, they can't know their child's experience of "the slings and arrows of outrageous fortune". For parents whose children suffer a disability, this necessary reality takes on an added resonance. A sense of entrapment or hopelessness, both symptoms of depression, are likely to be felt at times. They must accept that their child's condition sets them apart, even from their parents. It's a cliché that their 'child's mind is wired differently'; the perception and vision of parents and child are alien to each other.

Solomon reminds us that most children resemble their parents by calling on "the time-worn adage that says an apple doesn't fall far from the tree". He goes on to describe children with special needs, "but these children are apples that have fallen elsewhere, some a couple of orchards away, some on the other side of the world" (Solomon, 2013). As we know, an exceptional identity is isolating, sometimes shaming, and in the case of parents of children with ASD, this alienation can extend to them. These parents may also need to acknowledge that their combined genetic make-up has been the cause of the added difficulty their child is facing, despite creating other children that do not suffer in the same way.

Yet Solomon goes on to expound that "intimacy with difference fosters its accommodation" and that "myriad families learn to tolerate, accept and finally celebrate children who are not what they originally had in mind". I am not sure of the percentage of parents of children with ASD who would join in the celebration, although I have heard awestruck parents acknowledge their son or daughter's resourcefulness, bravery and sense of humour in the face of adversity. Their acceptance, which will hopefully join with their ASD child's recognition of his or her condition, if they have the necessary cognitive development to do so, is where couple psychotherapy can have a vital role to play. Clinicians use of transference and countertransference will support them as they wade through feelings of inadequacy, tolerate projections of envy, conquer their shameful fear of getting it wrong and share anger at injustice alongside parents but, most of all, intense sadness, as they contain the emotions of a couple working their way to this place of acceptance.

Perhaps this is not so different to other areas of the work of couple psychotherapy and requires, as Mason describes, both therapist and patient acquiring the position of 'safe uncertainty'.

> "This position is not fixed. It is one which is always in a state of flow and is consistent with the notion of a respectful, collaborative, evolving narrative, one which allows a context to emerge whereby new explanations can be placed alongside rather than instead of . . . a framework for helping people to fall out of love with the idea that solutions solve things."
>
> (Mason, 1993)

For these parents, there is no silver bullet magic solution. Their work will continue as they learn to conquer feelings of powerlessness, hopelessness and fatigue. It is important to create a space where they can enjoy aspects of their child as they are and live in the here and now rather than attempt to predict an unknown future. This work can begin within the secure setting of couple psychotherapy.

Co-creating a secure enough couple relationship, if parents can keep the boundary around it intact, is perhaps the best chance for parents and their children. Their relationship is the resource – to be turned to, to nourish them and to keep hope alive. For they, more than for the rest of us, must trust in a benign and generous world to continue parenting their adult child after they have gone.

## References

American Psychiatric Association. (2013) Diagnostic and Statistical Manual of Mental Disorders (DSM-5). Washington, DC: American Psychiatric Association Publishing.

Britton, R. (1995) Introduction. p. xi. In F. Grier (Ed.) Oedipus and the Couple, 2004 (p. 9). London: Karnac Books.

Cantwell, J., Muldoon, O., & Gallagher, S. (2015) The influence of self-esteem and social support on the relationship between stigma and depressive symptomology in parents caring for children with intellectual disabilities. Journal of Intellectual Disability Research, 59, 948–957. http://dx.doi.org/10.1111/jir.12205

Coleman, W. (1993) Marriage as a psychological container. In S. Ruszczynski (Ed.) Psychotherapy with Couples (pp. 70–96). London: Karnac Books.

Fisher, J. V. (2008) The role of imagination in the apprehension of difference. Fort Da, 14(17–35), 17–20.

Giallo, R., Wood, K., Jellett, R., & Porter, R. (2013). Fatigue, wellbeing and parental self-efficacy in mothers of children with an autism spectrum disorder. Autism, 17(4), 65–80. https://doi.org/10.1177/1362361311416830.

Griffith, G., & Hastings, R. (2013) 'He's hard work, but he's worth it'. The experience of caregivers of individuals with intellectual disabilities and challenging behaviour. A meta-synthesis of qualitative research. Journal of Applied Research and Intellectual Disability, 27(5), 401–419.

James, C. (2007) Cultural Amnesia, p. 258. London: Picador.

Kogan, M., et al. (2008) A national profile of the health care experiences and family impact of autism spectrum disorder among children in the United States, 2005–2006. American Academy of Pediatrics, 122(6), e1149–e1158. https://doi.org/10.1542/peds.2008-1057

Lovell, B., & Wetherell, M. (2016) The psychophysiological impact of childhood autism spectrum disorder on siblings. Research in Developmental Disabilities, 49–50, 226–234.

Mason, B. (1993) Towards positions of safe uncertainty. Human Systems: The Journal of Systemic Consultation and Management, 4, 189–200.

Milton, J. (1884) Paradise Lost: Book X, pp. 743–45. New York: J. W. Lovell Company.

Morgan, M. (1975) On being able to be a couple: The importance of the "creative couple" in psychic life. In F. Grier (Ed.), Oedipus and the Couple (pp. 9–30). London: Karnac.

Rodrigue, J. R., Morgan, S. B., & Geffken, G. R. (1990) Families of autistic children: Psychological functioning of mothers. Journal of Clinical Psychology, 19, 371–379.

Solomon, A. (2013) Far From the Tree, pp. 5–6, 95. London: Chatto & Windus.

Wolf, L. C., Noh, S., Fisman, S. N., & Speechley, M. (1989) Psychological effects of parenting stress on parents of autistic children. Journal of Autism and Developmental Disorders, 19, 157–166.

# Part 4

## Conflicted parents and their children

# Chapter 12

# "Good cop – bad cop"

## The challenge for parents of finding the middle ground

*Sophie Corke*

This paper is based on experience of working with what I will refer to as "good cop – bad cop" parents. These are couples or co-parents whose conflict centres around their management of and relationship with their child or children. Unlike in reasonably well-functioning families, where it might be openly acknowledged that one or another parent is a "soft touch" or parents may alternate their stance, "good cop – bad cop" parents feel trapped in rigid roles with each angrily asserting what is "best" for the children, unable to see the other's point of view.

Characteristically, the "bad cop", often the stay-at-home parent or main carer in a separated couple, feels compelled take total responsibility in regard to childcare. They become the designated keeper of boundaries and saying "no", freeing the "good cop" parent to have all the fun, even joining the child to undermine the "bad cop's" directives.

In this chapter, I will illustrate that these "good" and "bad" parenting roles often arise as the result of parents' own experience of being parented and are related to their unconscious choice of one another as partners. This selection of a partner may be viewed as an attempt to resolve their own childhood difficulties but instead can serve to reinforce them. Furthermore, this unconscious compulsion for a couple to split between "good" and "bad" can be seen as a faulty attempt to deal with anxieties about their role as parents. Finally, I will explore how, in their battle over parenting, couples may in fact lose sight of their child as a person separate to them and who needs their care. It is partly through starting to accept their child as having a mind of his or her own that parents in conflict can start to reconnect with their offspring and create a supportive parental relationship.

## Conflict over parenting

Parenting in today's world has increasingly become an anxiety-provoking business, with a confusing array of theories available as to what is best for the child. There is also greater awareness of how parental failures are likely to damage children. For parents whose relationship is in trouble or who are separated, feelings of failure are likely to be particularly strong, leading them, as we shall see, to adopt more extreme and opposing views.

DOI: 10.4324/9781003387947-17

The arguments that warring couples bring to the consulting room often centre around the tension between setting rules or boundaries for their child on the one hand and being "child-centred", following the child's wishes or demands on the other. The "bad cop" parent may be characterised by the "good cop" as overly traditional, strict or rigid. Conversely, the "bad cop" may accuse their partner of being cowardly in refusing to say "no" and of spoiling their children. One parent may have avidly read books on parenting, while the other may be more laissez faire.

While most couples will disagree on some aspects of parenting, what characterises "good cop – bad cop" parents is their absolute certainty in their way of thinking, with the "bad cop" parent often suffused with a strong sense of grievance at being pushed into their role and feeling abandoned by their partner. These couples believe that it is precisely their conflict over parenting that has driven them apart, whereas before having children, they were "on the same page".

In the case of couples who are separated or divorced, their co-parental relationship may be the only thing keeping them in contact with each other (see Chapter 14). Such parents may be particularly prone to using conflict over the relationship with their child in order to punish each other. The extreme states of mind that divorcing parents can find themselves in makes it particularly hard for them to separate what is best for their child from the continuing conflict with their ex-partner.

While "good cop – bad cop" couples may believe their differences to be solely about how to parent, on exploration in therapy, it becomes clear that their positions are also a way of dealing with deep unconscious anxieties about how to be a couple as well as being parents or how to be parents while no longer being a couple.

## The role of parents in psychic development – moving from dyad to triad

The move from being a couple to being a family, of two becoming three (and more), has been identified by Freud, Klein and their followers as a cornerstone of psychic development. The young child's wish to join up with one parent to the exclusion of the other is illustrated in the myth of Oedipus, which underlines the potentially catastrophic consequences of incestuous wishes being fulfilled (Grier, 2005).

By contrast, in healthy development, the young child's desire to have one, or either, parent to themselves needs to be gradually frustrated. A couple who can maintain a "couple state of mind", drawing on their couple relationship at the same time as being parents (Morgan, 2019), will help their child begin to tolerate exclusion from the parental couple. As Di Ceglie points out, summarising Britton, the triangular family situation has the potential to help the child move beyond the oedipal stage by providing the child with the following:

> *"three different and co-existent emotional experiences: based on (1) his separate link with each of the parents: (2) on being the observer and not the participant in their relationship: and (3) being observed by them (my emphasis)."*
> (Di Ceglie, 1995, p. 50)

Where parents can put a boundary around their relationship at the same time as holding their child in mind in this way, the child will be able to internalise their parents as a "benign parental couple" (Ludlam, 2007; Morgan, 2019). This internal couple then enables what Britton terms a "third position" so that the child can become an observer of his parent's relationship and so, too, of himself (Britton, 1989).

In the case of "good cop – bad cop" couples, where one partner effectively teams up with the child, oedipal realities are avoided. Unconsciously, these couples are denying the crucial reality of the gap between the generations and an acknowledgement of time moving on. Such couples instead resort unconsciously to an "oedipal illusion" (Britton, 1989) which, as we will see below in the case of Steve and Maria, can lead to a feeling of time standing still in the following:

*"domain . . . separated from the real external world . . . free from the demand of the exigencies of life, like a kind of reservation."*

(Freud, 1924; quoted in Britton, 1989)

Within this "reservation", reality is denied in favour of a stuckness or "psychic retreat" (Steiner, 1993) so that parents avoid working through their ambivalent feelings and are unable to either separate or move towards becoming a couple within their role as parents.

The stories of Maria and Steve and Neel and Maya are composites of couples I have worked with who have consciously or unconsciously adopted "good cop – bad cop" strategies. They illustrate couples who struggle to develop a "third position" either individually or in their couple relationship and are left feeling understandably at a loss as to how to parent. Their adoption of "good cop" and "bad cop" roles can serve as a defensive solution to this troubling situation.

## Maria and Steve – a parenting crisis

Maria and Steve came to therapy because of rows over the parenting of their daughter, Anna, aged 11, which seemed to be spiralling out of control. The argument which led them to seek help was about Anna tidying her room, a subject which had become a battleground between mother and daughter, with Steve apparently staying on the side-lines. On this occasion, Anna had talked back to her mother, provoking a furious response from Maria. A "tussle" ensued with both mother and daughter pushing each other, forcing Steve to separate them. I was struck by the contrast between Maria, who was grim-faced and full of remorse, and Steve, who had an evasive air, appearing curiously unconcerned, saying that he knew Maria was a good parent, and of course, he did not want to pass judgement.

When we explored a little further, it became clear that this was a pattern in their relationship, whereby Maria felt forced into always taking the role of "bad cop", whereas Steve rarely enforced rules and did not back his wife up in saying "no" to their daughter. Maria spoke plaintively about how she felt Anna and Steve teamed up and had fun together, leaving her on the outside. Steve said that he thought Maria was a good mother, but sometimes he felt she was too strict. Steve asserted that he was just an "easy-going" person, and to me, it felt there was something rather smug in the way he said this.

In early sessions with this couple, I found it hard to think in the face of Maria's tirades against Steve, whose efforts to appease his wife stirred up feelings of irritation in me, helping me to realise how angry he must have been feeling. I felt pulled between the couple. On the one hand, I thought that Maria set overly high standards for herself, her daughter and for them as parents. On the other, I recognised that Steve was subtly undermining his wife's efforts to keep order and to be a responsible parent, unconsciously leaving her with what has been referred to by couple therapists as a "double dose" of angry feelings.

I noticed that Maria expressed her view of parenting in a rather aggrieved and relentless manner, which felt similar to the way in which she tried to keep the house tidy, as if life were a series of tasks, one after another. Maria had put her incipient career as an interior designer on the back burner to devote herself to being a mother. However, despite some warm and loving moments with her daughter, where they did crafts together, mostly it felt that parenting was something of a drudgery for Maria, who often resentfully referred to herself as the "servant" in the household.

I also had the impression that Maria and Steve, although in their 40s, were very "young" in terms of their emotional development. Although apparently in a crisis, they would wander into the consulting room, taking their time to arrive and leave so that I had a feeling of time being suspended. I also experienced great confusion in my countertransference (the feelings evoked in me by the couple), which seemed to reflect the couples' own confusion about whether they were a couple or not. Since their daughter was born, their sexual relationship had faded, and they slept in separate bedrooms. While Steve expressed more of a wish to rekindle their physical relationship, things between them felt stuck, and Maria was of the view that this part of their relationship was over.

## Understanding parental history

As work with this couple continued, looked at through the lens of their parental relationship, it became clearer how the couples' adoption of "good" and "bad" cop roles tied in with their own family experience and their unconscious choice of one another or "couple fit" (Morgan, 2019). While initially reluctant to talk about their own histories of being parented, Maria and Steve gradually became more interested in how this might be connected to their current positions.

### The "bad cop"

Maria came from a traditional background in rural Spain. She gave a sense of a chaotic and frightening family home with a tyrannical father, who shouted and threw things. Maria said her mother was timid and often withdrew, keeping herself in the background. Maria thought that she, her mother and her younger sister were treated as second-class citizens, both in society and within her family. As was traditional in her part of Spain, she was given the same name as her mother, which added to her sense of not being recognised as a person in her own right. As a result, Maria struggled with self-confidence and had been attracted to Steve, who was eight years older than her and whom she believed had everything "sorted".

## The "good cop"

Steve was characteristically evasive about his birth family, describing them initially as "loving and supportive". However, in the course of a session in which I pointed out to him that he smiled even when Maria was shouting at him, we began to think more about his need to appease others and to push away his own angry feelings. Steve admitted that he could be "passive-aggressive" in leaving Maria to be the "bad cop". When we wondered why Steve felt he needed to appease everyone, he began to talk more about the difficulties in his upbringing.

Although Steve remembered his early childhood as warm and loving, this had changed when his father developed motor neuron disease when he was 11 years old. From this point on, Steve, who was the eldest of three, needed to help his hard-pressed mother, who became unavailable and short-tempered under the pressure of work and family. Steve recognised that he had to step into a parenting role, both for his siblings and for his father, leaving him little space to be a child himself.

Coming from a chaotic family background, Maria's conscious choice of Steve, who appeared to her to have had a "happy family", was in the hope that he could create the loving family life that she idealised and felt she had never had. However, unconsciously, Maria had chosen a rather absent person, replicating her relationship with her distant mother, whose demonstrative love she had desperately wanted. Steve chose Maria, who, as an interior designer, liked to make things "homely". He unconsciously looked to her for the thoughtful mothering and warmth that his own mother had withdrawn after his father became ill.

Through further exploration in therapy, we began to better understand Steve and Maria's couple "fit" through which each of them carried a disowned part of the other. Steve, who was invested in being the "good" child/parent, unconsciously projected his "bad" or angry feelings into Maria. Maria, who despite her efforts to make something of her life, tended to revert to feeling that she had nothing to offer, was predisposed to take on the "badness" or sense of failure in the couple.

## Different solutions to a joint defence

Maria and Steve both lacked a benign internalised parental couple which could have given them confidence in their parenting. As Maria herself put it, "How are we supposed to do this when no one ever did it for us?"

Couples are helped to parent effectively where they can draw on an experience of relationships being supportive so that doubts and uncertainties can be thought about and shared between them. Instead, Maria and Steve shared the unconscious phantasy (Bannister & Pincus, 1965; Hewison, 2014) that two people coming together would result in something catastrophic. For Maria, her parental home felt unsafe, and her internalised parental couple was one in which her mother subjugated herself in order to appease her tyrannical father. Steve also unconsciously felt that a couple could not come together creatively. His ill and depressed father created a gap in the family which Steve unconsciously tried to fill, leaving him and his mother "coupled-up". Complying with this precocious burden, pulled into a premature "adult" position alongside his mother, Steve had little room to be a child himself. The couple put me in mind of the "false self" couple described by Fisher:

*"Made up of the tyrannical self and the compliant object, or conversely, the compliant self and the tyrannical object, unable together to create the triangular space necessary for genuine mutual relating."*

(Fisher, 1993, pp. 164, 165)

Steve and Maria had become a couple partly in the unconscious hope of addressing their own lack of parenting. Their solution before having Anna was to create a fused relationship of total agreement that initially worked for them. Their wish to have children, particularly from Maria's side, was in the idealised hope of redressing the poverty of her own childhood, and she fully expected that having her own family would be like "one big love bubble". Their illusion was brutally shattered on discovering themselves miles apart over how to parent. What they couldn't understand at the time was that splitting their roles as parents between "good" and "bad" served unconsciously to preserve their "oedipal illusion", where their envious and attacking feelings could remain unknown to them.

The defensive mechanism of splitting was identified by Klein in her observation of infants. Klein described the infant's primitive feelings towards the mother (represented in the infant's mind as the breast) as veering between idealisation on the one hand and destructive feelings of envy or hate which were stirred up by the baby's anxiety or physical discomfort (Klein, 1946). The fear that he would damage his mother with his phantasised envious attacks led to the infant splitting mother into a "good" and "bad" breast, rather than being able to acknowledge that the same person could be the source of both bountifulness and of frustration (1957, pp. 191–192). However, alongside the wish to preserve the "good breast" on which he depended, the infant also feared that his aggression would lead to being attacked in return so that the bad breast became the persecuting breast. As Klein puts it:

*"The idealised breast forms the corollary of the persecuting breast; and in so far as idealisation is derived from the need to be protected from persecuting objects, it is a method of defence against anxiety."*

(Klein, 1952, p. 64)

Klein referred to this state of mind where splitting, persecutory feelings, denial and idealisation predominate as the "paranoid-schizoid" position, a state of mind which, she believed, is never entirely overcome (1957, p. 233). Instead, throughout life, and particularly at times of stress, we can easily revert to splitting when overwhelmed, apparent in the conviction that, for instance, one person or organisation or idea is entirely "bad" and another entirely "good".

Faced with the difficult and often conflicting demands of parenthood, it is not surprising that all parents, at times, find themselves in a paranoid-schizoid state of mind, where extreme emotions dominate and thinking seems impossible. Just as the infant fears that he will destroy his mother with his phantasised attacks, parents who are in this state of mind may fear damaging their child or children as they stir up feelings of hate as well as love.

I had the sense in working with Steve and Maria that in splitting into "good cop – bad cop" roles, they were defending against their joint anxiety about failing as parents. Steve, as the "good cop" parent, was more obviously defended from reality. With his tendency to behave like an adolescent and team up with Anna, his parenting seemed oblivious to his responsibility to help his child develop and enter the world, separate to her parents. He feared that saying "no" to his daughter would mean losing her love, and this put him in the dilemma of needing to choose between his daughter and his wife.

Maria was defending against the fear of chaos that was so overwhelming in her childhood and that was stirred up again when she became a parent herself. In talking about this in therapy with Steve, she came to understand that her strict rules and schedules were a way of trying to keep chaos at bay, especially since she felt that Steve abandoned her to make difficult decisions. A less evident aspect of Maria adopting her "bad cop" role was, as we came to realise in the sessions, that she was also defending against intimacy with her daughter, in her unsmiling refusal to join in "play", something neither parent had experienced themselves. Both were defending against coming together as "creative parents", who could draw on their parental relationship as a "third position" and could observe their daughter and think about her as separate but linked to them.

## Separated parents – difficulties in co-parenting

Separated or divorced co-parental couples for whom primitive feelings and defences are much in evidence are particularly susceptible to splitting into "good cop – bad cop" roles. Where one parent is the main carer, he or she may feel dumped with the responsible and "disapproving" role, while the non-resident parent may desperately attempt to "make up" and overcompensate, showering their child with treats or presents while at the same time continuing the feud with their former partner. Patchy communication between separated parents can also be exploited by children, leaving them in a powerful but also frightening position.

Where parents argue repeatedly in front of their children, this can be damaging to the child's sense of self and to their feeling of security as has been well documented (Clulow, 2019, pp. 40–41). In the case of "good cop – bad cop" parents, where arguments seem to be specifically about the children, it is not surprising that these children will believe they are the problem. Such children are then also more prone to difficulties in their own adult relationships (ibid).

I will now outline the case study of Neel and Maya, divorced parents whose efforts to co-parent led to furious rows between them, often in front of their two children. Their divorce had involved bitter battles in the courts over access to the children, culminating with Neel as the main carer and Maya having the children twice a week.

## Neel and Maya

Neel and Maya came to therapy to improve their co-parenting relationship because of their alarm over the behaviour of their son, Arkesh, aged 14 years. Arkesh had been getting bad reports from school and seemed set to fail some of his exams. He was also shutting himself in his bedroom playing computer games and, most recently, had been caught stealing a bag of sweets from the local shop. The shopkeeper, who knew the family well, let Arkesh off with a warning, but the incident led to even more conflict between the warring parents.

Their "good cop – bad cop" roles seemed fixed and inflexible. Neel accused Maya of spoiling Arkesh and always giving in to him; he claimed that she let their son spend too much time online and gave him treats rather than encouraging him to save up for things. He worried this was making Arkesh greedy and lazy. Worse still, Neel said that Maya was deliberately trying to sabotage his relationship with his son, turning Arkesh against him and encouraging him to choose to live full-time with his mother. Neel said his ex-wife wanted Arkesh to leave his elite private school and go to the local comprehensive, where he believed his son's laziness would be encouraged and he would end up a failure. Maya countered that Neel did not show his son affection and was overly harsh with him, only caring about his achievements. She believed their son was misbehaving because he felt rejected and criticised by his dad. By contrast, she accused Neel of idolising their daughter, Ella, who always did well at school. Maya said she did not want to repeat the mistakes of her own childhood, where she felt she was given no choices at all; she desperately wanted their parenting to be more child-centred.

## The forgotten child

While both Maria and Steve and Neel and Maya clearly cared for their children, there were times when it felt that the actual child or children were secondary to each parents' determination to prove the other one wrong, as if this was the only path to getting their own infantile needs met. At these times, it seemed, as noted by Target et al. (2017), in their qualitative study of child contact between separated and divorced parents, that the child or children involved were "everywhere and nowhere" in their parent's minds. The authors found that in the majority of their interviews with separated and divorced parents:

> *"their intense preoccupation with their ex-partner and the ongoing conflict compromised their capacity to picture the child's experience . . . so the real child was at times unintentionally "nowhere" in their minds."*
>
> (Target et al., 2017, p. 225)

As the same study notes, disputes over children can be hard to resolve because of the following:

> *"The child represents a living link to the couple and specifically their previous relationship and as such is a continuing symbol of their union, both physically and psychologically."*
>
> (ibid, p. 236)

While this "living link" may be used to continue the couples' former disputes, where couples can begin to come together in thinking about their child, there is also the possibility of finding a way back to a more collaborative parental relationship and a calmer psychic space for both parents. In sessions with Maria and Steve and with Neel and Maya, significant moments in the therapy occurred when the child seemed to be rediscovered in the minds of their parents.

## Maria and Steve – losing and finding Anna

While Maria and Steve seemed to become more reflective in thinking about their own parenting histories and how this might have affected their choice of one another as a couple and their division into "good" and "bad" cop parents, it felt that there was a continuing blindness at times towards their daughter.

Steve, while interested in the idea that he might be projecting some of his own "bad" feelings into his wife, still had difficulty being in touch with his ambivalence towards being a parent, tending instead to express this in a passive-aggressive way through "forgetting" and "withdrawing". Steve admitted that he had difficulties with time management and so would sometimes disappear from family life because he had become "caught up" in a particular task. This absence served to reinforce Maria in her "bad cop" role of dutifully and grudgingly attending to the details of their daughter's life.

When arguments flared between the couple, they would withdraw to different corners of the house, leaving Anna, as the "living link", carrying messages between them, in order to help them start talking to one another again. In these situations, it felt as if Anna was being put in the role of the parent. When I wondered aloud in sessions with Maria and Steve about what it might feel like for Anna to mediate in their arguments and the responsibility she carried because of them, the couple seemed unable to give this much thought, swiftly returning to blaming one another for not being good enough.

However, this changed after an incident around six months into the therapy seemed to bring the couple into reality with a jolt. Anna wanted to go shopping for a new coat, and Steve said he would meet her at a shopping mall in their local town after school. Maria felt anxious about father and daughter locating one another; however, Anna and Steve were united in dismissing her concerns. On the day of the outing, Maria, not trusting Steve to be organised, kept texting him to remind him to be on time. Steve was irked by this prodding and ended up leaving his office slightly late, "forgetting" his phone which he left at work. Anna, having arrived at the busy shopping centre, panicked when she could not find her father and called Maria in tears. Maria, unable to bear her daughter's and her own anxiety, started criticising Steve to their daughter, leading to Anna switching off her phone. For half an hour or so, Anna was "lost" with neither parent able to reach her. While Anna soon reappeared, the anxiety and guilt both parents felt at that point had a sobering effect.

In discussing this incident together, we were able to understand how, in adopting their familiar "bad cop – good cop" roles, neither Maria nor Steve was attending to the business of parenting and, crucially, of joining together to think about their daughter's best interests. Steve took on board, more fully than before, how he tended to get caught up in rebelling against Maria, joining Anna as another adolescent, rather than setting some firm boundaries for his daughter. Maria realised that she had also become caught up in her anger with Steve, rather than focusing on Anna and talking her through the various scenarios of the shopping expedition to establish what her daughter felt comfortable with.

### Neel and Maya – reconnecting with Arkesh

While attempts to explore Neel and Maya's past relationship seemed to lead into a cul-de-sac; bringing the focus back to their co-parental relationship, whilst challenging their "good cop – bad cop" roles, ultimately led to a shift in the work.

Initially, it felt the couple had great difficulty putting themselves in their son's position, even though both were convinced they were doing their best for him. When challenged on his tendency to view his son as "lazy", Neel began to recognise that in his own family, he felt that the only way to gain his parent's approval was through academic and later financial success. It dawned on Neel that he had always sought to be the "good" child by working hard, succeeding in exams and later gaining promotions at work. This was in the hope of getting his parents' attention. Their focus was on his elder sister, who was the "golden girl" in the family and could do no wrong.

Maya, who became more reflective while Neel was saying this, pointed out quite gently that this was a carbon copy of Neel's view of his own children, with Ella as his "golden girl", while Arkesh could not do anything right in his eyes. It felt that there was a moment of understanding between them when Neel said in a heartfelt way that perhaps he knew how much of a disappointment Arkesh must feel to him because this is how he still felt with his own father. Maya, for her part, began to understand that while in some ways she was standing up for her son in her arguments with Neel, she was also carrying on her feud with her ex-husband by trying to undermine him and by encouraging Arkesh to choose her over his father. Maya began to appreciate more how anxious she was at some level about losing her children. Both parents began to appreciate that under their fixed views, there lay a shared unconscious phantasy that only one could be accepted while the other would be rejected by their children.

## Repairing the parental couple

As I hope to have illustrated in describing some of my work with separated or warring parents, bringing the therapeutic focus back to the child can lead the way to something more hopeful between parents. My experience is that there is the potential for the parental couple relationship to be repaired, even where the couples' romantic relationship is over and where considerable bitterness remains. The beneficial effect of working with parents specifically on their parental relationship was noted in a study of 110 married couples, some of whom were seen in co-parenting groups while others worked only on their marital relationship. According to this study, the co-parenting groups were more successful so that the author concluded:

> *"helping parents work together on issues about rearing their children seems to have positive effects on their parenting and on the marital conflict."*
>
> (Cowan, 1996, p. 156)

In the case of both couples described in this chapter, it was their ability, ultimately, to stand together and *observe* their child that most of all brought relief from their battles with one another. As Winnicott pointed out, following his own study of parents and babies, parents' anxieties about the damage they might do to their child are soothed by the presence of the child himself. This is because the child:

> *"has an innate tendency towards breathing and moving and growing. The child as a fact deals, for the time being, with all the fantasies of good and bad, and the innate aliveness of each child gives the parents a sense of relief as they gradually come to believe in it."*
>
> (Winnicott, 1957, quoted in Abram, 1996, p. 228)

Winnicott here draws attention to the containment offered to parents by their child's resilience, something which felt to be a turning point in the therapy of both the couples in this chapter.

While Neel and Maya felt deep disappointment and shame about the failure of their marriage, in talking about their children in the therapy sessions, some more lively and hopeful feelings emerged. At times, they were able to laugh fondly together about one or other child's behaviour and to join together as a parental couple to think up strategies to overcome a particular problem. There was even an acknowledgement that Arkesh's truculence showed his ability to be separate and was evidence of a healthy resistance, unlike Neel who had always felt he had to comply with parental expectations. It was agreed that Arkesh would himself be asked which school he preferred to go to and that they would visit both schools together as a family.

Maria and Steve also shifted in being able to join together to observe and think about their daughter as a parental couple, even though the future of their couple relationship remained unresolved. Steve had a greater appreciation of how he could stir Maria up and leave her to carry his angry feelings, which made it more likely that she would explode. He agreed to take on more of the role of rule setter and saw that this was valuable to help his daughter feel safe.

At times in the therapy of both couples, it could seem that the "bad cop" was in fact the "good" parent or indeed, the only parent, as their partner seemed to abandon their parental responsibility. However, as the work with both couples continued, the contribution of the "good cop" parent came to be more appreciated. The two "bad cop" parents, Maria and Neel, both came to realise that they used their rather manic rulemaking and activity partly to stave off having more intimate playtime with their children, something their partners felt more at home with. Maria admitted that she envied Steve's ability to be playful and have fun with his daughter. In Maria's own family, play had been frowned upon, and unconsciously, although she had wanted her daughter to have freedom to play and be a child, in practice, it filled her with feelings of inadequacy and a fear of failing. Another unwelcome emotion that Maria began to acknowledge was her envy not only of her partner but also of her daughter being able to have a better experience than her. Maria began to take part more in family outings and "play" time, even though this felt uncomfortable for her. Neel similarly had not had much time for fun in his hard-working childhood, but he began to make efforts to do enjoyable things with Arkesh that neither had to do "well" at. Overall, in understanding the parenting stances they had been stuck in, both sets of parents felt able to alternate more in taking different roles, gaining a greater appreciation that the other had something to offer.

## Conclusion

The strategy of splitting roles and effectively denying reality, adopted by "good cop – bad cop" parents, is an unconscious and ultimately self-defeating effort to meet the challenges of parenting for which these parents feel ill-equipped. With support, even where parents are separated and disputes about children are underscored by the other disappointments in the marriage, couples may be able to start to think more about the impact of their arguments on their child. There is then the potential for them to acknowledge that, whatever they have lost in the marriage, consolation and even hope can be gained from the living proof of a child who is "moving and growing" and whom they have created together.

Couples who can increase their confidence in their ability to parent, while also becoming more realistic about it, may come to better appreciate one another. The shift that took place for the couples described in this chapter enabled them to relax their "good cop – bad cop" roles and to become more reflective, helping them to see that the other parent's role was important and that both needed to move towards the middle ground. In doing this, they were able to make room for mourning failures and acknowledging the damage caused by putting the children at the centre of their entrenched arguments. While the ability to relinquish a paranoid-schizoid way of relating is not permanent and needs to be constantly renegotiated, work with couples in conflict shows that there is a possibility for the parental couple relationship to survive or to be rebuilt. Parents can then begin to trust in their joint concern for their children as the basis for a constructive approach to parenting. This will, in turn, not only benefit their children but may also impact the next generation by helping their offspring in their own attempts to parent.

## References

Bannister, K. & Pincus, L. (1965). *Shared Phantasy in Marital Problems: Therapy in a Four-person Relationship*. London. Institute of Marital Studies.

Britton, R. (1989). The missing link: Parental sexuality in the Oedipus complex. In J. Steiner (Ed.), *The Oedipus Complex Today* (pp. 83–101). London: Karnac.

Clulow, C. (2019). Couples becoming parents. In A. Balfour, C. Clulow & K. Thompson (Eds.), *Engaging Couples* (pp. 34–47). London: Routledge.

Cowan, P. (1996). Being partners: Effects on parenting and child development. In C. Clulow (Ed.), *Partners Becoming Parents* (pp. 140–158). London: Sheldon Press.

Di Ceglie, G. (1995). From the internal parental couple to the marital relationship. In F. Ruszczynski (Ed.), *Intrusiveness and Intimacy in the Couple* (pp. 49–58). London: Routledge.

Fisher, J. (1993). The impenetrable other: Ambivalence and the oedipal conflict in work with couples. In F. Ruszczynski (Ed.), *Pscyhotherapy with Couples* (pp. 142–166). London: Karnac.

Freud, S. (1924). The loss of reality in neurosis and psychosis. James Strachey (Ed.) The Standard Edition of the Complete Psychological Works of Sigmund Freud: Vol. XVIII. (1920–1922). London: Hogarth Press.

Grier, F. (2005). *Oedipus and the Couple*. London: Karnac.

Hewison, D. (2014). Shared unconscious phantasy in couples. In D. E. Scharff & J. S. Scharff (Eds.), *Psychoanalytic Couple Therapy* (pp. 25–34). London: Karnac.

Klein, M. (1946). Notes on some schizoid mechanisms. In *Envy and Gratitude and Other Works (1946–1963)* (pp. 1–24). London: Vintage.

Klein, M. (1952). Some theoretical conclusions regarding the emotional life of the infant. In *Envy and Gratitude and Other Works (1946–1963)* (pp. 61–93). London: Vintage.

Klein, M. (1957). Envy and gratitude. In *Envy and Gratitude and Other Works (1946–1963)* (pp. 176–235). London: Vintage.

Ludlam, M. (2007). Our attachment to "the couple in the mind". In M. Ludlam & V. Nyberg (Eds.), *Couple Attachments: Theoretical and Clinical Studies* (pp. 3–22). London: Karnac.

Morgan, M. (2019). *A Couple State of Mind: Psychoanalysis of Couples and The Tavistock Relationships Model*. London: Routledge.

Steiner, J. (1993). *Psychic Retreats: Pathological Organizations in Psychotic, Neurotic and Borderline Patients*. London and New York: Routledge.

Target, M., Hertzmann, L., Midgley, N., Casey, P. & Lassri, D. (2017). Parents' experience of child contact within entrenched conflict families following separation and divorce: A qualitative study. *Psychoanalytic Psychotherapy*, 31(2), 218–246.

Winnicott, D. (1957). *The Language of Winnicott*. Abram, J. (1996). London: Karnac.

# Chapter 13

# Mentalization-Based Therapy – Parenting under Pressure (MBT-PP)

## What does it feel like? Does it work? How can it help?

*Honor Rhodes, William Walker, Maria Franchini, Sarah Ingram and David Levy*

## Introduction

You won't know Marie and Peter. They are a couple whose story is made up from so many of the parents we met. The quotes are real and taken from our notes and interviews with parents and the staff who worked with them.

> *"Why does the Department for Work and Pensions (DWP) want to know about my relationship? Why do I need to give you my national insurance number and my address? Why do you need to know our children's dates of birth?"*

Marie's questions were good ones. Many parents we met during this project had asked the same. The answer is that the DWP has responsibility for the long-standing government commitment to support couple relationships and had created a programme to test different ways of helping parental couples in conflict, whether they lived together or apart and for same and different sex couples. Each of the methods had good evidence showing they were effective in helping parents improve the quality of their relationship.

The details we wanted were for a large research project and the national insurance details were to ensure we were reaching 'real' people as an anti-fraud measure. We needed the address to ensure that Marie lived in one of the areas that the programme covered and the children's dates of birth established that Marie and her partner were parents.

Like many other 'free' things in life, we pay in ways that are not money. Marie and Peter would be paying with their information. Understanding this and agreeing to it was a vital part of this early engagement. Throughout the project, the vast majority of parents decided to proceed. This tells us something about the significant levels of relationship distress amongst parents nationally and the desperate scarcity of free or easily affordable help that is focused on the couple relationship.

DOI: 10.4324/9781003387947-18

Marie's first communication was a message posted on the website designed to guide parents to the help they wanted in January 2020:

*"Can you help? We are rowing all the time. The children hate it, Danny (8) gets really angry and it's affecting his brother, Thomas, who is 6 years old a lot too. We have tried talking but it makes things worse. Now we aren't really talking at all. Christmas was just miserable for us all."*

We telephoned Marie and gained her consent for the process and filled in forms to assess her view of the conflict. She hinted that she and Peter would be hard to help. She said she'd considered separating, but now they managed their conflict by avoiding each other.

Peter was busy when we phoned in his lunch hour the following day, but we managed to complete the forms and answer his questions about what the work might feel like and how long it would take. He was relieved that the work would last no longer than ten meetings.

Neither Peter nor Marie was surprised that we talked about doing the work in their own home. As a team, though, we were just getting used to it. Traditionally, relationship help is offered in quiet, soundproofed rooms in a building designed for the purpose of therapy or counselling.

Marie and Peter lived in a small village in 'Larkshire'. There was no library, and the nearest children's centre was five miles away. Danny and Thomas' school might have been a possibility, but they had no space free for a regular meeting. It was clear that the Tavistock Relationships' worker would have to come to them.

We had created home-based working processes to ensure we could keep workers safe in environments we did not know. We issued mobile phones, had a check-in and -out system and carried out preliminary safety checks. Marie and Peter didn't have a dog, and their scores on the standard questionnaire indicated that they were not likely to become overwhelmingly angry or violent. These forms also told us that they were not so depressed to make us anxious about a risk of suicide or other harms.

We had also thought about how it might feel for parents to have a worker in their home. When a professional visits us, we can easily feel judged. We can wonder if the house is tidy enough. Will the worker want a cup of tea? What will happen if a neighbour drops in?

All these things needed to be settled for the work to begin, as well as other things that parents might not have thought of. Workers needed to try to recreate the quiet space a therapy room offers, so we negotiated about televisions being turned off and finding enough chairs. We asked parents not to answer or even look at their phones and not to leave the room for a cigarette or a cup of coffee. All these things are impositions and not the sort of demands a usual visitor makes of their hosts.

The workers were not usual visitors, though, and were able to explain, to most parents' satisfaction, why the requests we were making would help and support the work.

We also explained that we needed to spend the first two sessions meeting the parents individually. These initial sessions are designed to outline what MBT-PP is and to agree the goals each parent wants to work towards, given that we can only change ourselves, but that any change allows the other partner the chance to change too.

We listened to each parent's thoughts and feelings about what is going on between them. This gives the worker a view of the parents' conflict and what happens when it occurs. The worker checked carefully to see if each parent felt safe enough in the relationship and that there was no domestic violence or abuse.

Marie had told us in her phone call that, on occasion, their arguments had escalated to shouting at each other, that the row at Christmas had led to her and Peter pushing and shaking each other. We needed to understand more about the physical nature of the argument. Was there an imbalance of power with one parent being hurt more than the other? Was one parent stronger and more physically forceful? We held these questions in our mind to ask Marie and Peter in turn.

The worker arranged to meet Marie first. Peter had suggested meeting the following week, as it was more convenient for him.

## Marie's story, February 2020

In the first session with Marie, the worker wanted to understand her side of the story and what her hopes or 'goals' were but also to make clear what Mentalization-Based Therapy for Parents under Pressure (MBT-PP) was, what it would focus on, how it might feel and how it could help. We also wanted to know more about Danny and Thomas and the impact on them of their parents' conflict.

This way of working, developed by Tavistock Relationships, is drawn originally from the work of Peter Fonagy, Anthony Bateman and Mary Target. They had looked for a way of working with people, and families, who were very emotionally 'unregulated', whose ability to think about how they, or someone else, might be feeling or thinking had been lost or never learned (Bateman & Fonagy, 2006; Fonagy & Target, 1997).

The worker began by explaining 'mentalization'. Under stress, all of us can find using our imaginations hard, whether that stress is coming from our couple relationship, our parenting or from some other source. The term 'mentalizing' describes the process and skills involved in understanding mental and emotional states, in ourselves and in others, and the vital connection between our mental states and our feelings and our behaviour.

The worker asked Marie to describe from her early life as a child to the present. The worker was struck by the matter-of-fact way she talked about being a premature baby who had to spend nearly two months in an incubator. She had, and continued to have, health issues that rose from this, breathing difficulties in particular.

The worker asked about her parents' relationship and whether her parents had angry, unresolved arguments. If we grow up seeing our parents argue in ways that are full of anger, not having the chance to see them coming back together to apologise and make up, we may not learn how to do this ourselves. A childhood full of our parents' conflict can have a long-lasting effect in other ways too. It can affect our learning at school and our emotional and physical health. It can colour all our other relationships, and we can carry it with us into our relationship with our partners (Harold et al., 2016).

Marie's birth family has a history of dissolving difficult relationships; her parents divorced when she was three, and she grew up with a step-father and half-brothers. Whilst there was conflict between her mother and step-father, her concerns seemed to focus on feeling the odd one out, as she didn't look like her half-brothers.

The worker asked how Marie and Peter met and what attracted her to him in the first place. It can help the work with couples if we can help them remember those first warm, loving and desiring feelings, even if they can seem hard to recall. To be reminded of a time when we were thinking about our partners with affection and mentalizing naturally as we wonder what they are thinking and feeling can help people recapture some of that necessary curiosity and interest.

Marie had moved from the north of England when she was 22 years old for work. She had got a good job with a transport company, where she met Peter. She said that she had been instantly attracted to him. He was handsome and full of energy. It mattered to her that he went out of his way to be kind to her and made her feel she belonged. They had started a relationship quickly and had decided within a year that they wanted children together. Marie went on to talk about the pregnancies, both of which she enjoyed and both boys were born around their due dates, healthy, happy babies.

The worker asked about Peter's state of mind during the pregnancies and births of the children. This simple question is one way to see mentalization at work. Marie was being asked to imagine what Peter would have been thinking and feeling, the idea of 'standing in someone else's shoes'. If she could bring into her own mind what she imagined were Peter's thoughts and feelings, then building a stronger bridge between them would be easier.

Marie found the question hard. She became anxious and a little angry. She said, *"How do I know? He doesn't talk about how he feels, or not to me. I think he was probably a bit anxious. I know he talked to his mum a lot during the pregnancies. It sort of drove me mad, all that advice she gave him"*.

The worker was struck by how Marie could allow herself to give a little *"probably a bit anxious"* but moved on swiftly to reflect on Peter's relationship with his mother.

Moving to the present day, the worker asked about their arguments and the message Marie had put on the enquiry form about *"rowing all the time"* and that *"Christmas was miserable"*. Marie said that she thought that, at the heart of it, they are arguing about how to parent the children properly. Peter was so soft with them. He let them have their way all the time. She felt that she was always put in the position of having to deny the children things, and she felt betrayed by Peter when he took the children's side. If Peter "gave in", Danny's behaviour became very difficult to manage, with a "melt down" involving screaming and, occasionally, hitting his parents and brother. Marie added quickly that they were taking Danny for an autism assessment soon but that she and Peter had found this very hard to talk about together and what it might mean if Danny did receive a diagnosis.

The worker asked Marie to talk more about the argument at Christmas when they had hit and pushed each other. The worker explained that he needed to be sure that they were all safe to be together and that it would be helpful to know how it started, who did what, how it ended and whether it, or anything like it, had happened since then.

The worker could see and sense Marie's discomfort as she outlined the argument. Peter had come home far later than she had expected, and she had been anxious about him and annoyed. Danny had started a row about the food on his plate, and Peter arrived just at the point where Marie was shouting at their son over not eating his supper and that she wasn't making him anything else. Peter hadn't greeted her but simply moved close to Danny and asked what Danny did want to eat.

Marie had been angry before, and now she was furious. She felt two things powerfully: both very undermined by Peter and very ashamed for shouting and being the sort of parent who might let her son go to bed hungry.

*"Neither of us were calm. I told Pete that he could do what he liked about the food but that it was his fault for coming home so, so late. I told him he was a shit. I pushed him away when he came over towards me. He was shocked because I pushed him so hard. He sort of fell and grabbed my arm on his way down. He grabbed it so hard I had bruises the next day. He got up and took my shoulders and gave me a hard shake, shouting that I needed to get a grip and calm down. I shook him off and left the room. It did calm down after that mostly. Danny quickly ate what was on his plate and Thomas just cried. I felt so awful and knew we couldn't carry on like this.*

*We've pushed and shoved each other before when we've argued but now I think we are both so scared that we don't touch each other when we are arguing, we don't really touch each other at all now. If you are asking if I feel safe with Pete, then I do. I'm the one more likely to do the hitting when I see red."*

The worker now had one parent's account of this event. He was concerned that it had happened in front of the children and that rows like it, with angry physical contact, had happened before. He noted Marie's use of the past tense "used to" and made a note to check this account carefully when he met Peter.

There were many things the worker could have said at this point, about not arguing in front of the children when the argument is about them or postponing the row until later. Neither would have been useful to Marie in that moment. He simply told her that she needed to know that he was not judging her as a bad parent or partner and that he could imagine how hard that experience was, for Marie, for Peter and for the children. Feeling he needed to leave her with some hope, he reassured her that these things can change.

The worker closed the session by asking Marie about the changes in her relationship with Peter that she wanted most. It is always helpful to have clear goals in mind when we are working for what is really a very short period.

Marie said that she wanted their relationship to improve by communicating more clearly and kindly, to be able to talk about their differences without getting so angry and for the boys to be happier.

## Peter's story, February 2020

The following week, the worker visited the family home again, this time to meet Peter, who was using his lunch hour for the meeting.

The worker, mindful of Peter's deadline, outlined what the meeting needed to cover, with the structure being the same as the meeting with Marie, ending with Peter's goals.

The session started with a question about Peter's family of origin. Peter said he grew up in London, where his mixed heritage was less of an issue for him than now, living as a bi-racial family in a very white town. He felt that growing up as a Black child in Bermondsey meant that he had never been encouraged to think about university as an option for him. He expressed sadness about this and said it had made him very determined that his boys would be encouraged to do whatever they wanted. He talked about his parents, his mother, of Black British/Caribbean heritage, who was a nurse at the local Guy's Hospital, and his father, a docker from a large white Bermondsey family. He talked about a generally happy childhood, that his parents didn't argue much, and when they did, it was mostly about religion and politics. He felt strongly that they loved each other and him, as well as his brothers.

Moving to the present, Peter explained that he is now the senior logistics manager at a transport company, where he works long hours and has to manage a great deal of pressure. He said that not being home when Marie expected him was a constant source of conflict between them. She got very tired and found the bedtime routine hard on her own, particularly managing Danny's behaviour. He said that it was hard to come home. He worried about what is waiting for him on the other side of the door; he knew that it would probably be a row.

'Managing Danny's behaviour' was a common thread between the couple; the fact that they managed in very different ways was a major source of their conflict. Peter wanted home life with Marie and the children to be a place of refuge and quiet joy. He felt she was very hard on the children, watched over them too much and interfered in his relationship with them. He felt that Danny needed more time and some calm around him to help him feel comfortable.

The worker asked about the argument that led to their referring themselves for help. Peter's story, including shaking Marie hard, was the same as Marie's. He had been anxious about her breathing, something Marie had not mentioned. He felt that Marie became breathless when she got upset, and it was one of the reasons he had tried to change, to reduce the rowing and try and remain calm. The worker asked i this was a successful way of managing in the moment of conflict, but Peter wasn't sure. He wondered if his pretended calmness sometimes made Marie more angry. In terms of his goals, he wanted to be the following:

*"more together with Marie about things like Danny's behaviour. We need to have more peace and we need more things to enjoy. I need it to be more give and take, but I do need Marie to understand that I can't just drop everything at 5pm on the dot to come home."*

Peter looked at the clock and said he needed to go, and yes, he'd probably be late back, with all the unhappiness that this would entail.

The worker drove away, this time thinking of Peter and his experiences. He thought of himself, as a white worker, offering help to a bi-racial couple raising mixed heritage children and what these differences might, or might not, mean to Marie and Peter.

## Session 3, coming together, looking at the 'dance', early March 2020

The worker opened the first joint session by saying that he knew Peter would need to leave very promptly, so it would be important to agree how to use the time. Also, that he wanted to talk through with them was his thoughts about their relationship.

He had found the idea of a 'dance' that Marie and Peter did together helpful as a way to think about their misconnections and the conflict that rose from them. Talking about it in this way showed Marie and Peter the 'dance' they did when things got heated ("stepping on each other toes") and when they became chilly towards each other ("refusing to join the other on the dance floor").

Marie and Peter tested the idea and felt it fitted them. They agreed that thinking about the 'dance' that they do with each other, how they communicated and related, would be a good way to organise their thinking and frame the way the further sessions would go. They all agreed that focusing on Marie and Peter's thoughts and feelings about their relationship would give them a chance of creating a new dance together, one that allowed and encouraged the understanding of misunderstandings.

The couple had needed to co-create this idea with the worker. He had only just met them, and Marie and Peter would need to make things clear that he had misunderstood. After all, they were the experts at being themselves and their relationship.

Generally, the worker wondered if a way of describing the problems Peter and Marie had talked about was to think about Danny and Thomas and what growing up in their family was like – and what it could be like. Could Marie and Peter spend some time trying to imagine what it must be like for Danny, with his special sensitivity to noise, and for Thomas, just moving into year 1 and "a worrier", as Marie had put it? They also needed to think about themselves and each other. How could Marie understand more about what Peter was thinking? And vice versa. How could Peter open his mind to what Marie was really feeling as she 'battled' her way through the evening without him? How could Marie feel both the things she was feeling when she was so disappointed that Peter was not home and also feel some part of his dread at putting his key in the front door.

The worker was trying to describe the complex web of thoughts and feelings that link together to make our behaviours. This process is happening at the same time for both people in a couple and for their children. Imaginative sympathy is a tall order when we are under pressure. It is a gift we may not feel able to give just at the point when it is needed most.

The service described in this chapter is called 'MBT – *Parents under Pressure*' for this reason and the worker's job is to help release some of that hot, scalding steam safely so that parents can learn how, or remember, to do so in the future when faced with complicated and painful issues to deal with, without a worker by their side.

Establishing goals was a slightly simpler task, as both parents believed that Danny and Thomas needed and deserved to have parents who could agree about how to handle things together, like family rules and expectations. The worker did not want to be too general, so he used the example of the mealtime that started the 'big row' as one of the things that needed to be thought about and how it could be different for them all in the future.

The worker, in his meetings with Marie and Peter, had used a variety of mentalization techniques. He had slowed the parents down when their thoughts raced ahead and had asked them to explain to him – and each other – when things seemed confused. He was deliberately offering the parents the chance to see how this way of thinking carefully about their thinking, of feeling a connection and looking at themselves from the 'outside in', could help resolve painful disagreements. In time, he encouraged them to try these new thinking methods themselves.

Marie mentioned that after Peter had met the worker, he was very late home but that she had thought ahead that this might be the case, given he had not worked through his lunch break as he often did. She moved on to talk about Thomas' friendship group, but the worker returned to this 'thinking ahead' as something important.

This small exchange had given the worker a chance to notice and appreciate Marie's useful mentalizing. She had thought about Peter's lunchtime session at home and had anticipated the consequences. She was right and he was late, but she had managed the children's suppertime without much difficulty. She had made sure she offered Danny something he really liked to eat and was able to spend some time with Thomas consoling him about feeling lonely at school.

The worker paid attention to this example, as he would to others as they came up in the conversation, and increasingly, as the sessions progressed, Marie and Peter started to notice mentalizing in themselves and each other.

The worker noticed that Marie rarely looked at Peter but that Peter kept his eyes on her, only looking at the worker to speak to him. Why was this? the worker wondered

> *"Peter looks at you, Marie, nearly all the time but you don't really look at him unless he is speaking to you directly. It is making me curious. I don't understand it. Peter, Marie, help me out here."*

Mentalization asks workers to become the opposite of experts, to become 'not knowers'. This gives the work a certain freedom. It means a worker can ask what might be thought 'stupid' questions and notice small, possibly 'stupid' things, like a couple who do not share the same way of looking.

Marie sighed, "*He's looking to see if I am still breathing. He can't help it.*" Peter grimaced. "*When you've seen someone's lips go blue because they can't breathe, then you look, you look a lot*".

Again, although what they were talking about was frightening. It showed a tender capacity to think of each other that the worker had doubted he'd find easily. He commented on their shared experience and had another wonder about where it left them. Did it annoy Marie to be reminded that she had a lifelong condition that was constantly in Peter's mind, or did she feel cared for? Did Peter feel Marie could not manage to breathe unless he was there to watch over her? Was this something that the children worried about? he wondered.

The worker asked if the Covid-19 flu, all over the news, was worrying them, given Marie's lung condition.

Peter and Marie nodded in unison. They were anxious, especially Danny, who would ask if she had her inhaler whenever they went out and made it his business to know where it was in the house. Danny had become very agitated during the week, as the inhaler had been temporarily lost.

Marie and Peter were left with the task of thinking together of a way to offer Danny some comfort, a joint task that they would need to agree and both stick to. It was a small but important job for them to do as loving parents.

## Session 4 in mid-March 2020

The worker arrived for the next session in March. Unknown to them all, this was the last time that they would meet together in person.

He was greeted at the door by Peter and Marie. Both looked drawn and said that they had not had much sleep, as Marie had a chest infection "*but not the flu, thank heavens*". Marie had her inhaler in her hand and used it during the session.

Things had been hard during the week. Danny had been in trouble at school. He had thrown a book at the teacher, and Marie had been summoned to the school for a meeting. She'd had to go on her own, as Peter could not leave his work. Her anger was easy to read, and she could not accept Peter's explanation that he could not drop everything at such short notice, even though he knew it was important.

The worker commented on their lack of mentalizing or 'meeting of minds' and pushed them to try and imagine what it was like for each other. If they could have the conversation about the urgent school appointment again, how could it go? Both tried and failed to come up with anything other than they had done, with shouting and blaming at the heart of it.

Peter said, "*This is hopeless, we are never ever going to be able to sort this out. I know that Marie thinks we might be better apart. I haven't wanted to think that.*"

Marie seemed pinned to her seat, unable to say anything. The worker paused and then offered a thought:

*"I wonder if you are both thinking the same thing but haven't found a safe enough way to talk about it. You might be right that this is hopeless and you'd be better parents apart from each other. That is one possibility. The other possibility is that you might be better together and that things are not as hopeless as they feel right now."*

Marie was convinced the worker was telling them that a separation was the right thing for them. Peter thought the opposite and said, *"I want it to work, I really want it to work, the boys want us to make it work"*. His firmness was a surprise to Marie, who said that she had never heard Peter say that so clearly before. She had imagined that he wanted to leave and was trying to find a time to tell her.

The worker pointed out that both kept some of their most important thoughts and feelings hidden from each other, hoping that the other person would be able to read their mind.

*"We are not mind readers, we can be really bad at it, it's why I ask you stupid questions sometimes, to help you speak about what is in your minds. It'll take some time and courage but I wonder if you can both begin to be more open about what is in your minds with each other, you might both be surprised."*

Peter and Marie understood but seemed reluctant to try. The worker suggested that they share a thought that they hadn't felt able to. Marie offered that she often wondered if her being a white mum to their Black boys was an issue, as it was something that they hadn't talked about for a long time. Peter was surprised by this and said that he wondered, a lot, about her feeling separate and different to him and the boys but worried it would make her feel anxious and left out, so he didn't.

The worker commented that this was one of the first times he had seen them show real curiosity about each other. Marie had wanted to know if race was a factor in Peter's mind when he thought of her as a mother and of her approach to the children. Peter had wanted to know how included or excluded she felt being white in relation to the children and himself. Being able to be curious about what is in someone else's mind is one of the key ideas in mentalization, and Marie and Peter had found a way to express it. This capacity – and ideas about their identity, both separate and together – would be something the worker returned to and explored each time it came up in future sessions.

### Sessions 5–10, March to July 2020

The nation went into lock down on 22 March 2020, and all work at Tavistock Relationship moved from in-person meetings to an online service.

For some workplaces, this was not such an upheaval, but for therapy and counselling organisations, moving to a platform like Zoom was a great deal of work and learning. Workers had to be trained to use Zoom, and we were worried that lots of parents would decide to withdraw.

Marie and Peter, though, were keen to carry on the work, as were other parents we worked with. Peter would join from work, where he still went each day, and Marie from home. The worker wondered what it would be like for them not be in the same physical space but accepted that this made the work a great deal easier for Peter, whose logistics company was now busy shipping NHS supplies.

The midpoint review, session 5, was the first on Zoom. The therapy had arrived at the halfway point, and both parents reflected on their goals of being more united in their approach to parenting, finding more peace and joy and working together to improve their relationship by sharing more of their thoughts and holding the children's minds in mind, as well as their own and each other's.

Both agreed that it had been easier to think about the boys than each other. There had been a couple of big arguments, but for the first time in a long time, they had agreed to wait to talk about it when the boys were not around. They had even managed to be friendly enough rather than withdrawing into a chilly silence like before.

The next two sessions continued to focus on moving closer to their goals. They thought together about the boys and what they needed and wanted from their parents and how to jointly manage the frustration of Danny's autism assessment being postponed for four months.

Marie and Peter made good progress, having some brave conversations and, they confided, having sex. Sex had felt impossible with so much distance, anger and disappointment between them. It now felt like something that they could share together, and the worker was quietly confident that they would manage to hold onto these gains and rebuild something that had meaning and enough value to work for.

Just before session 9, the worker had a text from Peter to say that they would miss the next session, as Marie was in hospital. The worker called Peter, who was tearful and said that Marie had been admitted in the night to the intensive care unit with Covid-19. They had tried really hard to shield her. Peter had worked from home, and the boys stayed at home, too, but it hadn't been enough.

The worker could only say that he was so sorry and that he would be holding them all in his mind. He asked about support for Peter, as he struggled with parenting the boys on his own. He recognised how hard it must be for Peter in not being able to see Marie, given the complete restriction on hospital visits. The worker asked Peter to tell him how things were going when he felt able to.

During the next six weeks, the worker had more texts and calls from Peter. Sometimes Marie was making good progress, and sometimes it seemed that she might die. Peter was left to manage this seesaw of emotions but was glad when his mother decided to come and live with them as a part of their household. The worker listened and thought with Peter about the painful task of hearing the boys' feelings of desperation for their mother, when he was feeling so desperate himself.

The work was formally suspended, of course, but this worker, like the others with parents in a similar position, continued to be present for Peter.

Finally, in mid-June, there was good news, Marie was going to come home. Peter's elation was clear over the phone. The boys had decorated the outside of the house, his mother had batch cooked and he had shaved his lockdown beard off.

Peter was tempted to book an appointment for the work to continue, but the worker, whilst delighted with the news, suggested he wait till Marie was home and they could talk about the right time.

## Sessions 9 and 10, July 2020

Marie contacted the worker, saying that she and Peter had agreed that they wanted to meet. The couple had found a great deal of time for reflection and taking stock of their lives, as so many people did, during this serious illness.

The session after Marie's return home was complicated by Peter's grief that she had been so ill and his despair that she would die. For Marie, her experience had been so different. She could remember the ambulance ride but not much more given that she was immediately sedated and ventilated for over six weeks, as the hospital staff fought to save her life.

The final session allowed for a full review of where the work has got to, measured against the goals that they set and the 'dance' they had developed. Both Peter and Marie felt that their lives had been completely changed by her hospitalisation and – Peter hesitantly suggested – the sessions too.

The worker asked them to focus on what they had learnt from this time they had worked together.

Without Marie at home, Peter had become fully responsible for the boys at a dreadful time in their lives. He had understood the boys' terror at the thought that their mum might die and had suffered with them but shielded them from it. He had allowed himself to recognise that his relationship with Marie was the central pillar of his life and had been able to tell her. She had been able to tell him how much she loved him in return, something that had not felt possible, or perhaps even true, when the work began.

For all parents, there are 'bumps in the road' that need to be managed; it is easier if we have planned for them and thought together about how we might tackle them. So while Danny's behaviour had settled a great deal and Thomas was enjoying online schooling, it was plain to both parents that this was only a temporary respite from a future that would include Danny's autism assessment and what it might mean for Danny and for themselves. What they had learned, they said, was a way to parent more collaboratively, more able to talk about their differences in thought and feelings in a measured and kinder way, leaving enough space to find out what the other person's thoughts might mean and how they felt.

The worker gathered all the changes he'd seen and offered them back to the couple, noticing how far they had come from the first session and much he had learned from working with them. He admired their courage and persistence to se this work through to the end when it would have been easier, and understandable, to stop after Marie's hospitalisation. Marie said that she was glad they had worked through to the end, that there was still a lot to do but that they had remembered how to be together.

It is worth pointing out that Marie and Peter did make significant changes. They improved their relationship quality, improved their own mental health, reduced the conflict between them and improved their children's wellbeing. We know this as we measured their relationship satisfaction, depression and anxiety again at the end of the work, using the same tools as before.

Their story is unique to them, but they belong to the thousands of parents whose lives changed for the better, thanks to investment from the government's DWP, to end where we started.

## References

Bateman, A.W., and Fonagy, P. (2006). *Mentalization-Based Treatment for Borderline Personality Disorder: A Practical Guide*. Oxford, UK: Oxford University Press.

Fonagy, P., and Target, M. (1997). Attachment and reflective function: Their role in self-organization. *Development and Psychopathology*, 9, 679–700.

Harold, G., Acquah, D., Sellers, R., Chowdry, H., and Feinstein, L. (Eds.) (2016). *What Works to Enhance Inter-Parental Relationships and Improve Outcomes For Children*. London: Early Intervention Foundation. www.eif.org.uk/report/what-works-to-enhance-interparental-relationships-and-improve-outcomes-for-children

# Chapter 14

# From partners to co-parents

## Treading a new landscape after separation

*Joanna Harrison*

A metaphor that often comes up in my work with separating or divorcing parents is that of find themselves in a new land. This is a landscape, whose contours and customs are unfamiliar at best and terrifying or stressful at worst, sometimes steep to climb and sometimes giving way under parents' feet. As they tread through this alien landscape of separation, most parents express a hope to protect their children and yet sometimes struggle to do so or struggle to know how to do so.

Approaching separation, both parents will most likely have different ideas of what this landscape might hold, both in the external practicalities of how life is arranged and in their imagined ideas of how it may feel between them. They may feel they have no model of how it will work. Perhaps experiences of their own parents' divorces will inform their expectations, or maybe images of high-conflict divorce they have read about in the newspaper or seen depicted in films. Alternatively, they may have an idealised image of an 'amicable' divorce, where there are no bumps in the road and everyone gets on perfectly.

Everyone's divorce or separation resonates individually, but what I hope to do in this chapter is describe my experience of working in the field of divorce and separation, conveying some of the familiar themes and issues that often crop up and, in doing so, to give parents a 'lie of the land'. I previously worked as a divorce lawyer before retraining as a couple therapist. As part of my current practice, I work with separating parents, both at Tavistock Relationships and at Family Law in Partnership, a central London multidisciplinary divorce practice, where lawyers work alongside therapists.

## The different domains in which divorce takes place

I am talking about divorce as a new landscape, but within this landscape, there are different domains in which a divorce takes place (Shmueli, 2012). One domain centres on the practical and financial aspects of separation (e.g., where people are going to live and how the arrangements for the children are going to be worked out). The other domain, often overlooked but which can affect how the practical

DOI: 10.4324/9781003387947-19

aspects play out and how everyone feels about the situation, is that concerning the emotional and psychological consequences of divorce.

It is crucial to remember that *both* of these domains need tending to when facing a separation. If we see being separated as a new landscape for parents, we might think that the choice of route, the terrain, and the weather are the practical aspects to contend with, but the attitude and health, both physical and mental, of the people finding their way through will affect *how* they manage the navigation of this new space. I think the metaphor of a journey is also appropriate. Processing the end of the relationship takes time and has different stages, some predictable, some unpredictable. We know divorce to be stressful; parents may feel their most vulnerable, incompetent, and inexpert at a time their children need them the most. As has been said "parenting is most under threat when, arguably, it is most needed" (Vincent, 1995).

Each of these domains, practical and emotional, affect the other. For example, difficulties in the financial domain can cause upset in the emotional domain. Equally, feelings of resentment and hurt between a couple can impact the practical domain in relation, for example, to finances. A lack of goodwill can find an easy stage to play out in the practical arrangements between a separating couple.

> *"Composite case example 1: Max and Maggie were divorcing and seeking help through a mediator to work out their financial situation. The main point of conflict appeared to be over whether Maggie and their two children should stay in their home and Max rent a flat, (Maggie's wish) or whether the house should be sold and they both downsize, (Max's wish). These options represented issues in the practical domain of their separation but had deep emotional resonance for both. Max was worried that, if he had a much smaller place than Maggie, he'd be viewed as the lesser parent and the children would not want to visit him. Maggie protested that she hadn't chosen the divorce and, as Max had initiated it, why should she have to change her life and risk upsetting the children by moving?"*

If this problem is only tended to in terms of the concrete practical domain, as in what the law says or what is actually affordable for them, then important emotional aspects can be lost from sight. Max's fears about his relationship with the children diminishing and Maggie's objection to the end of the relationship and her fears about the children's wellbeing are all aspects that could benefit from being aired and understood in order to support the separating couple find a creative solution.

> *"The mediator referred Maggie and Max to a relationship therapist. Initially Max was sceptical. "Why would I see a relationship therapist when our relationship is over?" The mediator explained that it could be helpful to look at some of the underlying feelings that they both had about the ending of the marriage and about their future process."*

### Tending to the breaking-down relationship

Max's scepticism about seeing a relationship therapist links to a common confusion for separating parents. There is an idea that now their couple relationship is over, what is important for them to focus on is their individual relationship with their children rather than their relationship with each other. Of course, it is important for them to focus on their individual relationship with their children, but thinking that relationship therapy is only for couples who are trying to save their marriage may deprive them of opportunities to attend to the difficult feelings and dynamics that affect their relationship in the present. This idea is echoed in the Resolution Parenting Through Separation Guide for Parents[1] which helpfully suggests that "Parents may often find it difficult to separate their couple relationship feelings from their parenting feelings and it is this clash that can get in the way of allowing an ongoing relationship with the children".

> *"In their sessions with the relationship therapist, Maggie and Max spoke about the ending of their relationship. Their relationship therapist heard their different accounts of why they split up and the disagreement over where each was to live. She felt a pressure coming from them to judge that one was right. She resisted this pressure and instead spoke about how difficult it was for both of them to face the reality of their situation and to come to terms with the end of their relationship and all that this entailed. She suggested that they took some time to think together with her about what had happened to end their marriage. Over the sessions that followed, what emerged was that Max had ended their relationship suddenly and without explanation which had left Maggie in profound shock. Time was needed for a better understanding between them about what had happened. By being more in touch with what had gone on between them, it felt that they were more able to appreciate where the other partner was coming from with regard to their concerns about the future. This created a more compassionate atmosphere in which to work creatively and to find practical solutions regarding their situation, although this wasn't a simple matter."*

Facing up to the disappointment of a relationship failing and the pain associated with it is extremely challenging. There's often an attempt to manage it through blame and by seeking a judgement that the other person is wrong. In my experience, however, it is when the disappointment and pain can be given more attention that the parental couple are more likely to be able to move forward in a more constructive relationship. This space allows separating couples to understand each other's experience as opposed to focusing on their own individual survival. The depiction of parents in conflict is often that they should be able to automatically switch off their hostile feelings or put them to the side and think about their children. However, without support at a deeper level, it may not be possible to flick that switch.

There will be some separating couples who literally cannot stomach the idea of sitting in the same room with their partner or do not feel it is safe. Since working online, I have found that some of these concerns have been mitigated by the reality of partners not having to be in the same room together. Of course, where it is not safe enough for them to be together or where things between them can seriously escalate, then individual therapeutic support is more appropriate.

### Who do I need to help me?

It can be very confusing for people separating to know who to consult or what help or protection is needed. At a point at which they may feel very vulnerable, unsure, and anxious about an uncertain looking future, there may be different ideas about what is appropriate. If therapeutic support is needed, should that be individual, relationship, or for the children? Within the legal framework, there are different processes that can be used to deal with the situation, the choice of which can feel overwhelming. Well-meaning friends and family will also make their own suggestions of who or what may be needed. In this unfamiliar landscape, it may feel like standing at a signpost with many different directions that could be followed and no clear idea of which one to take.

Professionals working in the different domains may have different repertoires for responding to the situations in which they find their clients.

> "Composite case example 2: Chris sought a solicitor as he was worried that Fran was preventing him from having proper contact with his young son, Billy, aged 18 months. Fran felt that their son was too young for overnight contact and that this was something they could build up to. Chris didn't trust her to follow through on this and that it was important to have his son stay overnight as soon as possible. His solicitor advised him that he had options through the court system to seek contact. He also advised that Chris first try to speak with Fran with a professional or with a mediator.
>
> However, Chris felt attracted to what he perceived as the concrete security of the court process and had the resources to use it. He liked the idea that there would be an end date and a court order in place to protect his position. He didn't feel much trust in Fran to work with him and he wanted his son to know that he had done what he could to ensure he spent as much time with him as possible.
>
> A court application followed with an initial hearing and meetings with a Cafcass officer.[2] The communication between Chris and Fran reduced to a minimum and increased between solicitors. Both made statements about what they thought was the best situation for Billy. These statements pointed out the shortcomings they felt about each other, resulting in a very hostile atmosphere between them. At the end of the court process, an order was made for a joint contact arrangement with Billy but relations between his parents were at an all-time low. During the time of the court process both had felt they needed to be on their best behaviour; there was a fear that anything they 'did wrong' would be

*used against them. There was very little goodwill and when it came to putting the order into practice it didn't go as smoothly as Chris had imagined."*

There are situations where a court process is required, but often, the experience of going through it will take its own toll on the parental relationship and destroy trust that is hard to recover. What may have supported these parents more would have been an intervention in their parental couple relationship to help build trust in each other and create an atmosphere that would be attuned to Billy's needs. This could perhaps have provided more of the security Chris was looking for than a court order.

## What divorcing parents might look for in the professionals working with them

A helpful professional will be able to think with their client about what support might be needed in the different domains of their divorce. Whether the professional works in the legal domain and is giving them an idea of how they might get help in the emotional domain, or vice versa, it's essential that the professionals have a working knowledge of each other's terrain.

There can be a real pull on the professionals to join their client in criticising their ex-partner and to buy into the narrative of one person being to blame. If the professional gets caught up in this, unsurprisingly, this can escalate matters. It may feel to a parent that a professional has got their back or is on their side if they are willing to join in blaming, but in fact, the wellbeing of the family may actually benefit from the professionals retaining more of a couple state of mind in order to support de-escalation.

Taking this into account, there are new initiatives in the legal system aimed to de-escalate the polarisation that can happen for separating couples. New 'one-lawyer-one-couple' models[3] are of interest because rather than pitting one person's narrative against the other, both parties receive the same advice and are encouraged to resolve things together. Other models go further and attempt to address both the legal and emotional domains simultaneously by having the different professionals working alongside each other, such as mediation taking place alongside relationship therapy. The new 'Language Matters' project[4] aims to engage legal professionals in thinking about the accusatory language they may be drawn into using.

## Common areas of difficulty

I'm now going to consider five different areas that often cause issues for parents as they transition out of a couple relationship and into a co-parenting relationship. I hope that in doing so, parents may gain some confidence that the difficulties they find themselves grappling with are perhaps an understandable feature of the new landscape they are in and 'go with the territory'.

I also hope to provide a lens through which parents can look at the situation they find themselves in to comprehend the inherent difficulties they have to manage.

This can provide a context to help understand that the transition to shared parenting is inevitably difficult and takes time to adapt to (an experience that may echo the difficulty of transitioning to becoming parents in the first place). There is a need to mourn what is lost, and I think it can be helpful for parents to have a sense that the transition to being co-parents is not something that can happen overnight. This state of mind can alleviate the tendency to persecute themselves or each other for not getting it 'right'.

The transition to becoming co-parents also occurs in the fluid and constantly changing backdrop of the developmental demands of the children involved. The age and stage of the child will be important to bear in mind when thinking about what might be most supportive for them at a particular time as well as what they might struggle with.

1. How do we tell the children?

Often, this is the question that is uppermost in parents' minds when they initially seek help about splitting up. Parents are concerned about the significance of the moment of disclosure and have a wish to minimise any upset for their children. It may also relate to their own reaction to facing up to the situation they are in.

Parents can feel very preoccupied with what narrative to give to their children about what has happened – a preoccupation that reflects what will be going on for them as a couple. Often, children are told early in the separation process when raw, angry, and blaming feelings ricochet between the couple. Where one parent feels that the relationship ending is not their fault, creating a shared narrative can be harder. For example, they are less likely to be able to tolerate that "mum and dad have decided to end the relationship because it's not working anymore" and opt for "dad is leaving because he has met someone else". Conversely, dad may believe "he has met someone else because mum stopped listening to him years ago and his affair was symptomatic rather than causal". There is real work to do for parents to think together about what is helpful for their children to hear, all of which needs to be thought about in the context of their particular developmental age. Where there are children of different ages, this requires a delicate balancing act as parents think about what each sibling might be able to manage and what is age appropriate for each of them as well as how they as parents manage this together.

Some of the complexities of how and what to tell the children are encapsulated when the singer Adele spoke to *British Vogue*[5] about her divorce and the album she had written:

*"My son has had a lot of questions. Really good questions, really innocent questions, that I just don't have an answer for. Like? Why can't you still live together? . . . I just felt like I wanted to explain to him, through this record, when he's in his twenties or thirties, who I am and why I voluntarily chose to dismantle his entire life in the pursuit of my own happiness. It made him really unhappy sometimes. And that's a real wound for me that I don't know if I'll ever be able to heal."*

So much of what a parent has to contend with on separation is encapsulated in her visceral and honest statement. It alludes to a hope that, in due course, a child might come to a better understanding of what happened. It also encapsulates the internal conflict that might be felt by the parent in taking the step to separate and the hurt that may be caused by the divorce. When a parent asks, "How can we tell our children we are separating?" The real feeling underneath may be "How can we tell our children we are separating and make it not hurt for them?"

Information is widely available on phrases to choose when talking to children of different ages. These concrete resources can provide a helpful scaffolding for parents to hold as they try and think together about how to support their children with the news about their parents' separation or divorce. However, what is important is perhaps not so much getting the words right as having the capacity to think together how to minimise the hurt and ensure as much continuity, reassurance and security as possible for children. It is a conversation that is likely to need to be repeated, to evolve and to develop over time and that needs to respond to the way in which the child responds to it.

2. How is life going to work?

On a practical level, the shift to living in two different households rather than one can present real everyday challenges. Even in relationships where perhaps one parent does far more of the 'hands-on parenting' (perhaps itself an area of conflict that has affected the breakdown of the relationship), there will be moments where the loss of 'two pairs of hands' is felt, even more so with younger children or those with special needs. Part of transitioning to co-parenting means transitioning to a new way of parenting, one that doesn't involve the other's 'pair of hands' so much and of finding ways to deal with this. All this at a time where a parent is likely to be feeling more vulnerable emotionally.

There will be much to work out in terms of day-to-day practicalities: living arrangements, both temporary and permanent, and the financial settlement and care of the children, including each parent's involvement. Understandably, there can be real tension as the couple negotiate their differences with regard to these vital aspects and come to terms with the reality of the situation. A colleague of mine described a client who said that he had not considered the reality, before separating from his partner, that he would only see his son half of the time.

In order to make the practicalities work in this new separated landscape, there is more need for co-operation than most parents envisage. Where relations are poor between them, the absent parent can feel robbed of their relationship with their child. Where there is more goodwill, parents seem more able to give each other the sense that they are being held in mind by their child by sending photos or messages about what they are up to, which can help lessen feelings of loss.

*"Composite case example 3. Ritchie and Linda had decided to separate but were still living in the same house. They had developed a timetable for who did what and when with their children. This somewhat rigid structure was threatened,*

*however, after Ritchie, whose turn it was to do breakfast for the children, had found that there was no milk in the fridge. He thought that it would have been reasonable for Linda to tell him that the milk had run out. She said that it had slipped her mind but, in any event, it was 'his problem' now as she sorted out food for the children for her meals with them and he could do the same. Ritchie seemed surprised and saddened by this new state of affairs while Linda felt it was realistic that she no longer had to think about this sort of stuff on his behalf."*

Ritchie and Linda were not the only couple I have worked with who, following a separation, would report conflict concerning practical minutiae, such as milk bottles or school packed lunches. They seem to symbolise how the very basic workings of domestic life have to change. The conflict between Ritchie and Linda drew attention to their need as separated parents to create a new shared system for parenting.

Their difficulties at this time also convey something of the practical challenges at the beginning of the process of separating when realistic arrangements haven't been worked out and feelings are raw. There may be ambivalence about taking the step towards living apart, especially if there is not enough money to move into separate accommodation. My experience of this kind of situation is that it is a pressure cooker that brings its own conflict. Often, I will work with parents to create ground rules about what this phase is going to be like. It can feel alien for them to navigate rules about living in the house in which they had lived freely for many years. The pressure involved in adapting the familiar environment into an environment with new unfamiliar ways of being can sometimes be too much for couples to bear, and they express relief when they are able to move into separate accommodation and report less annoyance and frustration with each other.

Composite case example 4. Leszek was a client who came to work with me on his own following a separation from his wife, Hannah. He came with different ideas between him and his wife about arrangements for the children which required attention.

*"Leszek said he was finding it difficult to make arrangements with his ex-wife, Hannah, over care of their twins aged 8. He thought she should be more supportive in encouraging them to come and stay with him. Although they had agreed that the twins could stay over with him every other weekend, often, at the last minute, Hannah would tell Leszek that they didn't want to come and that she wasn't going to force them. He wanted her to insist and accused his ex-wife of purposefully making life difficult for him. I felt pressure coming from him to agree that Hannah was the one who was to blame for this whole situation.*

*I asked whether Hannah had raised any specific concerns with him about their children coming to stay. He said that she was very controlling about what he could feed them and was always complaining about the amount of screen time he gave them. Leszek thought it was none of her business and that when they were with him, she should trust him, especially as he cared about their health just as much as she did.*

*I spoke about how little appetite he seemed to have to speak to her about these issues. He was surprised by my comment. He said that their relationship had ended and that he wanted little to do with her. He found Hannah difficult and frustrating which was why he had wanted to end the relationship. He also hadn't agreed with the way she parented and felt relieved that now he could introduce some useful boundaries for his children.*

*I wondered if it was really too painful to co-operate with her but, by refusing to engage with her, it further blocked the channels needed for them to build trust in their new roles."*

It can be really difficult for parents who feel hurt and betrayed by their ex-partner to collaborate and manage practical details in regard to their children's lives. Ensuring that the right things are going into the schoolbags on the right days when a child spends different days of the week with each parent requires a greater degree of organisation and communication between a couple than perhaps existed before, particularly if previously only one parent assumed responsibility for the schoolbag. Essentially, to 'make things work', parents need to 'upgrade' their way of communicating with each other.

When there is little communication between separating couples, there is more scope for misunderstanding and unhelpful assumption that can seriously impede their ability to work together for the sake of the children. For instance, in Leszek's case, it seems that he had little understanding or acceptance of Hannah's concerns relating to his time with their children, a factor that may reflect difficulties between them that ultimately led to the breakdown of their marriage. If Leszek can be supported to think about Hannah's concerns and reassure her that he understands and respects them, it may contribute to building trust between them for the sake of the children.

Children and screen time seems to be a particularly thorny issue for separated parents to negotiate. It may embody the lack of control parents are feeling in all aspects of their lives due to so much change. It is an area where experts at the World Health Organisation have issued guidelines about recommended amounts of screen time, and this may relieve parents from arguing who is 'right' or 'wrong'. I have also noticed that the parent who is not physically present with the child is often concerned that the child is being neglected when 'left on a screen' at the other parent's house. This may speak to their own concern about the new reality of only one parent being around in the new setup. Where parents are able to voice these concerns, then they are more able to attend to each other's fears rather than feeling 'neglected'.

3.  How are our wider families going to be involved?

One of the things that a person who is separating might be helped to think about is the support network they have around them as they make the shift to being on their own in both the practical and emotional domains. Extended family and friends can often provide crucial support and help take care of their children. This network can become problematic, however, when the extended family becomes (what a solicitor colleague of mine refers to as) a 'chorus of voices' that serve to magnify and polarise the issues between the parents and where the needs of children get lost.

Grandparents and relatives adopting a more neutral position can be more helpful, offering a stable structure to separating couples, both during the breakdown and as they attempt to rebuild their lives. A grandparent who is able to remain steady and involved with their grandchildren and who is supportive of both parents can offer a vital source of consistency for all concerned.

Wider family and friends understandably can feel a loyalty to one half of a separating couple, wanting to show support for their friend or relative by agreeing with all of their grievances about their ex-partner. However, the neutrality of a professional may enable these narratives to be challenged, although professionals themselves are not immune to the pressures of a particular narrative. Avoiding polarisation and blame will be helpful to the separating couple and provide role-modelling for what they need to achieve themselves.

Composite case example 5. *Tommi's parents had had a 'messy divorce' leaving her and her brother feeling 'emotionally scarred'. They had always felt a tense atmosphere in the family home, but when she was 10 and her brother 13, her parents announced that they were divorcing and that Tommi would be staying with her mother whilst her brother would live with their father. Tommi believed that her relationship with her brother never really recovered from this rupture and that her relationship with her father also deteriorated. Why didn't he choose her?*

*As an adult Tommi sought therapy as she felt unhappy within her own marriage, feeling unloved by her partner. This had developed when her youngest child started secondary school and she had taken on a larger role running art workshops in the community. She had really enjoyed the sense of doing something useful for the community and contrasted this with her dissatisfaction in her relationship. Her presenting problem in therapy was how to end her marriage in a more positive way than her parents had done. She was concerned for her children but was also concerned that, if she stayed married to their father, they were witnessing a poor example of a couple relationship. Her partner was apparently unaware that she planned to end the marriage.*

Being in therapy gave Tommi room to make links between the *unloved* feelings she had felt growing up with the *unloved* feelings in her own relationship. In one session, she said it felt so overwhelming trying to deal with her sadness about her childhood experiences alongside trying to protect her children from pain relating to the separation from their father. Sometimes, she said, it was hard to know what belonged where. Over time in therapy, she became more aware of how her childhood experiences were affecting her ability to move forward. As her therapist, I felt cast in the role of 'magician', helping Tommi find answers that would take away the pain of her experience. Once this was acknowledged, she began to think about the possibility of her and her husband seeking a joint referral so that the trouble in their relationship could be thought about, rather than her feeling she had to solve it all herself.

4.  How are we going to manage the children coming and going between us?

> Composite case example 6. *Nick and Bradley were finding the handovers of their daughter Olivia, aged 4, difficult and had asked their solicitors to recommend some help. Olivia often found it hard to say goodbye to the parent she had been spending time with and would become quite upset. Nick wanted to be pragmatic and quick about these goodbyes and then comfort her after. Bradley felt it was important to slow things down and sit with her while she was upset. What usually happened was an argument erupted between Nick and Bradley on the doorstep about how best to deal with the situation. Both felt increasingly tense about the handovers but agreed they needed help.*
>
> *After much toing and froing about making an appointment, they arrived for a consultation. It seemed that both had an expectation that the therapist would solve their problem and tell them how to deal with this situation. Their therapist asked them to describe their current relationship, and both said they were trying hard to be as positive as possible about the breakdown of their relationship. Nick said that he didn't want to talk about their relationship; what he wanted was an expert to tell them what was best for Olivia. She would be starting school soon and he was concerned about how she might manage the increased separation from home, with more drop offs and pickups.*
>
> *The therapist picked up on Nick saying that he didn't want to discuss their relationship and wondered with them just how difficult they had found it to come to the session. Clearly, they were both concerned about Olivia and wanted to find a way to protect her but perhaps it felt really difficult to contemplate the idea of sitting in a room together and to confront the intimacy of that. The therapist wondered if they were caught in a conflict themselves of whether to be pragmatic and business-like with each other, or whether to be more emotional about the end of the relationship. Perhaps they were all struggling with the separation, not just Olivia.*
>
> *Nick was sceptical about this as an idea, but Bradley said that it was true that he had been dreading the session and was worried that if they started talking about how they were doing it might become overwhelming. Nick wasn't sure that going over old ground was helpful, but he trusted his solicitor and would do whatever it took to try and help Olivia.*
>
> *When they came back a week later, they both said that had found the session helpful and that they would like to continue for Olivia's sake. As time went on, they seemed more able to convey their own upset feelings about the ending of their relationship and the separation that they were having to*

*tolerate. They also felt less need to argue on the doorstep as they knew they had the session coming up. After some time, they reported that Olivia was finding it much easier to go between them and they noticed that they both felt less tense about it.*

One might speculate about what it was that had helped Olivia to feel more relaxed about going between her parents. Perhaps her age, perhaps her parents getting on better, perhaps their being able to express some of their feelings about the end of the relationship and their having used some of the time in their sessions to reflect on the reality of where they were instead of the future they had imagined. It seemed though that they had made use of the sessions, and paradoxically, it was the intimacy of the sessions that had enabled them to separate.

5. When to introduce a new partner?

Composite case example 7. In my experience, no issue causes as much rage and upset as an ex-partner introducing a new partner to the children prematurely, at least in one parent's view, or without any notice. The primitive fears attached to the involvement of another adult in parenting proximity, encapsulated by the wicked stepparents of fairy tales, can be stirred up viscerally.

*"When Jane's solicitor, Rohan, opened his email on Monday morning there was an urgent message asking him to ring her. When she spoke to him, Janie was extremely upset. She said that her two children, Vic, aged 13, and Georgie, aged 11, had returned home following a weekend stay with Patrick, their father, and had told their mum that they had spent the weekend with him, and a lady called Claire, "Daddy's new girlfriend". Jane was devastated and couldn't believe that this had happened without prior warning. She instructed Rohan to write a disapproving letter to Patrick's solicitor. The response she received set out to justify Patrick's actions on the basis that the children had got on well with his new girlfriend and given that a year had elapsed since the breakdown of their relationship, he saw nothing wrong with them meeting her. Furious and concerned about her children, Jane threatened to stop the kids staying at their father's home."*

The introduction of another adult into the privacy of family life can feel intrusive, and parents can feel deeply concerned and protective. Of further shock to parents is that suddenly, these sorts of highly personal issues might become debated and argued publicly through solicitors.

*"The circumstances of Jane and Patrick's breakdown had been hostile and there was little goodwill between them. They had briefly tried relationship therapy, but Jane had felt that Patrick wasn't willing to give it a go while Patrick maintained that Jane was over-reacting to issues between them. Following their split, they had found a way of parenting their children which was very much at arm's*

*length, with little communication between them. They stuck to the structure of the contact schedule, and it mostly worked. However, when the issue of Patrick's new girlfriend arose, their shared parenting was thrown into turmoil, and they experienced a resurgence of hostility similar to the feelings expressed at the end of the marriage and manifest in the solicitors' correspondence."*

Whilst Jane and Patrick seemed to have defensively managed a way of being that worked in the external domain of their contact schedule, which their children had got used to, when a new partner was introduced into the picture, the somewhat defensive structure gave way to hostility and distress. Although their solicitors advised them to seek help together, there was little interest in being in the same room.

What had really caused a problem was Patrick's *unilateral* action in introducing the children to his girlfriend without first discussing it and its implications with their mother. Whilst it may feel to someone who is separated that they can now act separately in relation to the children, and in doing so avoid having to deal with their partner whom they find difficult, the reality is that avoiding thinking about something together with their ex-partner can cause more difficulty than they had envisaged. However difficult it may be to 'be in the room together' and to 'think together' about, for instance, the introduction of a new partner and the plans around this, this can support their children and their co-parenting relationship. I have worked with parents where both are in new relationships and respect each other's privacy but can also bring up concerns or feelings about the new partner in relation to their children. These are very delicate conversations to have, but there is a sense that the children will benefit from the engagement of their parents over such matters.

## Conclusion

Every parent going through a divorce or separation has their own particular experience. Their journey through this new landscape will depend on many factors including but not limited to their setup, their resources, the dynamics of the relationship with their ex-partner, their own personality, the personality of their children, the age and stage of their children, and the path that they choose to follow through the landscape.

From my experience of working in the territory of divorce, it is where separating couples can be supported to work together and to think about the impact they each have on the other that can, in turn, create an atmosphere that also enables them to think about the impact their ongoing relationship has on their children. Where they are more able to get in touch with the sad and disappointed feelings about the end of their relationship and what wasn't possible between them, it may be possible to move on from polarised narratives about one person being to blame.

What can be surprising is that separating parents often need to work together more than they imagined in order to manage the problems, practical and emotional, that can arise in the new landscape. Just at the point they thought that they would be separating from each other, in fact, because they are no longer in the working couple relationship, there is more that they need to do to co-operate and contain the anxiety that differences between them or issues with their children throw up. We cannot forget also that these are two people who have, at some level, found that they can't work together, at least not as a couple, causing them to separate. There may be real and long-lived difficulties in the way that they operate together, and it may be that therapeutic support, as well as other expert help, in both the practical and the emotional domain is needed in order to scaffold two parents as they move towards a new way of being. What we do know is that if they remain stuck in intractable conflict, their children will suffer as a result.

## Notes

1 Resolution Parenting Through Separation Guide. https://resolution.org.uk/wp-content/uploads/2021/05/Parenting-through-separation-guide.pdf
2 Cafcass stands for Children and Family Court Advisory and Support Service. Cafcass represent the interests of children and young people in family court cases in England and seek to independently advise the family courts about what is safe for children and in their best interests.
3 For example https://resolution.org.uk/news/resolution-reveals-innovative-new-model-to-help-couples-divorce-amicably-with-just-one-lawyer/
4 Language Matters Project. www.familysolutionsgroup.co.uk/language-matters/
5 Interview with Adele in British Vogue, November 2021. www.vogue.co.uk/arts-and-lifestyle/article/adele-british-vogue-interview

## References

Clulow, C. and Vincent, C. (1987). *In the Child's Best Interests – Divorce Court Welfare and the Search for a Settlement*. London: Tavistock Publications.
Shmueli, A. (2012)."Working therapeutically with high conflict divorce. In A. Balfour, M. Morgan, and C. Vincent (Eds.), *How Couple Relationships Shape Our World: Clinical Practice, Research, and Policy Perspectives*. London: Karnac; Routledge.
Vincent, C. (1995). Consulting to divorcing couples. *Family Law*, December. London: LexisNexis UK.
Weiss, R. (1975). *Marital Separation*. New York: Basic Books.

# Index

For Product Safety Concerns and Information please contact our EU
representative GPSR@taylorandfrancis.com Taylor & Francis Verlag GmbH,
Kaufingerstraße 24, 80331 München, Germany

Printed and bound by CPI Group (UK) Ltd, Croydon, CR0 4YY
08/06/2025
01897002-0013